Shepton Mallet Local

'A Town Alive'

Shepton Mallet and District during World War II

Compiled by Alan Stone
and the Members of the
Shepton Mallet Local History Group

*

Published in 2004 by
Shepton Mallet Local History Group
10 Society Road, Shepton Mallet, Somerset, BA4 5GF

Dedicated to the memory of those who gave their lives

"Bid them rest in peace"

Printed by Creeds the Printers, Broadoak, Bridport, Dorset. DT6 5NL

ISBN 0-9548125-0-6

Subscribers

We would like to thank the many people who showed enough faith in this project to purchase a copy of the book before it was even written. Without them we would not have been able to arrange the finance for printing.

Mrs Maureen Shearn

Richard (Dick) Male (in memoriam)

Edmund Harold Norman (in memoriam)

Paul Brayton

Rob Hunter

Peter Morley

Septimus George Lemon (in memoriam)

K – P & S Turner

Moneycare Financial Planning Ltd

Mrs Christine Marshman

Richard Raynesford

Mr & Mrs R A Stone

Mrs P M Robertson

Mrs E Jones

K Whitcombe

Mr & Mrs B Neill

B J Padfield

David Vagg

Douglas Moore

F J Disney BEM

Jim Doble

Mr & Mrs Percy Higgins (in memoriam)

Christine, Richard & James Stone

Mr & Mrs Dymond

Fred Merrit (in memoriam)

Mr Ken Moores

Chris Phillips

Peter Clark

Gordon Turner

Amy Frances Lemon (in memoriam)

Mrs Sheila Bays

Mrs Jean Chapman

Peter Bould

'Dick' Griffiths

D R Willis

John G S Maidment

Lionel Pearce

Arthur Thomas Ware (in memoriam)

Miss S B Bristow

Derek Warren

Paul Treby

Richard Witcombe

David P Williams

Mrs A Symes

Margaret Drew

Mr R A Carley

The King and Queen and Winston Churchill –
inspirational throughout the war.

Introduction

The Shepton Mallet Local History Group had evolved during 2001 and 2002. Once it was up and running I had to ask the question – which aspect of the vast and unexplored history of Shepton shall we research first? The answer came strongly from the members– they wanted us to look at Shepton Mallet in World War II. Ken Moores was amongst the keenest. He was typical of many other members. They had been children or young people during the war years, many in Shepton itself. They saw it as a special time in the town's history and wanted it recorded before the memories disappeared.

Although I took on the role of coordinator, someone has to pull it all together, this was very much a collective project. Probably more than 100 people have contributed over the two years of research. A core group evolved which included Ken Moores, George Bartlett, Mrs E Jones, Maureen Shearn, Jim Doble, David Williams, Brian Neill, Francis Disney, Stan Blacker and our superb roving interviewer Colin Ryall.

There are so many more who have helped with their time, their memories, and letting us borrow their photos and artifacts where possible this has been credited in the text. It has been a fantastic experience to meet and work with so many Sheptonians.

I must pass a special thanks the Brian and Pam Neill and Jim and Diana Doble who undertook the proof reading. What with my transcriptions of others words and a constant muddling of tenses and Capitals this was a horrendous task. That it is now moderately consistent is down to them although I have retained some of the questionable wording from the originals. Brian also, very bravely, pointed out that there should be some maps, and found himself agreeing to producing them at the last minute!

We must also thank all those who have materially helped with the publication of this book. The many people who have subscribed in advance to a book that didn't exist. Also to the Town Council who found my request baffling - for a short term loan to cover the difference between our reserves and the cost of printing whilst we sold enough books to cover all costs. Fortunately they had the vision to agree.

Many thanks also go to Mr Philip Welch the editor of the Mid Somerset Series of Newspapers for permission to photograph some of the advertisements from the wartime editions and to the staff at Wells library for their cheerful tolerance of me ever changing the times of my numerous sessions looking at the old newspapers on their micro film reader.

I would also like to thank Lorraine Pratten and her staff at the TIC who in their enthusiastic engaging in conversation of visitors to the town have unearthed a number of stories.

Alan Stone
June 2004

Methodology

I originally thought that this book would be a theme based study, taking different topics and piecing together people's memories into them. However my self-imposed task was to go through the local papers for Shepton Mallet during the War years to find out what information was stored there.

In some ways the papers were a disappointment – they didn't actually say much directly about the war. However I soon discovered I was gaining an understanding of what made the town tick. The snippets in the paper reflected the experiences people were going through and the changing times they were living in. A new framework suggested itself, a chronological journey through the war fitting in thematic topics and peoples' memories to fill out this picture. I am quite excited by the result, I feel it makes the town come to life and the tales suggest plots for any number of new wartime dramas and comedies.

The Shepton Mallet Journal was four pages of closely set type each week. Of this probably a page was given over to Wells and to the nearby villages, Nearly a page was given to advertisements and nearly another page for national information and orders and guidance for farmers. It still managed to pack in a lot of local news and opinion.

Much of it was rather routine reporting on births, deaths and marriages. I have had to edit out much fascinating information of historical importance to Shepton but not relevant to the war years. The reports of Council Meetings and the Courts may not have been exciting but have contained some gems. The number of ways that people could end up in court during the war has never ceased to amaze me.

Shepton Mallet Journal.

One of the most important things about the newspaper reports is that they are in the main indisputable. The paper was reporting things as they happened at the time. Into this structure I have woven the huge number of memories I have been given. These have either come as written memories, through interviews undertaken by Colin Ryall, myself or others, or in snippets grasped from meetings and any number of chance encounters. It is quite clear that the memories are sometimes amended by subsequent knowledge. In the case of the very elderly the memories were sometimes muddled and from those, who were young at the time, were somewhat vague. However against the framework of newspaper reports they help build a very rich picture.

I have tried to let the memories and paper reports provide the picture and to keep annotation and explanation to a minimum. For example I had intended an essay on farming during the war – however I found that much of it had been covered in the memories of Norton Corp. Chris Challis has been working on the history of the shops and rationing. However as this was such an integral part of war-time Shepton much appears in the text. I am sure these areas will be fully explored in a subsequent publication. Volume Two looks very much a possibility. I am waiting for the deluge of – 'oh, why did you miss out this?' Or 'didn't you know that?'

Most of the newspaper reports have had to be paraphrased and edited for reasons of space and interest. However, I have attempted to include enough of the original wording to give a flavour of the language the paper uses. I have enjoyed the results – I hope you will.

Chapter One

Shepton Mallet at the Outbreak of War

The Second World War was a highly active period in the history of 'Sleepy Shepton", a town which it had been said only awoke once a year for the Mid-Somerset Show and then went back to sleep. The war changed that in a big way and the foundations were laid for a period of prosperity into the 50s and 60s – which when looking at the long pull of Shepton history, it has to be said, is the exception rather than the rule,

Although Shepton remained uniquely Shepton throughout, the war period rapidly bought changes, many of which were to be of considerable duration. New people and jobs flooded into the town and at the same time young men moved out to join the armed forces whilst other young men arrived to man newly set up military establishments. Buildings that had long remained empty and redundant found themselves fully utilized.

The years between the Great War and the outbreak of the Second World War had been years of great economic depression and hardship for the country as a whole. Shepton, with its industrial heritage had probably suffered worse than most. In 1939 there were small signs of recovery but these were slight. In 1931 the census had shown the town as having a population of 4108. This was the lowest figure since censuses begun in 1801 when the population was 5104. Throughout the Nineteenth Century it had usually been a little higher than this reaching a peak of 5500 in 1891. By 1921 it had fallen to 4295 and the decline had continued.

So in 1939 Shepton was a small rural town of about 4000 people. In terms of housing it probably covered less than one third of the area the town does today. In the north there was no Hillmead. In the east there was little housing other than Victoria Grove beyond the Charlton Cross Roads, To the South there was no Ridgeway development and only the first houses and bungalows were being built on Compton Road. To the west there was nothing on the St Peters development, Shaftgate Avenue and Wickham Way. However, the increased availability of Mortgages and Council House building by local authorities meant that the building industry was one of the few activities leading the way out of the depression. There had been building in Westfield and the first inhabitants had recently moved into Cornwall Road. There was private building along West Shepton and the first houses of Southfield.

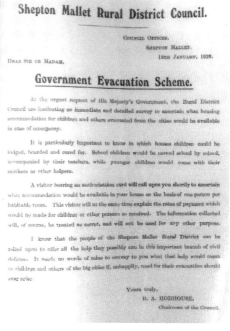

Evacuation Request Notice.

8

However the developer had found that he was unable to find a buyer for these.

Although the area covered was less and in general the density was less there were areas that would have had a denser population of small workers' cottages which have since been swept away. Old maps and photos show the cottages and mills in Draycott which were demolished in the sixties when Hillmead was developed. Garston Street and Town Lane had more buildings and there was a lane in between, beneath what became the massive Showerings factory in the 1950s.

Elderly residents memories are not of one town but of identifiable communities such as Kilver Street, Garston Street, Leg Square, Draycot, Charlton, Bowlish and Darshill. Those separate communities spread along the River Sheppy with the limited area of the town centre around the Church and Market Place. They also remember it as a town very much divided on class lines with the wealthier inhabitants certainly having very different social circles.

Virtue Bakery Invoice for Charity Loaves.

The depression of the early 1930s had been a time of few jobs and general economic hardship. Local veteran Stan Blacker can remember those times well. He recalls the bread rooms where his gran used to send him to collect the Charity 4lb loaf on a Saturday morning. Everyone was in the same boat so there was no question of pride. The loaves were freshly baked by Mr Virtue in his bakery in Leg Square (now flats). Stan recalls that it smelt so good that he could not resist pulling off the corner to eat. He got a clout around the ear for that!

The Employment Exchange in the 1930s was in 8 Market Place which was about where the north end of Regal Road now is. Apparently the queue used to stretch form there down to the Pack Horse Pub in Town Street where Martins is now situated. For some claimants this was appropriate as once they had got their money this was where it was going to be spent.

According to Stan, Clem Reed was the relieving officer in Leg Square in the 1930s and he was very hot on making sure the money was not spent on drink, instructing wives not to give it to their husbands. Apparently there were more than 300 families on the dole. Later the Labour Exchange moved to the top of town at the south end of the High Street.

A Mr Matthews was in charge. One Perc Vining was on the dole for so long that Mr Matthews gave him a job.

Shepton Mallet was an interesting town economy wise. It had long been an agricultural town with a livestock market, agricultural merchants and industries associated with agriculture. Farmers' invoices of the period show that for a wide area around Wells, Midsomer Norton and south to Ditcheat, Shepton Mallet was where farmers came for their market and to buy agricultural supplies. Wainwright, Laver and Crees ran the Livestock Market at Townsend and were one of the major Land Agents in the region. Allen and Foster ran a Corn Mill in Park Road – now the offices of accountants Tenon. Examination of cheese-making equipment on most of the farms locally would show that much of the equipment had been made in the town. Cary's Cheese Factors had premises down in Draycot and bought and traded cheese from many local farms. Plus the town was home to one of the leading Agricultural Societies in the region, the Mid Somerset Agricultural Society who held their annual show at Field on the second Tuesday in September every year – probably the major annual event in the town.

But it was not just supplying and servicing farmers that was a feature of the town. Retired farmer Alan Hoskins came to the town as a boy when his father J Hoskins took on Park Farm in Bowlish. He suggests that at the beginning of the war there were 19 Dairy Farms or Dairies in Shepton Mallet. Mrs E Jones of West Field can remember as a girl going to Tilleys at Ivy House Farm to buy Milk. Ivy House Farm was in Board Cross only a couple of hundred yards from the town centre. (There was another Ivy House Farm in Kilver Street.)

Local Farms listed in Kellys Directory for 1939 include:-

- Percy Applegate, Stomacher Farm, Downside
- William Baulch, Kent Farm
- Charles Banks, Foss Lane
- Walter Britten, Pitts Farm, West Shepton.
- Louis Defage, Rosamond Green, Winsor Hill
- Benji Francis, Cannards Grave
- Henry Godfrey, Lower Downside Farm
- John Hoskins, Park Farm, Bowlish
- Harry Maidment, Warren Farm, Maesbury
- Edward March, Gore End, Cannards Grave
- Cyril Mitchell, Kingdon Farm, West Shepton
- Edmund 'Harry' Norman, Cannards Grave
- John Oram, Winsor Hill Farm,
- George Pearse, Bullimore Farm
- George Perkins, New Road Fm, Downside
- Sutton Perkins, Yew Tree, Downside.
- Reg Pike Ivy House Farm, Kilver Street.
- William Rugg, Barrendown, Leg Square
- Robert Snelgrove, Millbrook Fm, Downside
- Harry Swain, Woodlands Farm, Charlton
- Arthur Tilley, The Ivy House
- Reg Vagg, Field Farm
- George Weeks, Millhouse Farm, Winsor Hill

If we add to these farmers their families and the large number of farm workers it can be seen that a good number of the population were still firmly agriculturally based.

However, then as now the townscape was dominated by large industrial looking buildings. Some of these came from the legacy as a textile town which had been the basis of the town's wealth up to the beginning of the 19th Century. However the textile trade had all gone. There was only one small glove making factory left at the outbreak of war at the southern end of the High Street and in Townsend where Chantry Digital is now. The massive Jardine's lace factory in the Mill in Kilver Street had closed in the interwar period. Other mills stood unused or semi derelict at Charlton, Draycott, Coombe Lane and Darshill.

The Prison with its massive walls in Town Lane had shut in the early 1930s and was empty.

There was still a considerable brewing industry in the town. There was a large brewery at Charlton and Showerings both brewed and made Cider in Kilver Street. However, the town's biggest brewery and most prominent building, the Anglo (Bavarian) Brewery had ceased to brew in the early 1930s although the Anglo Cider Mills still operated on a much smaller scale from the site. In terms of manufacturing industry the town was very nearly dead.

As a commercial centre Shepton Mallet was still a lively little town. It was considered in those days to be in a good situation for communications. It was at the focus of a number of main roads and had two railway lines. The Somerset and Dorset Railway, a major connection from the Midlands to the South Coast had a station at Charlton Road on the eastern side of the town, the mighty viaducts that carried it down from the Mendips forming a northern boundary to the town. The GWR 'Strawberry Line' from Westbury and all points east ran through the town on its way to Wells and Cheddar. The GWR station at Townsend was at the south end of the High Street. Together, the railways represented one of the larger employers in the town.

There had been signs of new industry in the shape of the Co-op Bacon Factory which was set up in the town in 1936 to process the pigs bred on local farms. Stan Blacker remembers that this was considered a major boost to the town and that it provided a number of extra jobs. The buildings in Charlton Road are now used by Framptons.

At that time Shepton Mallet was the shopping centre for both the town and the surrounding villages. There were upwards of 100 shops in the town centre and the surrounding streets. Most of them were small family businesses but some boasted several different departments. The shops kept the town looking busy and with shop assistants and delivery boys, contributed significantly to the employment of the town.

One of the features of Shepton Mallet at the outbreak of War was how self-contained it was. Today it is difficult to appreciate the extent to which Shepton Mallet was responsible for running itself. Today the Town Council is responsible for street lights, footpaths and maintenance of the Park, and even the latter they have put out to tender to a company aligned with Mendip District Council.

In the 1930s Shepton Mallet was run by Shepton Mallet Urban District Council and the surrounding villages by Shepton Mallet Rural District Council. The latter covered Ashwick,

Batcombe, Binegar, Bradley (West), Cranmore, Croscombe, Ditcheat, Doulting, Downhead, Emborough, Evercreech, Holcombe, Lamyatt, Lydford, Milton Clevedon, East Pennard, Pilton, Pylle, Stoke Lane, Stratton on the Fosse. In 1931 the SMRDC area had a total population of 10,126. Both Councils operated from the Council Hall in Market Square which stood where the 'Amulet' is now.

They covered the sort of functions that Mendip District Council now does for a much larger area, housing, refuse collection, street furniture etc. In addition they seem to have had responsibility for the Fire Brigade, a surveyor responsible for the roads of the district and a role in health provision. As will be seen, the outbreak of war added considerably to their duties.

It was not only at Council level that Shepton Mallet was more responsible for itself. Gas was provided by the Shepton Mallet Gas Company from the gasworks in Cowl Street. Water was provided by the Shepton Mallet Water Company whose secretary was local surveyor Geoffrey Budd. In health provision, the town was responsible for running its own hospitals – The Shepton Mallet Hospital Board, and they had to raise their own funds. The nurses in the town worked for the Shepton Mallet Nursing Association. Today it is difficult to conceive this level of self responsibility in the running of public affairs in so small a town.

All these functions were run by local citizens and the same names keep on cropping up again and again as they will throughout this history.

Edmund 'Henry'' Norman. A tall grey-haired farmer of Cannards Grave. Chairman of the Town Council.

Berkley Hall. Bowlish Villa. An accountant who had come to the town in the early 1930s and as well as setting up his accountancy practice had very much involved himself in town affairs. In his 40s married with two daughters. Vice Chairman of the Town Council.

Miss E E Allen. Highfield, Park Road. The last of the family of Allen 'the Snow Drop King' who lived in Highfield House now occupied by Mendip District Council.

J H Addleshaw. Ridgeway, Compton Road. One of the leading Solicitors in the town aged in his mid 40s Born in Cheshire he had married Elsie daughter of Harold C Allen of Shepton Mallet. Was Clerk to the Shepton Mallet County Justices and Clerk to the Commissioner of Taxes Shepton Mallet District.

Sir Frederick Berryman. DL. JP Barrister at Law of Field House. In his seventies but still very much the most distinguished resident of the town and active as Chairman or President of many organizations. Born in Shepton, son of Frederick Berryman, he was a JP and from 1927 – 1932 had been chairman of Somerset County Council.

Harry Britten. Frithfield, Paul Street. A local Butcher.

Geoffrey Budd. Princes Road. HC Budd and Son Auctioneers and Surveyors.He also ran Shepton Mallet Water Company.

Charles Burnell. Charlton House. Ran the Charlton Brewery. Another of the distinguished residents who was President of many societies.

Reginald Byrt, Eden Grove – a lovely house in Leg Sq. The Byrts had a long association with the Church. They had founded the Shepton Mallet Journal and ran a stationers and printers business in the town.

Rev William Crawford (Roman Catholic) Old Bowlish House.

Dr Alexander Finch. The Shrubbery. Doctor and Medical Officer for the District.

Major A Garton Pylle Manor. Of the family who used to own the Anglo Bavarian Brewery where Archie had helped run the Fire Brigade. He was a Vice Chair of the Shepton Mallet Rural District Council, keen promoter of Rural Crafts and an Expert in Somerset Dialect.

Rev A S Gribble MA Rector. The Rectory. This was the massive old Rectory which was demolished to make way for Rectory Road to take traffic out of Town Street and the Market Square. Rev Gribble was a relative newcomer to the town taking over from Rev Landeman who had been Rector for nearly 50 years. The Rev Gribble was introducing some new ideas.

Dr Annie Hyatt, Merrymead, Charlton Road. A retired Doctor who had been born in the town and had given many years medical service.

Wyndham Laver, Guest House Downside. A partner in the town's leading Land Agents Wainwright, Laver and Crees.

Frederick Luff, The Laurels, Bowlish. One of the Luff family who mainly lived near Evercreech and were involved in the local Quarry industry.

Thomas Melhuish, Park House, Park Road. Local Builders.

Ingleton Rowe. The Priory, Commercial Road.

H Showering, 13 Charlton Road. One of the Showering Family. Owner of the Kings Arms, and the Brewery in Kilver Street.

C R Wainwright. Summerleaze. A grand old house which was demolished for the building of the now redundant ICI Factory. 80 years old, JP and Land Agent of a long-standing Shepton Family. **C D Wainwright.** Westleigh, Hitchen Lane. JP and Land Agent. Son of CR Wainwright.

Shepton Mallet had a range of Churches functioning in 1939. The fine Old Parish Church with Saxon origins and there were also church rooms in Cannards Grave. St Michaels Catholic Church was at Townsend. A very active Baptist Church who worshipped in the corrugated iron chapel in Commercial Road which is now used as industrial premises. The Congregational Chapel was in Cowl Street while the brethren Methodists worshipped at the Ebenezer Chapel in Paul Street with a Methodist Mission at Downside. The Salvation Army barracks were in Draycott. Finally there were the Unitarians who worshipped in the marvellous Chapel in Commercial Road which is now used by the Baptists.

The townspeople had very active social lives. There were numerous clubs and societies. There was the Regal Cinema which put on two different programmes a week. In these pre-television days, the Cinema was a major draw. The Pathe News reels which were shown were a major – if edited – source of news information. Stan Blacker remembers how alive Shepton Mallet was on Saturday evenings. People used to shop late and the butchers would be trying to sell off all their meat before Sunday. There would often be dances or bands playing and the pubs would be packed out.

Although there were not as many pubs as there had been earlier in the town's history there were still plenty, especially when you think the population was only half of today.

According to Kelly's Directory there were the following pubs in the town in 1939.

- Bell Hotel, 3 High Street
- Black Swan, Market Place
- Bunch of Grapes, Market Place
- Cannards Grave Inn
- Charlton Inn, Charlton Road.
- Crown Inn, Draycott
- Downside Inn, Downside
- Field Inn, Field
- Hare and Hounds Hotel, Commercial Road.
- Horseshoe Inn, Bowlish
- King William, West Shepton.
- Kings Arms, 1 Garston Street
- Pack Horse, 62 Town Street
- Railway Inn, 25 High Street
- Red Lion Hotel, Market Place
- Royal Oak, Commercial Road
- Ship. 40 Kilver Street
- Victoria Inn, Board Cross
- White Hart, 58 Garston Street
- Wine & Spirits Vaults, 10 High Street
- York House, 45 Town Street

The overriding picture of Shepton Mallet is of a town in which people lived, worked and socialized. A town which meant a lot more to its inhabitants than today because so much more of their lives was tied up with it. Young people joining the forces probably started the social revolution that led to a rapid change in the old order but it is interesting to note the large number of family and business names as we go through this history that are still present in the town today.

Preparations for War

Shepton Mallet was far from unprepared for the war. It is believed that planning will have dated back to the early 1930s. There may have been an 'Invasion Book' but despite the best endeavours of Chris Challis this has yet to come to light. There is no doubt that the large number of empty buildings in the town had resulted in Shepton Mallet being earmarked for special preparation. An Observer Corp had been set up and operating since 1938.

The town was designated as a reception area for evacuees. Notices had been sent out by the Councils at the beginning of 1939 to identify where evacuees could be placed. Evacuees arrived in their hundreds within hours of the start of the War and in their thousands within weeks. Whole schools together with their teachers were evacuated from the East End of London.

The Public Record Office moved large quantities of their records to the former women's wing at the prison including a copy of the Doomsday Book and the Magna Carter. Gordon Vincent can remember seeing the vans arrive. Bailey's of Great Ormond Street in London were the removal company used. Prison Historian Francis Disney has been responsible for much research into whether the Crown Jewels were at the prison. The official line is that the whereabouts of the Crown Jewels is a well-kept secret. It is not possible to deny that they may have been at the prison but it is not thought to have been the most likely location. He can however prove that the Doomsday book was there as his photograph of it being handled by curators in a cell shows.

The National Deposit Friendly Society moved into the empty Jardine's Mill in Kilver Street bringing a large number of employee's with them. The Air Ministry took over the Anglo Brewery for a supply depot.

The Military also arrived in force. The Hampshire regiment was within days setting up an army camp where the Clarks Factory used to be in grounds owned by Wainwright of Summerleaze. Many local builders were ordered to stop what they were doing and get on with building for the army. The rest of the prison was taken over as a military prison and shortly the Royal Navy were to arrive with a team who rebuilt and tested marine engines – although it has been suggested that they may also have been testing destructive weapons.

All of these arrivals bought extra people who needed somewhere to live, eat and sleep. Within a very short time the town had been transformed – in many ways for ever.

Mr. Johnson and Mr. Collie with the Doomsday Book in Shepton Mallet Prison.

Chapter 2

1939

- On September 1ˢᵗ German troops crossed the Polish frontier and German planes bombed Warsaw.
- That same day in Britain the evacuation of 1 million children from 'vulnerable areas' began. The cabinet sent an ultimatum to Germany.
- "I have to tell you that no such undertaking has been received and consequently this country is at war with Germany" (Chamberlain)
- November. Russia invaded Finland.
- December. Much merchant shipping lost to U-boats

8 September 1939

Editorial. Dark and difficult as may be the days that lie ahead, we feel confident that as in the days of the Last Great War – the war waged to end all wars – there will appear a silver lining; indeed it has already shone through in our midst and was evident on Friday evening last when the whole town made ready to accord a hearty reception to approximately 800 school children evacuated from London.

Note – Already the Shepton Mallet Journal had been cut in half due to restrictions on fuel for heating, gas for lighting and power and paper for printing. Railway and bus timetables were to be dropped to save space.

Letter – from Mr H Clifford appealing for gifts of toys, games and clothing for evacuated children to be sent to Mr Whittock, Waterloo Road School.

Note – The paper was full of national notices. These included this week small bits on

- Soldiers to help in harvest
- Cereals to be requisitioned
- Local Food Control Committees
- Control of Meat and Livestock
- Paper supply controls
- Rationing of Coal, Gas and Electricity
- Petrol Rationing Scheme

The Journal continued to be used for national notices of this sort throughout the war. Unless there is a particular local impact we will not be repeating these.

Things started to happen extremely quickly in Shepton Mallet. The following gives a fascinating insight into the arrival in Town of the National Deposit Friendly Society.

Jardines Mill. Kilver Street, Shepton Mallet.

By Joyce Hanton née Cartwright. Notes collected by Audrey Symes.

"One day during August 1939 the staff of the National Deposit Friendly Society, Queens

Square, Holborn, London, were called together in each department to be told that property had been purchased in Shepton Mallet, Somerset, and in the event of war being declared, the offices would be moved to Shepton Mallet. After the meeting, we in our department looked in our reference books to see what information we could find out. This told us that Shepton Mallet was a market town in Somerset with a population of 5,000.

Subsequently on 4th September '39 we were told that the office would be moved to Shepton Mallet, and we had the choice of going to Shepton, or we would lose our jobs. After talking to my parents it was decided I would go, and on Sept 13th 1939, the majority of the female staff met at Paddington Station. After tearful goodbyes to our also tearful mothers, but still feeling excited, we left for Shepton Mallet, and arrived after a long journey at High Street Station.

I think some of the male staff had moved to Shepton a few days before us, as we were met at the station by several of the male staff. I cannot remember how we were divided up, but the older girls, over 21 were taken to houses in West Shepton which had just been built, and were empty. The younger staff were to be placed in Jardines Mill in Kilver Street, an old lace factory.

We followed our guides in one long line, through the High Street into Peter Street, Leg Square, Town Lane and our first sight of the 'mill'.

This as I have said was an old derelict Lace Mill, purchased by the NDFS and partly rebuilt

Evacuees. Alf Taylor is on the far right, Bill Hogwood front row left.

into living accommodation, and offices. We were taken up a flight of stairs, and into the dormitories, which were on two floors, a toilet block at each end, with wash basins, toilets and a bathroom. The floor was sectioned off into rows of beds. 8 or 12 in each section. Gradually groups of friends placed luggage on their chosen beds. My friends and I followed to the end, found another small flight of stairs, into an end room with just 4 beds, this was just right for the four of us, and we claimed these while the rest of the girls went on to the other section of dormitories until most beds were taken. We had been told to take two days 'iron rations' until the canteen was organized. Memory fails me as to what we had to drink, though that first evening I was in a group taken to the 'Ship Inn', and others to the Charlton Inn', great excitement to be going to a pub!!

We had two days to settle in and to inspect the other parts of the mill which were to be our offices. The 'mill' was in two buildings, connected with a covered walkway. When we looked into the office space, some of the old machinery was still in place and being moved. After a couple of days, tables, chairs, files and all the paper work of those days, were put in place, and we were able to start work, plus overtime to catch up on the days lost.

We all soon settled down together, not far to go to the office, instead of the trains, tubes or buses we were used to. My mother came to see me for my 18th birthday in November and was horrified to see all the wet washing hanging up to dry, but I don't think we came to much harm.

There was a "Matron" in charge of us, she had rooms on the ground floor near the canteen. We were supposed to be in by 10 o'clock pm, unless there was a dance, but as in those days we had 'Market Hall' at the top of town, 'Central Hall', Drill Hall, Council Offices and after a while our canteen was opened up for dancing, there was a dance on most evenings. Plus of course the Regal Cinema , and Penny's Fish Café, so we were not short of entertainment.

I remained in the 'mill' until November 1940 when our house in Walthamstow was badly damaged, and my parents joined me, and we lived in furnished accommodation. Despite wartime, a few happy memories remain of Jardine's Mill. Especially trying to find your 'date' for the evening, in the blackout making sure you picked the right one, of all the chaps lined up in the lane."

Joyce still remains in Shepton Mallet. She is one of the many incomers who remained. She married locally to a Soldier, Percy Hanton, who died in 2003 during the preparation of this book.

15 September 1939

Shepton Mallet Urban District Council. EH Norman (Chairman) Berkeley Hall (Vice Chair) Miss E M Thorne, Sir Frederick Berryman, W H Lintern, C B Witcombe, F J E Pullen, E J Hardwidge, W A Price, W E Hayes, H Askey, C Penelhum. Officers Mr H Belchamber, Clerk and D T G Brown, Surveyor.

Items discussed included

- £6 to fit a lightning conductor to the band stand.

- Compton Road. A proposal to name the new property of Sir F Berryman at the north end of Compton Road 'Compton Corner' approved.
- A guard-rail to be fitted to stop children running out into road at a the blind corner in Board Cross near Heard's Paddock where the road suddenly widens.

The big debate was on public provision of Air Raid shelters in Urban Districts. Mr Pullin reported that there was an excellent cellar at the Bunch of Grapes but the police would not pass any cellar unless it had two exits. He suggested putting steps in to make the coal shute an exit.

The surveyor reported two approved places: Messer's Allen's Highfield (now part of Mendip District Councils offices) and Cary's in Draycott (former cheese factors converted to flats in 2003). He pointed out that the council were under no obligation to provide shelters 'except for those in the street'.

Mr Price expressed the opinion that he considered the medical officer's report 'that ARP work in the district is in a fairly forward condition', open to serious doubt. At present they had a paid man at the 'post' for eight hours a day but during the most necessary period of all, the night, they had no-one there at all. Mr Hall explained that it was down to the Control Officer and the council had no power.

Mr Witcombe expressed the opinion that it was about time everyone had a gas mask. He was told that they had 'run out.' Mr Hall said Shepton had got the number they had asked for. The long and the short of it was the census was not complete.

Touching on the subject of Air Raid shelters Mr Pullen remarked that in Shepton Mallet they were particularly fortunate in their stone-built houses. A table placed alongside one of the thick walls would afford excellent shelter.

Regal. Showing 'The Saint in New York.'

22 September 1939

Shepton Mallet Rural District Council

R A Hobhouse (Chairman) Major J A Garton (Vice Chair) Commander RJB Hippisley, Major H K Shore, Col H G Spencer, Mrs B M Sword, Miss M Bethell, Rev E Ogden, J Matthews, W C Britten, S W Golledge, A G Barber, J P Luff, C Neale, A J Whitehead, J Sealy, J H Sperring, W H Bond, A Gilson, W W Gilson, R J Britten.

Major J A Garton, Area ARP Controller appealed for as much voluntary work as possible in order to conserve finance and manpower. He considered ' the rush to paid labour was very unpatriotic.'

Regal – 'Hey, Hey, USA' with Will Hay

Note- there is a quite marked difference between the make up of the Urban District and Rural District council. The Rural District was very much made up of the 'county' set. (The local if not the aristocracy the next set down. The Hobhouse's and Hippisly's and Luff's etc, backed by a large number of the local farmers.) The Urban District council had a farmer Mr Norman as its chairman but was largely made up of the local professional and trading classes. It included Berkeley Hall an accountant as vice chairman, Miss Thorne, a local shop keeper, and the energetic Mr Pullen a builder and decorator.

Major Archie Garton of Pylle a descendant of the family associated with the Anglo Brewery appears to have been everywhere in the first few weeks of the war as the local ARP controller. He soon disappears and it later transpired that he had regained his commission in the army.

29 September 1939

Voluntary Aid Detachment (Red Cross). The First Aid Parties of the VAD (Somerset BRC no 13) were inspected on Sunday at the Grammar School by ARP Area Controller Major Garton MC accompanied by deputy controller Mr Berkeley Hall. There was a Demonstration of stretcher drill. The controller expressed his appreciation of the smartness and keenness of the men. It was regretted that they were unable to raise sufficient funds to equip and clothe the parties. Although they were engaged on essential ARP work no assistance could be made by the government but should be made the subject of local effort.

"I am sure Shepton Mallet people fully appreciate what is being done for their protection."

Advert – 'For the dark evenings, A large selection of games and jigsaws. A Byrt and Sons 47 & 48 High Street Shepton Mallet.

Advert – Blinds Rollers and Fittings. Easy fix runner curtain rail, expanding curtain wire, blackout shutters, blackout paper, paints and lathes and all ARP requisites. C, Amor 27 Draycot Road, Shepton Mallet.

6 October 1939

AGM of Shepton Mallet Chamber of Commerce held in Peter St Rooms. Mr F Luff President, Berkeley Hall Chairman executive committee Mr L E Rickards Hon Sec, Mr S G Lemon Treasurer. Discussion was on plans to promote Shepton Mallet as a 'holiday haunt' which had apparently met little enthusiasm from the public, hotel owners etc.

Football. Shepton Mallet 1 Evercreech 7! The team played football in Whitstone Park.

Adverts. Special Notice. Just arrived at Henley's A large Quantity of Blackout Materials. Henley's 22, 22a & 23 High Street, Shepton Mallet.

A Dance will be held every Wednesday and Saturday until further notice at the Market Hall, Townsend, admission 1/- 6.30pm – 10.00pm. Percentage of profits in aid of the Shepton Mallet Red Cross Units.

13 October 1939

Urban District Council. 'Southfield Road' name approved for the road formed by Mr C Zwarts off West Shepton.

Repair of War Damage. Committee has notified local builders that they will require their immediate service to repair any damage from aerial bombardment.

Petrol. Committee recommended that a license to store 1,000 gallons of petrol in two underground tanks on premises at Darshill be granted to Mr F W Bennett.

There is a reference to the County Education Committee buying part of Whitstone Park as a site for a new senior school. Note. It would be more than 30 years before Whitstone School was actually built!

ARP – Anderson Shelters. The County Council says it is unable to obtain Anderson Shelters as all had been reserved by the Home Office.

On Instructions from the Ministry of Agriculture as much land was to be made available for allotments as possible. The council was to advertise for applicants.

ARP – It was proposed that the Swimming Baths should be used for decontamination of ARP personnel.

Auxiliary Fire Service. The council have put a submission to the Home Office for the full time manning of one fire pump and eight whole-time firemen but they do not think it is necessary. They recommend that Mr C Pursey, the second fire officer, be appointed as Temporary Whole Time Officer of the Brigade at £4 a week. They also need a more suitable fire station and have been instructed to look for premises.

Letter. Dear Sir, May I through the hospitality of your columns thank those who worked so hard and gave so generously to the Flag Day…. The splendid sum of £25 was raised…. Yours faithfully Elsie Addleshaw, Commandant VAD Somerset Y8, The Ridgeway, Shepton Mallet.

20 October 1939

Advert. ARP Volunteers are needed in the Sub Control Centre Shepton Mallet for duty as:

- i)   Telephonists (men or women)
- ii)   Messengers (Young men between the ages of 16 and 19.) Apply to the ARP office No 5 Area. J A Garton Sub Controller

27 October 1939

Lighting Offence. Arthur R Marry, Hairdresser, 23 Town Street, Shepton Mallet fined 10/- for permitting a light to be visible from a building during the hours of darkness.

Advert. Shepton Mallet Co-operative Society. Important notice re rationing. Dividend rights fully maintained. Statements have been circulated to the effect that Co-operative Societies will not be allowed to pay dividend on purchases when rationing schemes are in being. These statements are entirely false and baseless.

3 November 1939

The National Deposit Central Social Club has now been running successfully for over three weeks in the rooms over the Market Hall. The club was opened by the National Deposit head office staff now working in Shepton Mallet entirely on their own initiative in order to provide themselves with some place for rest, recreation, comfort and warmth. All communication should be addressed to the Social Secretary at Jardine's Mill.

Wells and Shepton MP Col. A J Muirhead has died in 'tragic circumstances' only in his mid 40s. There was a letter from Col. Garton who had been a friend since Eton.

Advert. Poppy Day. Earl Haig's British Legion Appeal Fund - Wreaths and Crosses from 4/- each. Make 1939 a bumper year and give all you can for our disabled men. Entire proceeds sent to head quarters. Official agents for the District where a large selection may be seen. Thorne and Thorne, High Street Shepton Mallet.

10 November 1939

Advert. War Time Requirements. Gas Mask Carriers assorted colours 2/- and 2/6d. Ration Book Containers and Identity Card Holders 2d each in strong Manila. 'Lumo' Badges to wear at night 1/- each. A Byrt and Sons 47 – 48 High Street Shepton Mallet.

Letter from EH Norman about the 200 Evacuees from the 'very poor districts of London' and the problems of clothing them. 'Boys' overcoats and shoes are badly needed…. Contributions of money, clothing, boots and shoes will be gratefully received by Mrs Nalder representative of the Women's Voluntary Services of Civil Defence, Tall House, Park Road, Shepton Mallet. (Note. Mrs Nalder was the widow of Mr Nalder a prominent local solicitor and citizen who had died in the previous August.)

Below are a few of the memories of the early part of the war by evacuee George Bartlett. George is a member of the Local History group and has been a keen supporter of this project.

A thankful Evacuee

"Lots of memories of the 2nd World War are locked in the mind, but I would like to recall in writing the adventures of one of many evacuees who left London just as the war started. I do recall before we were evacuated, the guns being put into place, shelters being built, and those wondrous Barrage Balloons – I was 8 years of age at the time.

Leaving Paddington Station with the crowds of other children, the thrill of a steam train and being put into the train for a journey to where? Most of us wore labels with our names and carried most likely a pillow case with all our worldly goods. I remember as we sped along the track the song ' Wish me luck as you wave me goodbye,' and to this day it recalls vivid memories.

We eventually arrived at Shepton Mallet High Street station (GWR). I can vaguely recall it being dark. We were then selected to be placed in our billets. My brother and I went to Charlton Road (the houses are no longer there) and stayed with a very nice family.

My brother and I stayed with this family for some time. We were billeted later on to Board Cross owing to the lady having her first baby. After a few further years we split up and I finished up in Evercreech: An incident of pure impulse happened one day. School was out and as we were escaping the gates a lorry went slowly by, there were very few vehicles on the road during the war, we hung onto the tail board. We, three of us, finished up at Milton Clevedon, a distance of a few miles from Stoney Stratton where we were billeted. When we arrived home, an offer of no tea or supper, or a whack with a cane. We all chose the cane. The other memory is of scrumping. This happened where the telephone exchange area is, bottom part of Church Lane. Two of us walked through a gate into an enclosed garden belonging to Mr. Butler (the Florist), filled our pockets with delicious apples, but as we were leaving the garden Mr. Butler appeared at the gate . No escape – offer of visit to the police station or a clip around the ear. We chose the latter."

Another evacuee who stayed locally is Alf Taylor whose children and many grandchildren have no trace of the slight London accent he still retains. He also has memories of the move from London.

"We were at school in Clarkson Street School, Canning Town, London when these red double decker buses came and took us to Paddington Station where we were put onto trains. Most of us were aged between 8 and 12 years old. We were all given a bag with Barley Sugars in it.

The train arrived at Shepton Mallet in the late evening and we were taken along Station Road to the old glove factory which is now part of the Haskin's complex. Local people came to take us to their homes. My brother and I went to Mr and Mrs Bristow at Field View where we were made to feel very welcome.

The next day we all met at the Market Cross when we were told where to go. Some of us went to Kilver Street School where we were taught by Mr Whitock, headmaster and Mr Golding, teacher. Some children were homesick and went back to London.

Four of us passed our 11 plus exam and went to Newquay in Cornwall to the school which had been evacuated from Plaistow in London."

17 November 1939

At Wells petty sessions. Percy Turner an Insurance Agent, Park Road Shepton Mallet pleaded guilty to failing to obscure the front lights on a motor car. Fined 10/-.

Urban District Council. Bowlish Lane in disrepair. The Council not prepared to do anything about it as they thought it was up to the hospital. Mr Pullin disagreed and said that he could remember when it had been maintained by the town. (Note. The course of Bowlish Lane can still be traced as a footpath through the St Peter's Estate on the west side of Shepton.)

The Council was worried about the state of the Factory at Darshill. Barrels etc. scattered around. The matter was taken up with Mr F Bennett. (Note Mr Freddie Bennett had had to give up the Anglo Trading Estate, the former Brewery, to the Air Ministry at the start of the War. He had moved his Cider Mills down to Darshill where they stayed until they closed in the late 1950s. The Air Ministry continued to occupy the Anglo Brewery well after the war, only finally leaving in the early 1960s.

Light Rescue Party Depot – The County Council have approved the adaptation for this purpose of a shed in Mr Pullen's yard.

Chief Fire Officer reports that they are training a party detailed by the National Deposit Friendly Society. Mr Price believed that 60 people were working on one floor at Jardine's Factory and was worried about lack of escape routes.

Gas Masks. Mr Witcombe said it was a disgrace that German Prisoners of War had gas masks but some residents of the town still had not.

24 November 1939

Advert. A Grand Social and Dances organized by St Michael's Entertainment Committee. 'Palais de danse,' Shepton Mallet on Thursday November 30th in aid of evacuated children. Music by Billy Lukins Tor Dance Band. Tickets (and refreshments) 1/6d.

1 December 1939

Women's Volunteer Services. WVS working party meet each week knitting garments for evacuee school children. Smaller clothes sent to Cranmore Hall Maternity Hospital.
    Clinic held three times a week by the Women's Section of the Red Cross
    Members of the Women's Branch of the British Legion knitting comforts for the services.
    Members of the WVS also helping at the Telephone Sub Control office in the Council Hall. Mrs Nalder appears to have been the driving force.

British Legion – Information is received that there are talks about Home Defence Battalions (to replace the called up territorials)

Advert. Friday December 15th 1939, Market Hall, Shepton Mallet. Christmas poultry Show and Sale. 1000 specially fed Christmas Cockerels, Hens, Turkey, Geese and Ducks. Wyndam Laver Auctioneer.

8 December 1939

Mrs Bessie Brown of the King William fined for selling adulterated Whiskey.

Test of the Air Raid Warning Siren in the Council Hall will be made on Tuesday next at 11am.

Whist Drive held in Cannards Grave Church Room on Tuesday with 12 tables in play. Mr WG Norman held the whistle and kept the games going well. (Note. Whist Drives were exceedingly popular at this time with scarcely a week during the winter without notice of at least one drive. The church rooms at Cannards Grave were a regular and seemingly popular venue.

Shepton Mallet Choral Society presided over by Miss E M Thorne unanimously decided to 'Carry on'.

Advert. Ballroom Dancing. Miss Monica Byrt AISTD (Ballroom Branch) West of England Professional Champion begs to announce that she has commenced her Winter Dance Sessions. Private Lessons by appointment. For full particulars apply Miss Byrt, The Rectory, Shepton Mallet. (Note. The Rectory at that time was the very large house demolished in the 1970s to make way for town centre redevelopment.)

15 December 1939

Shepton Mallet Scouts and Wolf Cubs annual general meeting. Report on a good year. A number of evacuees had been drafted in and others had attended other meetings at headquarters on special nights. Also a branch of the pack had been started at Ivy House School. Six scouts had passed their Red Cross exam and valuable assistance had been given to ARP control and to wardens during black out.

The Regal. 'Inspector Hornleigh' starring Gordon Hawker and Alistair Sim.

Shepton Mallet Post Office Christmas 1939. Work will be harder because of reduced trains so post early in the week before Christmas. Sunday 24th One delivery, usual dispatch in the afternoon. Monday 25th Xmas day. One delivery of letters and parcels throughout the district. Country letter boxes will be cleared about the time of delivery.

Rural District Council. Evacuees. A nurse from West Ham had spent a fortnight in the area and stated that the children had benefited considerably because of the attention they were getting.

Special Excursion train from London to Shepton Mallet on December the 17th to enable parents to visit children.

Waterworks protective clothing stored at the premises of Mr Budd.

Urban District Council. Poultry keeping encouraged – even on council estates.

Firefighting. On advice of 29th of November from the Home Office they had dispensed with a whole-time fire officer.

Note. The Fire Station in Shepton Mallet was next to the police station. Throughout the majority of the war it was under the control of local shop keeper Arthur Hobbs who is well remembered. Apparently the first time the fire brigade were called out to deal with an incident following bombing in another town, they discovered that all the fittings on their hoses were incompatible. Something that had to be put right very quickly.

WVS responsible with the billeting officer for evacuees' entertainment at Christmas.

Vandalism in the Park during the blackout. People had been carving in benches and lifting off gates.

A car load of books and magazines for the troops had been donated following an appeal in Shepton Mallet. Taken to the Red Cross in Weston-Super-Mare.

Letters of complaint about cars parked in the Market Place without lights during the blackout. People were bumping into them.

22 December 1939

Children's Christmas treat. 'Few towns have given a more hearty reception to the London children than has Shepton Mallet. Right from the first never-to-be-forgotten-night when the little ones arrived in the drenching rain and blackout there has been ample evidence of a desire to make the young visitors happy and at home.'

Advert. H Britten. The Oldest Established Family Butcher, begs to announce that with his usual good judgment he has purchased the usual supply of Christmas Beef and Wether Mutton. Geese and Turkeys to order. 54 High Street, Shepton Mallet.

The Regal. 'Keep smiling' with Gracie Fields.

Football. Shepton Mallet easy 8 – 0 winners over the CWS Tannery Street.

Letter. From J A Bew, Air Ministry, Shepton Mallet 17/12/39 complaining about rip off charges being made for empty rooms while the staff were away over Christmas. More than a luxury hotel in London. Four girls sharing a room being charged 10/- each.

REGAL
SHEPTON MALLET
PHONE 107

Thur. & Fri. at 7 p.m.   Sat., Matinee at 11 a.m. & 2.30 p.m.   Evening Con. from 5.45 p.m.
Jean Arthur, Melvyn Douglas & Fred McMurray in MY TWO HUSBANDS.
Also Jean Parker and James Dunn in SON OF THE NAVY.

Week Commencing Monday, March 3rd.

MON. & TUES. One House Only at 7 p.m.	THURS. & FRI., One House only at 7.0 p.m.
WEDNESDAY, Matinee 2.30. Evening 7 p.m.	SATURDAY, Special Children's Matinee at 11 a.m. Also Matinee at 2.30. Evening 5.45 continuous. Last performance 8.30 approx.
HARRY KORRIS, FRANK RANDLE, with PERCIVAL MACKEY and his Orchestra in	ARTHUR LUCAN & KITTY McSHANE IN
Somewhere in England	**OLD MOTHER RILEY JOINS UP**
ALSO	ALSO
GREEN HELL WITH	**CONVICTED WOMAN** WITH
Douglas Fairbanks, Jnr. & Joan Bennett.	Rochelle Hudson and Glenn Ford.

BOX OFFICE OPEN FROM 10 a.m. TILL 1 p.m.

Regal – the weekly advertisement.

29 December 1939

Death of Mr A J Allen, eldest son of W H Allen. Funeral in the Cemetery. Killed by a double decker bus in the blackout in Bristol.

Reports of the Christmas celebrations in the local hospitals.

Isolation Hospital 14 patients, Children's Home 26 little ones, West End Institute 127 patients, District Hospital, 11 patients.

Mrs Prince, now over 90 and her daughter Joan Hayter remember the isolation hospital well.

> Mrs Prince lived in Shepton – Cornwall Road throughout the War. Her husband Sid had war exception as he worked in the quarries. He did Fire Warden Duties throughout the war two or three nights a week.
> Mrs Prince had two children Joan and a boy. She also looked after two nephews Ron and Pete who were evacuated from London. Ron had St Vitas Dance and had been in Dartford Hospital. He had to come out when it was needed for soldiers coming back from Dunkirk.
> At one time all four children were in the Isolation Hospital at Shepton. There were three wards: Scarlet Fever, Diphtheria and Consumption. The two nephews went in with Scarlet Fever. The son went in with this as well but it was discovered he actually had Diphtheria. Joan also went in with Diphtheria when she had a sore in her nose.

Children's Christmas Party. 700 evacuated and local children entertained at Waterloo Road senior and junior schools, Kilver Street and Bowlish schools. The community singing went well with the latest hits 'The Siegfried Line' and 'Run Adolf Run.'

The solicitors Nalder Littler and Addleshaw (now Dyne Drewett) replied on behalf of Mrs Brooks against Mr Bew denying the 10/- charge suggested by the girls and that they would like the address of the first class hotel in London.

Chapter 3

1940

- January, Food Rationing began
- April 8, Hitler invaded Denmark and Norway. Britain's expeditionary force to Norway was a shambles and was withdrawn on May 8
- May 10, Chamberlain resigned. Winston Churchill became PM assured of Labour support.
- May 10, Hitler invaded France, Belgium, Luxembourg and the Netherlands.
- May 28, Dunkirk Evacuation began. Success exceeded all expectations, in all 338,226 men were recovered
- July 19, Hitler offered peace. The offer was brushed aside. Debate as to whether Britain, now standing alone, could survive the next few weeks.
- Hitler directed that preparations for the invasion of Britain should commence. The first stage was the destruction of the RAF by the Luffwaffe. The Battle of Britain was on.
- September 17, Hitler postponed invasion as he could not gain air superiority. He now tried to bomb Britain into submission
- September to November – The Blitz.
- December 8, North Africa. The British Army's 7th Armoured Division under General Wavell of 25,000 completed the destruction of the Italian army which collapsed. 40,000 prisoners taken.

1 January 1940

'Wintry weather since Christmastide has been severe and has tried the strength and physical fitness of young and old alike. The former however have been afforded some measure of enjoyment in the Park, where, well wrapped up in mufflers and coats they have enjoyed the lake, which is frozen over to the full. The footpaths too have made gorgeous slides.

Walter A Foxwell, farmer of Middle Thrupe Farm Croscombe, was summoned for permitting a number of cows to be driven on the highway without a light at front and rear.

Shepton Mallet Urban District Council. Notice is hereby given that the Chief Constable having temporarily withdrawn permission for cars without lights to stand in parking places. Until further notice cars cannot be parked during hours of darkness in front of Lloyds Bank in the Market Place Shepton Mallet without conforming with the requirements as to the showing of lights.

Recipe of week – roast rabbit!

12 January 1940

Shepton Mallet Urban District Council. Quibbles over new house numbers in West Shepton.

Evacuees. Very few have gone back to London but more are arriving.

War Charities Committee. Rev A Gribble, Rev Adams, Mr SG Lemon, Mr C B Rodway, W Shepherd, R G Byrt, Miss E M Thorne, Mr E J Hardwidge.

Shepton Mallet British Legion Annual Dinner in the Grammar School. Old soldiers bemoaning that they couldn't get into the services by reason of their age but pointing out that they were doing solid stuff with the ARP.

Shepton Mallet Rural District Council. Doulting Vicarage had been let / requisitioned for a nursery school by the Ministry of Health Regional Inspector for £150.

Major Garton ARP was complaining that the siren was not loud enough. How could he gather the necessary services when he had no method of communicating with them? This may be very important for life saving, they may be needed in Bristol or Yeovil.

19 January 1940

Salvation Army. A New Years free tea was provided for 80 people in the Salvation Army hall in Draycott.

Letter of appeal for ARP's. 'More volunteers are required to keep the Sub Control Centre efficiently manned in Shepton Mallet. Centre for the whole of the ARP services in the area depended on for a preliminary warning of an air raid and to co-ordinate the services if an air raid does occur. No 5 Area ARP, Council Office, Shepton Mallet.'

26 January 1940

An appeal. Will any members of the Mothers Union willing to work once a week at the Military Canteen, Liberal Club from 8.30pm – 10pm please send their name to Donald Wainwright as soon as possible.

National Savings War Campaign. Savings in the Shepton Mallet Urban District for the week ending January 20th 1940 were as follows. Savings Certificates purchased £911 pounds, Defence Bonds Purchased £1,710. Deposited in National Savings Bank £484. Total £3,105. (Note. Although this seems a rather exceptional week there was an almost weekly report on the savings deposited throughout the war.)

Commissioned. Appearing amongst the long list of officers commissioned in the London Gazette dated 23rd January is the name of D M B Durie younger son of Mr and Mrs C Durie. Mr Durie is no stranger to local sportsmen for as a keen rugger man and player of repute he helped Shepton Mallet Rugby Club on many occasions.

The Regal. Charlie Chan in 'Honolulu' the first film with Sidney Toler carrying on the tradition of Chan.

Grow more food. A meeting arranged by the Council to further local food production was held in the Council Hall. In short there was not an allotment holder in the town who could not well have profited by attending the lecture and yet only 11 enthusiasts were present.

Letter from F J E Pullen, Percy Villa supporting 'Grow More Food.' The Society of Friends were supplying seeds at reduced prices to unemployed, widows, impoverished persons and OAPs. Information from W A Witcombe 39 Garston Street.

Advert. England Needs Men. Does this Concern You? Thousands of men are needed – urgently- for the great county army on which England depends for the protection of her railways and roads, her ports and vulnerable points, her industrial and agricultural areas.

This is not a job for young men. It is a job for YOU, the men between 35 – 50 years of age, whether you have previous military experience or not. Your county regiment, like every other, now has its Home Defence Battalion. By joining it at your nearest recruiting office you will set free a younger man to serve his country overseas and you will find good company and a Man's Job of Work. England again needs men. Enlistment for the duration of the war. Details with British Legion Branches. (Note. This was not the Home Guard but an attempt to recruit older full-time soldiers.)

1 February 1940

Somerset Comforts Fund. A second parcel of knitted comforts has been sent to Taunton by members of the Shepton Mallet Women's Voluntary Service Detachment. We understand that a third consignment is almost ready. Mrs Nalder will be glad to receive the names of any who are willing to help in the military canteen which it is hoped to open shortly.

Regal. 'Jamaica Inn' starring Charles Haughton and Maureen O'Hara.

Advert, For sale. Pure farm Cider Old and New, Delivered, Stone, Lamberts Hill.

Advert. Huge stocks of Rudge – Whitworth, BSA, Elswick and Sun lightweight Cycles now on show at Vowles, 55 High Street, Shepton Mallet.

9 February 1940

Advert. Edwin Henley's, Costumiers and Milliners. Annual Winter Sale, Starts today (Friday). Prices have risen and are still rising but we have big stocks ordered before September and while these last we shall be happy to sell during the sale at Reduced Pre- War Prices.

Ancient Order of Druids. To the large number of visitors to the town it may not be generally known that it possesses quite one of the most ancient Lodges of Druidism in the County. It is number 412 in the Union and the brethren meet on alternate Tuesdays at the Bell Hotel. To those who have now come to reside in the town and who belong to a branch of the Ancient Order the officials extend a most hearty invitation to join them.

Regal. 'Suez' with Tyrone Power and Loretta Young.

Shepton Mallet Rural District Council. The return home of unaccompanied children (evacuees) has reached about 50% in Shepton Mallet District.

16 February 1940

Town Band Meeting to report a successful 1939, Mr H Weston in the Chair, Mr Short Secretary, Mr Pullen Treasurer, Mr C E Burnell President, Mr R Marsh Bandmaster. Unfortunately the band has had to face the loss of several members who have been called to The Colours and also the loss of the Band Room. They are now using the Mid Somerset Agricultural Society office in Park Road.

Shepton Mallet Urban District Council. Still debating the house numbers in West Shepton, and after dark parking in the Market Place. Street lighting at £1 per lamp for 15 Watt lamp not to be entertained. Decided it would be too expensive to have ARP controlled blue light in the Market Place. Mr Pullen was disappointed.

Swimming Baths. The Military are using the shower and a dressing room and are providing at their own expense the necessary fuel as well as a man to look after the plant.

The Food Office is being moved from the Council Hall to the Museum Room, the museum being closed for the time being.

23 February 1940

Bull sale. Mid Somerset Shorthorn Breeders Association, improved quality compared to previous years. John Day of Stone House, East Pennard gained an award for each of his entries.

Regal. 'Feather in your nest' with George Formby.

Advert. Ploughing and all kinds of Agricultural work all done with horses, apply J Denning, Woodside, Neighbourne.

For sale, New Galvanised Chicken Coops. E Hobley & Son, Ironmongers, Shepton Mallet.

Allotment Gardens to let in centre of town and at Charlton. Apply L J Allen. Garage, Commercial Road.

Advert. Cook General Wanted early in March. Three maids kept Mrs Finch Shepton Mallet. (This was probably the wife of Dr Finch, after whom Finch Close is named. At that time they lived in what is now the Shrubbery Hotel.)

1 March 1940

Advert. To Knitters Working Parties etc. Knitting wools will probably be much advanced in price in the near future. Buy now. We hold stocks of all service colours. Thorne and Thorne, High Street, Shepton Mallet.

Letter. Sir, I desire to support the appeal made by the Ministry of Supply for the recovery of waste materials which are urgently required for war purposes e.g. bones, paper, scrap metal and rags. Each of these plays an important part in our war economy and every ton that can be recovered for use in industry sets free shipping space and foreign exchange for imports from abroad …….. your obedient servant, Bath, HM Lieutenant, Longleat, Warminster.

Tom Vincent the well known elderly farmer of Lower Wraxall Farm in the Police Court for selling adulterated milk. Tests suggested that water was leaking from the taps on the milking machine. He denied neglecting mending it. In September last, one of his men had been called up and since then he had looked after the machine himself. When the machine was stripped down it was found a pipe had cracked in the frosts. The whole problem was down to frosts and he was not aware of it. The bench knew Mr Vincent as a man of good character and were satisfied it was not done intentionally. Defendant fined £1 on each of two counts and two guineas advocates fee.

Shepton Mallet District Hospital Annual Meeting. President Mr C E Burnell. Existing Trustees Mr A F Somerville, Mr J A Garton and Col Spenser. Mr Ingleton Rowe elected to fill the vacancy left by the death of Mr Nalder. Berkeley Hall Auditor.

Football. Waterloo Road Boys School v Highbury (London) Junior XI evacuated to Midsomer Norton, lost 2 – 3. The whole game was fought out in excellent spirit and enjoyed by both players and spectators alike.

Advert. (Note. This is one of many that appeared during the war in space provided by the Brewers Society. Most were on similar themes but well worth a read.)
"Hush, Hush. If you wished to draw a distinction between Britain and Germany it might well be on sense of humour. The new posters telling us to 'hush hush' warning us not to help the enemy by careless gossip – are an example of our incorrigible cheerfulness. Imagine Goebbels putting up posters of that sort in Germany!
You may see the same good humour in the pub. Indeed it is difficult to tell that we are engaged in a major war, when glasses of beer are filled and a game of darts is going. Beer must have a lot to do with our health and humour. It is a hearty drink. It makes for good health and good appetite. Its' barley malt and hops the very foundation of cheerfulness.
And that cheerfulness is going to win the war. A great country does not advance to victory beneath the shadow of a Gestapo. It wins cheerfully – or not at all. And in the pubs these days around the glasses of beer you may see how cheerful Britain is. Stick to beer. Beer is best."

8 March 1940

Appeal by Mr Gordon Perry secretary of the Mid Somerset Agricultural Society for people to continue subscriptions to recover funds lost by the show cancelled when the bulk of expenditure had been made. (Note. The Mid Somerset Show of 1939 had to be cancelled at the last minute with the tents already up due to the declaration of war two days before it was to be held.)

AGM of Shepton Mallet Cricket Club. 'Play to continue' Hare and Hounds Hotel.

15 March 1940

Air Raid Alarm. A test of the air raid siren was made on Tuesday morning, when it was heard to very good effect. Later in the evening there was a full dress rehearsal of the various ARP organizations when a very useful practice was fulfilled.

Note. West Shepton Resident Ken Norman can remember the air raid siren tests well. In the early part of the war he worked on the bacon counter at Levers which was in the High Street where Dredge and Male is now. The bacon counter looked out across the back. The siren was near the Anglo. He says that when it went off he got the full blast.

Mr William Hobbs of Hobbs Bros died having traded in the town for 65 years.

Advert. Midland Bank advertising Wills and Trusts in Peace and War'. Midland Bank

Executor and Trustee Co Ltd. (Note. From here on there are numerous advertisements from the Banks trying to cash in on people's fears.)

Shepton Mallet Urban District Council reported the receipt of a certificate from the Military Authorities for the opening of the cinema on Sundays. It had been deemed that the town had a high level of military presence. The Town Councillors were very hot under the collar that they had no say in imposing terms and conditions. Some wanted the proceeds to go to charity. (Note. In fact it doesn't looks as if the Regal ever regularly opened as a cinema on Sunday's throughout the war though it was sometimes used for special concerts or variety events – usually for charity.)

Regal 'Gunga Din starring Cary Grant and Douglas Fairbanks Jnr.

Advert. Girls wanted – we accept learners for machine sewing of leather gloves, paid whilst learning. Soon able to earn good wages. Apply to W E Gloves Ltd, Waterloo Road, Shepton Mallet. (Note. From the tone of advertisements it was becoming apparent that there was less labour available.)

Advert. Wanted Temporary clerk to the ARP. Salary £1 - £2 a week depending on experience.

Advert. Dig for Victory and increase your crops by using our Horticultural Manure – recommended for Potatoes and all Garden Products. Allen & Foster Ltd.

22 March 1940

Regal. "The Story of Vernon and Irene Castle' starring Fred Astaire and Ginger Rogers.

Shepton Mallet ARP was amongst squads from all over the area who went to Bristol for an exercise to deal with an imaginary air raid.

29 March 1940

Eastertide. The festival locally passed off very quietly; there was not even the usual run of railway excursions to break the monotony of everyday routine. There were however many visitors to the town – parents chiefly came to see their evacuee children.

Advert. Shepton Mallet Urban District Council. Waste Paper. Persons requiring sacks for the collection of Waste Paper may obtain same from the Surveyors Department Council Offices. Arrangements will be made to collect these when full.

Advert. Lorry Driver Required. Apply Showerings Ltd, Shepton Mallet.

5 April 1940

The Circus comes to town. Paulo's famous London Circus will pay its first visit to Shepton Mallet and will pitch the big top in Cook's Paddock on Saturday next for one day only…..
Featuring Asian Elephants, 6 Argentinos the fastest riders in the world, trapeze flyers, acrobats, monkeys, dogs and pigeons, dancing horses, midget ponies, famous clowns etc. The finest tonic you can get is to visit the Circus. (Note. Cooks Paddock was off Petticoat Lane. It had long been the stopping place of fairs and circuses.)

Mary C Williams of Cannards Grave Inn was fined 10/- for failing to get an alien to complete form AR.E. An Hungarian had stayed at the Inn on the 27th of October 1939. (Note. Hungary was not actually in the war at that time.)

Shepton Mallet Rural District Council. Supplementary Scheme for potential further evacuees. 4500 circulars had been sent out but only 150 householders were willing to take more children.

12 April 1940

Shepton Mallet Urban District Council. Utilization of Waste Foodstuffs for Pig and Poultry Feeding. In a recent circular from the Ministry of Supply Local Authorities are urged to co-operate in the collection of waste foodstuffs. Committee making enquiries to ascertain what is being done.

Mr Pullen asked questions about the control of food and fuel. He knew of a case where poor people with illness in the house were without coal for two days and were unable to get any. He asked why with coal pits so close to the town could our local merchants not get any. Mr Jordan the local fuel control officer thought that the Ministry must have taken the coal from local pits to cover shortages in other parts of the country.

Letter. From the Newsagents of the Town A Byrt and Sons, W Chalker and G Biggins explaining late delivery of newspapers asking for patience and understanding. New regulations of the County Council prohibited the use of school boys and war had taken the most eligible young men and it is almost impossible to replace the boys.

Rose Ware (née Brooks) can remember that after leaving school her first job was delivering papers – she did two and a half rounds with two big bags, She is quite a small woman and it must have been quite tough for a girl of 14/15. She started her round in Board Cross, went out to the GWR Station and the signal box. Then on to Compton Road and Field House – she says Sir Francis Berryman was a miserable old sod who told her off for being late when it was the trains late bringing the papers. She then went back to Board Cross to collect the second bag. She did Westfield and Cornwall Road out to West Shepton and down Coombe Lane. Her Mum got her a cup of tea when she got home which she really needed.

19 April 1940

Charlton House Gardens are to be thrown open to the public on Sunday 21st April on behalf of the Somerset Nurses Association by the kind permission of C E Burnell Esq.

Advert. Shepton Mallet Urban District Council. Swimming Bath Attendants. Applications invited from married couples.

Advert. "You Were Warned' Get some coal in!' Coal merchant Harold Oatley pointing out how good his warnings had been last winter and suggesting people get some coal in over the summer.

26 April 1940

ARP Notice. Inspection of respirators by ARP Wardens will be started forthwith in Shepton Mallet. Residents are asked to give every assistance to the Wardens who will instruct them on what to do if their respirators are defective in any way.

Regal. 'Stage Coach' starring Claire Trevor and John Wayne.

Advertisement. H G Fish have moved to 24 High Street, Shepton Mallet. Lately occupied by Mr G Vincent. Tailor, Clothier, Hosier, Hatter and Juvenile Outfitter.

3 May 1940

Smoking Concert – An informal smoking concert was held by the Red Cross detachment in the Council Hall on Wednesday evening. The programme included Mr Foster – monologues, Pte Jones - baritone songs, Pte Noyce - violin solos (accompanist Miss Gay Pursey), Miss Thorne - dialect readings, Pte Jones - accordion solos, the Misses Hall and Gordon - dancing, Mr J Phelps - songs, Pte Mayer - pianoforte solos, Mrs Bodley - soprano songs. Sketches by members of the Men's Red Cross Detachment.

Regal. 'All at sea' starring Sandy Powell.

Advert. Assistant Laundress Required, West End House. Resident staff at these institutions receive allowances in lieu of rations during annual holidays. Particulars from the Clerk of the County Council, County Hall Taunton.

10 May 1940

Shepton Mallet (Pigeon) Homing Society opened the season on Saturday with a race from Ashchurch 59 miles.

Shepton Mallet and District Wheelers Club Racing Section. The racing section of the club participated in their first actual team trial of the season on Sunday 28th April.

Goodbyee! Without the slightest warning and devoid of all ceremony a heavy motor vehicle in negotiating the High Street corner turning into Paul Street contemptuously swept aside the traffic lights by the Westminster Bank together with the whole box of tricks. Constables of the Special Police War Reserve have since been controlling the traffic there.

Cricket Shepton Mallet 101. Midsomer Norton II 25 all out. P Hodges 5 wickets for 5 runs,

Advert. Next Saturday 18th May. Genuine and unreserved sale of furniture and effects The Old Grammar School House. Wainwright Laver and Crees on behalf of Mr J A Evans for whom they have sold the house. (Note. This is the extremely attractive historic house on the north side of the church which until recently has been used as the Rectory.)

Advert. Tomato Plants for sale, Good sturdy, pot grown, suitable for cold houses. 2/6d per doz, Gane, 4 Draycott Road.

17 May 1940

Advance announcement. A Fete will be held in the grounds of Summerleaze House by kind permission of C R Wainwright on Wednesday June 19th in aid of the War Charities Fund. (Note. Summerleaze House was on the site of the former ICI/Huntsman factory.)

Shepton Mallet Urban District Council. (after a considerable period of debate) Agreed to Tarmac Bowlish Lane as far as the hospital gate for £150.

Summerleaze House.

Concern about Council House Tenants who have taken in lodgers without permission. (Note. it was very obvious that given the huge influx of people accommodation in Shepton Mallet was very much at a premium and many people were tempted to cash in.)

Park – The Committee recommended that subject to the Band giving not less than eight performances during the present season they should be paid the sum of £10 as before.
    The head teachers have been asked kindly to do what they can by instruction in school and otherwise with a view to the lessening of the damage so frequently done to the flowers and shrubberies. (Note. A campaign that appears to still be ongoing!)

Swimming baths opened for the season on 11th May

ARP. Miss Thorne asked if 'the powers that be' were satisfied with the ARP turnout last week. Mr Lintern ' I cannot give information on everything that was done. There were a few things not quite as they ought to have been…..' Mr Pullen 'On the whole the practice was fairly satisfactory, and after all a practice is a practice….. I know one or two bloomers occurred but that is bound to happen.' Miss Thorne……'May I ask Mr Lintern if we can have some more practice.' Mr Lintern, 'I hope that we shall.'
    Mr Price said that one of the things the ARP practice had disclosed was the fact that we

were unfortunately under-staffed in the matter of first aid workers. There was a dearth of volunteers in Shepton Mallet. At present there were only 9 first aid men. Need some older men to come forward as younger men being called up which will leave us with nothing.

Mr Pullen. In the demolition section you cannot have old men. It is dangerous work. Last week only five men turned out and some of these will be called up. It was decided to look for men aged 35 –55.

Regal. Louis Hayward and Joan Bennett in 'The Man In the Iron Mask.'

24 May 1940

Parent's visits to the wounded. Cheap rail tickets. The use of railway concession vouchers has been extended to include mothers, fathers, sisters and brothers who wish to visit unmarried soldiers lying ill or wounded in British hospitals.

Local Defence Volunteers. Somerset British Legion saying they are keen to support the scheme and pointing out their branches represent experienced bodies of men to convert to military units. (Between the lines it read as if they were very disappointed that it hadn't been handed to them to organize)

Local Defence Volunteers – the beginning. By George Witcombe as told to his daughter and son in law, Local History Group member Ken Moores

"Arthur Whittle and myself were both employed at the Charlton Brewery and were fully aware that we were not exempt from the National Call-up. However in the meantime we decided to join the Local Defence Volunteer Organisation.

The Headquarters of the LDV was the quarry office of Wainwright's at Windsor Hill, Shepton Mallet, and a Mr Norgrove the Manager of the Charlton Cross Roads garage was Captain in charge and Albert Dix a quarry foreman was our Sergeant in charge. I think that Stan Woolard may also have been a member but I am not sure about this.

Our uniform at that time was quite basic, made up of canvas suiting and ill fitting. Not much attention was paid to size and I finished up with a canvas top with the neck far too large and trousers far too long. On querying this I was informed that on no account was this uniform to be altered in any way as when I was eventually called up to the regular army this uniform would have to be handed on to someone else. All had to be tucked up – sleeves, trousers etc. However my wife did alter it!! The badge of authority was a wide white armband with black letters L.D.V.

At that time our equipment was a couple of shot guns, air rifles and anything that could be acquired in the form of a truncheon.

We went out on nightly patrols and at that time invasion was always a threat and our nightly route to patrol was on the Somerset and Dorset Railway line. We would proceed through the two Winsor Hill tunnels and up over the other side of Ham and continue in twos spread out over the fields. We would return over the top of the tunnels and proceed on the S & D line to a point halfway along the Kilver Street Viaduct. At the halfway point we met by arrangement with the S & D station personnel who used to patrol down the line towards

Evercreech.

The highlight of the LDV was the news that rifles from the USA had arrived for us at the local Police station and we were ordered to go to the police station and unpack these rifles and collect ammunition for them. Arthur and I had time off from the Brewery to visit the Police station and we saw these packing cases which were unopened and proceeded to jemmy them open. We did not know what to make of the arms at first glance as all we could see was thick heavy grease. Anyhow, we tentatively put our hands in and found the rifles. They were a P 17 model firing 300mm cartridges. We also collected at that time the canvas bandoleer (cartridge holder) holding 50 rounds. Before we could use the rifles we had to thoroughly remove the grease by taking the rifle apart and putting the parts in boiling water and also with the use of numerous 'pull throughs' clean the rifle barrel. The rifle and the ammunition had to be kept at home – mine was propped up in the bedroom behind the door.

We then attended firing practice on an established range at Beacon Wood. Starting at 200 yards the marksmanship was very good but as we extended the range it was eventually discovered that no hits were being made at all! On this being queried we walked from the 650 yd position towards the butts carefully studying the ground and found a line of bullets which had not reached the target, The eventual answer to this was the fact that these rifles and ammunition had been in store for an unknown number of years by the American Army and the charges had leaked away.'

The LDV was superseded by the Home Guard and they had much better uniforms and equipment. I was called up into the army in July 1940."

24 May 1940 (cont)

Message from the Archbishop of Canterbury. "The full glory of war is upon us. At any moment it may reach over our own doors……. So I bid you all keep calm and resolute in the midst of struggle. Be not distressed by disappointment or even reverses."

Even in this issue where it is apparent that the war is hotting up, the main front page long report is on the AGM of Shepton Mallet Nursing Association.

Advert. Motor Coach Tours Every Sunday Evening. 6.50 Circular Tour 1/6d. 4.00 Longleat and Shearwater 2/6d. Fry & Son, Stratton-on-Fosse.

31 May 1940

Shepton Mallet Rural District Council. Local Authorities being charged with the responsibility of removing carcasses (contaminated or otherwise) other than food animals killed on the Highway. Inspector instructed to collaborate with National ARP Animals Committee.

Air Raid Casualties. District Council to undertake work of recording and notifying air raid casualties.

A day of prayer. Members of the Urban District Council attended a service at the Parish Church on Sunday, the day set apart as one for National Prayer. Other bodies attending were Shepton Mallet Fire Brigade and Auxiliaries, ARP Wardens, Red Cross Nurses and members of the Men's First Aid Detachment, Women's Section British Legion, Girl Guides and Cubs.

Kathleen Joy Eames, Old Grammar School House and Gladys Templeman, 2 Church Lane fined 10/- each for causing light to be visible from the outside.

Letter in paper from Mr W A Price 63 High St, Shepton Mallet on the urgent need for first aid volunteers. ' It is YOUR mothers, wives, sisters and children that we have been formed to care for and you must realize NOW that your responsibility is as great if not greater than ours.'

7 June 1940

'Home and Welcomed. A Shepton Man's Experience. A Shepton man of the BEF writing home says 'Just a few lines to let you know that I arrived back in England safely after a very severe time, especially at the port of embarkation. Never mind we got back ..... we have to be reorganized before we do anything else…. As a matter of fact the people all the way from our station of arrival the whole way here gave us food, chocolate, cigarettes and tea, cheering and welcoming us home. It was very good and it inspired us more so to fight for freedom and win."

> Note. Call me a cynic but this strikes me very much of a piece of propaganda to keep the national spirit up in the face of the Dunkirk evacuation. National news. 400,000 now in the Local Defence Force.

Former Home Guard officer Alan Hoskins can recall the arrival of the troops from Dunkirk back to Shepton Mallet. They came into Weymouth and were put onto trains and taken off at Shepton. They were filthy and there was mud and dirt everywhere. (No comparisons with a wet Glastonbury festival please.) He says there were a lot from Scotland known as the 'kosbies.' (Kings Own Scottish Borderers) Apparently they broke the windows of an Ice Cream Shop in the town as they thought it may have something to do with Italians.

> The soldiers were lying all around Collett Park and in the Market Place totally exhausted. Alan has been told that Bill Hayes the landlord of the Bunch of Grapes bought them out a barrel of beer.

Kings Moving Message. Disaster into Triumph. A moving message of admiration and sympathy for the heroes of the Flanders rearguard battle has been received from the King by the Prime Minister Mr Winston Churchill.

> "I wish to express my admiration of the outstanding skill and bravery shown by the services and the Merchant Navy in the evacuation of the British Expeditionary Force from Northern France. The measure of its success greater than we dared hope…..
> We think with heartfelt sympathy of the loss and sufferings of those brave men whose self-sacrifice has turned disaster into triumph."

14 June 1940

Shepton Mallet Urban District Council. Collett Avenue. Weeds on the vacant building plot are again causing annoyance and the owner has been asked to agree to the Council having the weeds cut at her expense.

Lots of directives to the ARP – not all sufficiently practical to be put into operation.

Worry about the possibilities of Air Raids on schools. The only protection is to get under the desks. The Council understood that the County Architect was coming to go into matters.

Lance Corporal Harry Sweet 39 who had lived in Shepton Mallet before the war had been killed in an accident when controlling traffic in Frome. He had only returned with the BEF to this country Friday last. Mr Sweet before joining the forces had been the AA patrol man at Cannards Grave for 11 years.

Advert. Shepton Mallet Waterworks Company asking people not to leave hose pipes running overnight.

21 June 1940

Notice. Shepton Mallet Area Schools' Sports, Grammar School Field, Friday June 28th. Racing, Hurdling, Jumping, Team Games.

Garden Fete at Summerlease, War Charities Benefit. In the pleasant grounds of Summerleaze kindly lent by Mr C R Wainwright on Wednesday afternoon it was as if the tension of the past year had suddenly ceased and if, as of old, one and all met in happy social intercourse. The pretty grounds and Rose Garden lend themselves admirably for such an occasion.
> Mr S G Lemon Chairman of the War Charities Committee presided and in the unavoidable absence of the Chairman and the Vice Chairman of the Urban Council Miss Thorne welcomed Mrs K Durrant, better known to Shepton as Miss Dolly Wainwright.
> Children of the Convent gave excellent entertainment in the Rose Garden and a concert was given in the garage.
> The gross taking amounted to approximately £200.

Shepton Mallet Swimming Club Inter Club Contest. Diving display by the Greenbank Club of Street. Polo match with grim determination. Won 3 –1 but 'all in' by the finish.

Regal. Dickey Lupino and Fred Emney in 'Just William'

Advert. The head pest problem. Since the evacuation of children in the early days of the war the subject of head pests has been treated as a social disgrace whereas all children are liable to pick up Pediculus Humus Capitis despite utmost cleanliness.
> Recommend short hair and washing with Jeyes Fluid.

Voluntary Land Club. Hoped for volunteers who will visit farms to help in their spare time. Run by the Urban District Council.

28 June 1940

Miss Watkins has taken over the old established Chemists Business Formally carried on by Mr A W Halsted at 53 High Street, Shepton Mallet. Dispensing private and health Insurance. Toilet goods, films and all medical supplies.

Shepton Mallet Rural District Council. R Hobhouse Chair (presumably Colonel Garton had rejoined forces.) A hostel equipped to cope with Evacuees now complete, handyman and Cook housekeeper appointed. Equipped to deal with up to 50.

Fourth evacuation scheme contemplates another 1000 children and helpers arriving in the Shepton Mallet District.

South West Air Raids Victims report. Monday night in a south west town. Five dead and many hurt, fires started and private houses damaged.

Air raid censorship explained. 'Bombs were dropped on Blankshire in an enemy raid during the night;' a phrase to become familiar 'Keep the Nazi's Guessing'. Reports are vetted to make sure no information is included which could help the enemy drop his bombs more accurately next time.

People were warned against gossiping in the cinema or pub.

Advert. Lost, Royal Signal Cap Badge with pin at back (brooch-like) Small reward. Mrs Hedley Dodimead, Charlton, Shepton Mallet.

5 July 1940

Sunday Schools Outing. Blessed with true July weather on Wednesday, the children attending the Congregational and Wesleyan Sunday Schools journeyed by train to Weston-super-Mare for their annual outing and spent an enjoyable day. Accompanying the party were the Rev & Mrs Williams and the Rev A E Laws. Home was safely reached at 10pm.

12 July 1940

Shepton Mallet Urban District Council. Street Parties for First Aid and Fire. 20 stirrup pumps had been purchased for 24/6d each for use by parties formed for streets or other areas. It was left to Mr Lintern as Head Warden to get wardens together with a view to organizing suitable parties.

Mr Lintern said that 20 stirrup pumps was not enough. He recommended the purchase of another 50.

No response to press notice asking for Volunteer Farm Labour as suggested by the Somerset War Agricultural Executive.

Waste Paper arrangements now made whereby with the help of the WVS and Boy Scouts and Girl Guides the collection of waste paper from every house in the town should be assured.

Council Offices. The Council Hall home of both Shepton Mallet UDC and RDC. Pictured before demolition in the 1960s.

Recommendation to partition the Council Hall for Offices. Mr Price protested about doing anything which would interfere with social functions.

> Mr Pullen, 'As against that I think it is entirely wrong at the present time to congregate people together; in fact I think that we as a Council should consider how not to bring large numbers together at all.
>
> Mr Hall I am definitely against dances.
>
> (Note. We here see a two-fold issue. The work of Councils had expanded beyond belief and finding room for offices was a problem. However the anti social gathering feeling was not one that gained momentum. In fact quite the reverse would appear to be the case.)

Railway. Members believed the light from trains may serve as a guide to enemy aircraft; a letter on the subject has been sent to the Ministry of Home Security.

Regal. Edward G Robinson in 'Confessions of a Nazi Spy'.

Advert. Dispel your War Blues by visiting Lord John Sanger's Royal Command Circus, Shepton Mallet (Cook's Paddock) Tuesday 16th. 'The cheeriest war time show.'

19 July 1940

Don't go Bomb Sight-seeing. In recent raids over the south west bombs have been dropped in open country. Everyone should know that they can be fined £50 for trespassing on agricultural land on which is growing any crop other than grass.

> There has been an instance of an entire wheat crop of 25 acres being completely ruined by being trampled on by sightseers.
>
> Hindrance to ARP work has also been caused by sightseers in towns.

Mrs Prince who was a mother with two young children and two evacuated nephews can remember the bombings and plane crashes. They were obviously of great interest.

> The Princes had an Anderson shelter at Cornwall Road. They only used it twice as they got used to the bombs. 'The kids used it as a den.' They like watching the bombings over Bristol – 'like fireworks'
>
> When a plane crashed at Maesbury the children were told not to take any bits. Mrs Prince saw a small boy with a bit. A soldier told him to put it down, 'shan't,' said the boy. The soldier pointed a gun at him and the little boys brother said ' If you shoot him I'll get my father up to see to you.'
>
> Mrs Prince and family cycled out and about to see the crash sites, Maesbury, Castle Cary Station (the nearest bombing fatalities) and Doulting.

George Bartlett as an evacuee also has memories of the crashes.

> "As many people will recall, bombs were dropped onto Shepton Mallet. One area was Bullimore Farm where a bridge was bombed and destroyed. This carried the rail traffic to Charlton Station (Somerset and Dorset). Some of the surrounding fields were bombed and it was great fun looking for shrapnel a few days later.
>
> I remember a German plane crashing at Maesbury Ring. We were taken up to see this plane crash and walked from Board Cross to Maesbury Ring and back again. This really was a great adventure. One more of many memories, this being a dog fight over

the Collett Park when the townspeople were attending a war day. The German Plane was eventually shot down. The empty shell cases landing almost hit Mr Dunkerton while he was gardening in Board Cross next door to where I was billeted."

Advert. ARP. Now a vital need. Specially prepared Gum strip for sticking to Glass. Transparent Window Fluid. Sand bags, 1 inch wire mesh. C Amor all your ARP supplies, The Wall Paper and Paint Store, 27 Draycott Road Shepton Mallet.

Wanted Boys and Girls for work in Brewery. Apply Showerings Ltd, Shepton Mallet.

Shepton Mallet and the Most Secret Auxiliary Units of World War II – Tim Wray

Over the past few years there has been much media interest in unearthing the 'Secret Army' which operated in England during the war. Ordinary men sworn to long term total secrecy who had been trained in 'terrorist activities' to make life difficult for the Germans if they were to invade. They kept their secrets well for many years and even now finding information is extremely difficult.

Tim Wray of Shepton Mallet has carried out a substantial piece of research into this subject for his Open University studies. We are very thankful to him for permission to reproduce such a significant portion of his work.

"In Somerset, around 350 men were actively involved in the Auxiliary Units patrols in 44 patrols operating from around 50 hidden bases. The resistance operation in Somerset was run as two distinct areas, with each area under the command of a Scout Officer with a Scout Section of 14 men to instruct the Auxiliary Unit patrols and help construct the Operational Base. Captain Ian Fenwick of the Kings Royal Rifle Corps, and later Commanding Officer of 1 SAS, was the Army officer entrusted with establishing the guerrilla network in the county.

The Scout Section for North and East Somerset was based in the stables of Southill House, West Cranmore, a few miles east of Shepton Mallet. This unit was responsible for instructing and assisting the Auxiliary Unit patrols in the Yeovil, Frome, Bath, Long Ashton, Weston-super-Mare, and Wells Battalion areas. Its first Scout Officer was Lt John A McCue of the Wiltshire Regiment. In 1941 he was replaced by Lieutenant Keith W. Salter of the 6th Battalion Somerset Light Infantry. In those days, the owner of Southill House was Colonel Huntley Gordon Spencer, T.D., D.L, J.P, an ex - North Somerset Yeomanry officer, and Road Reconstruction quarry owner. He got very inquisitive about the activities of the Scout Section until Lt McCue told him to quieten down and made him sign the Official Secrets Act.

The Scout Section team was drawn from the Welsh Regiment, and included Sergeant Freddy Chapman (a well - known Wells hotelier after the war), Ron Garnham, Tommy Webster (who later became Mayor of Wells), Privates Gracey, Griffiths, Kitts, Rootes and Driver Townley of the RASC. The men were billeted in the stables at Southill House, and they took it in turns to cook. Lt Salter was billeted with Mr and Mrs T Gane in Lynnfield Guest House, half way between Doulting and Cranmore. Mrs Gane was, by all accounts, an excellent cook. The Scout Section personnel were attached to the military prison in Shepton Mallet for pay and rations, and drew petrol for the Motor Transport from local garages.

The men of the Scout Section had to build their own underground Operational Bases. The first was in Cranmore Woods, which was large enough to accommodate 10 bunks, all the Section explosives, 14 days worth of rations and a keg of Navy rum. A couple of Observation Posts were built nearby, smaller in size than the OB, but both also hidden below ground. These were linked to the OB by field telephones. Cranmore Woods was an area the Scout Section used to teach the civilians in the patrols how to build and camouflage their own OBs. The Cranmore Scouts had another OB, hidden in a particularly good location on the railway embankment at Bramble Ditch near Doulting. According to Mr Keith Padfield, who grew up at Brottens Farm during the war, there were also two Observation Posts in Bramble Ditch, part of a small network of trenches dug into the land, overlooking the road bridge and railway line. It remains unknown whether the Cranmore Scout Section OB in Bramble Ditch and the two Observation Posts 450 yards away were in any way connected, but this possibility has to be seriously considered. Once the German Invasion had come, the 'Cromwell' alert would have sounded, and the men in the Scout Section would have gone to ground, lying up during the day in the OB, only emerging at night to make an attack. As a roving daytime observer was not yet standard operating procedure in the Auxiliary Units, so a static observer was needed to watch for suitable targets. Where better than high above a railway cutting? Mr Padfield remembers that the men who used the Observation Posts sometimes drove a big old quarry lorry onto the bridge and chained it there, effectively putting the bridge out of action. It is thought likely that the lorry was packed full of explosives, which when detonated would have destroyed the bridge and put the railway out of action.

Strangely, all this secret activity was happening less than a mile from another wartime secret operation – the Meacon station near Doulting. German bombers flew into Britain from France following radio beams directing the aircraft onto the target. The Meacon or Masking Beacon received the enemy radio beam at one station, and re-transmitted the same signal several miles away, sending the planes off track. The signals received at Doulting, by the RAF radio counter measures personnel Reg Parkinson, 'Slim' Wood, and others, were re-transmitted at Lympsham.

It is known that the Cranmore Scouts abandoned the Bramble Ditch OB, and moved to a very good base on Creech Hill, outside Bruton. Just why the men chose to relocate remains a mystery, but it might have had something to do with Bert Williams, farmer and owner of Bramble Ditch. Even today, he is remembered as a 'bit of a case, who talked a lot, and wasn't the kind of man to keep a secret long.' Perhaps he spotted the soldiers on his land or discovered the location of the underground OB, and from then on was considered a security risk.

There was an Auxiliary Units patrol based at Bruton, led by Captain Albert Harry 'Dickie' Hunt, farmer of Dropping Lane Farm, Bruton. This patrol worked from three underground Operational Bases, one high up on Creech Hill outside Bruton, another in Raggs Copse, a small wood on farmland belonging to Dickie Hunt, and a reserve OB buried in Milton Wood, Milton Clevedon.

Wartime schoolboy Robin Dunford and his pals Nobby Pitt and Tom Green knew all about the Milton Wood base. Exploring in the woods one day the three boys came upon an underground concrete bunker, and venturing below ground found bottles with candles in, and about six bunks set up along one wall. Robin Dunford had tried to find this hide again on another occasion, but was unable to find the entrance. The Auxiliary Unit men who used the OB realised that unauthorised visitors had paid a visit, and incorrectly assumed that it was boys from the King's School were responsible. Apparently the trap-door was carefully modified to prevent another security breach, and the method of entry was to insert a long metal key of a yard in length into a particular broken tree stump, and lift the catch.

The hide on Creech Hill was a huge cavernous 'Elephant' shelter, built by a party from the Royal Engineers. Inside was sleeping space for up to 25 men, and enough stores and food to last for a month. Scout Section Sergeant Ron Garnham was good at making furniture, and it was he who made the trap door for the Creech Hill OB. It slid up and down instead of tilting as was usual. Just like the Milton Wood OB, this Creech Hill hide was also 'found' by a schoolboy, the son of the farmer at Creech Hill. The men of the Bruton Patrol frightened the boy into silence by telling him he would be thrown in jail if he talked. After the Auxiliary Unit stand - down on 31 December 1944, the Creech Hill OB was blown in.

The OB at Raggs Copse, Dropping Lane Farm was much smaller affair, with access to it via a hole dug into the side of a pond. The entrance was simply covered over with a straw bale.

Part of the secret Bruton patrol were two men from Shepton Mallet; Albert Edward 'Bert' Baker, the farmer at Ivy House Farm, and one of his farm workers, Archie John Roberts. These two men would regularly drive over to Bruton, in the farm truck, to train as saboteurs. The unit would meet up either in the outbuildings at 'Dickie' Hunt's farmhouse, or in one of the pubs in Bruton High Street. Archie Roberts remembered the day he was asked to join the Auxiliary Units. "I had already joined the Home Guard as a youngster, and one day my boss, Bert Baker, who I learned later was the Corporal of the Bruton patrol, asked me if I would volunteer for work of a different kind – work that might be dangerous. That was all I was told. Two weeks later I went to see Mr Radway, the Lloyds Bank manager in Shepton, he was the Lieutenant in the Shepton Mallet Home Guard. This was to arrange my transfer to this other unit. After this I had to visit Captain Hunt in Bruton to finalise everything."

Archie Roberts had worked at Ivy House Farm before Bert Baker took over as manager, but not at the time when Reggie Pike was there. After Reggie Pike died of cancer a farmer called Abbot took over for a short time, and Bert Baker came as manager after him. Bert Baker was originally born at Batch Farm, Lamyatt, and married in 1943. According to his son Philip, Bert Baker was a hard working farmer, always busy about the farm, milking and whatever. He was extremely good at working with horses, and could 'talk' to them. During the war he actually farmed with Shire horses, although a number of German prisoners of war were sent to Ivy House Farm to help. The farm also had a number of Land Army girls sent from London. After the war, during the 1960s Bert Baker bought some race horses that he then set about training. He was also a regular judge in the horse competitions at the

Shepton Show. It is not precisely known how Bert Baker became involved with the Auxiliary Units but he may well have known 'Dickie' Hunt through farming, or through family connections in the Bruton area.

The BRUTON Auxiliary Unit Patrol:

Corporal Albert Edward **Baker**	Farmer of Ivy House Farm, Shepton Mallet
Sergeant Edward Alexander **Edmondson**	Timber Haulier of Berkley House, High Street, Bruton
Robert **Francis**	Motor Mechanic of Fry's West End Garage, Bruton
Captain Albert Harry 'Dickie' **Hunt**	Farmer of Dropping Lane Farm, Bruton
George **Hutchings**	Farm labourer of Dropping Lane Farm, Bruton
Thomas Leslie **Luffman**	Baker of 19 High Street, Bruton
Archie John **Roberts**	Farm worker, Ivy House Farm, Shepton Mallet
John Albert George **Steeds**	Farmer of Steps Farm, Wyke Champflower
Edward **Smith**	Lorry driver for Vineys Quarry Haulage, Bruton
Tom **Symonds**	Fish Merchant of 86 High Street, Bruton

Today, whenever the activities of the wartime Auxiliary Units and the town of Shepton Mallet are mentioned in the same conversation, one name continues to crop up – Frederick George 'Coffee' Parfitt. It is known that 'Coffee' Parfitt was born at Priddy in 1912, lived in Shepton Mallet, and died in 1997. He was a one time lime kiln worker, horse dealer and casual worker at several farms situated between Shepton and Wells. People who knew him always recall that whatever he did for work, it was always with an eye to animals, especially horses. Shepton Mallet resident, Mr Stan Blacker recalled that his elder brother and 'Coffee' were Territorial soldiers in the 374th RA Battery of the North Somerset Yeomanry. He said 'Coffee' married a girl from the travelling family of Loveridge, who came to Shepton every Christmas, to stay in the building above Ivy House Farm on Kilver Street. This house was part derelict and part inhabited by the Shore family. There was a good paddock at the back where the Loveridges parked their caravan. They used to walk down and collect drinking water from the tap in the wall at Ivy House Farm.'

It is also known that Coffee Parfitt was a member of the Auxiliary Units, and 'shared' training with Harry Edward 'Bryan' Green, a farmer of Dudwell Farm, Chewton Mendip. However it is not certain whether Coffee was part of the same Wells patrol as Bryan Green, or whether he was in another patrol operating nearer to Shepton Mallet. It is believed that there was an Auxiliary Unit patrol located in Stoke Lane, now called Stoke St Michael, and perhaps another working from an Operational Base hidden in Beacon Wood, within sight of the earthworks and standing stone. The Beacon Wood OB was seen by several schoolboys during the early part of the Second World War. Francis Laver, witnessed the underground shelter during construction in 1940 as a 12 year old. Then living in the Downside area of Shepton, Francis Laver walked up to Beacon Hill one day with a few pals and their ferrets to hunt rabbits for the pot. The boys came across some rifle butts on the rifle range and spent some time collecting spent rounds. Then they came across a freshly dug hole of about fifteen feet long, ten feet wide and six feet deep. When he was next in the woods this hole had disappeared, but upon searching Francis Laver found a trap door leading down into the gloom. Below ground was a small room with racks bearing Molotov cocktails and small arms. After returning home he reported this 'find' to his father, Wyndham Laver, the auctioneer and valuer, who in turn contacted the police. That evening the Laver family were visited by an Army Intelligence officer, who gave the boy a serious lecture about what he had seen, and the importance to the war effort of 'keeping Mum.'

During the war Gerald Rodway's father farmed at Beacon Farm, close to the Operation Base. He recalled seeing the hide during the war, and he well remembered an exercise carried out by unknown armed men, who effectively 'took over' Beacon Farm for two days in order to test out the responses of the Local Defence forces. He suspected these were the men associated with the underground base. Mr Rodway thought that the hide would have been ripped out of the ground and destroyed when the Forestry Commission deep ploughed the entire crown of Beacon Hill in May 1953 for tree re-planting.

In spite of such excellent eye - witness accounts and countless hours of research, detailed information about the patrols linked to Beacon Woods and Stoke St Michael has remained frustratingly elusive. At this late stage in the game, almost six decades after the event, it may be that this information may never be uncovered. Out of the 350 men once involved in the Auxiliary Unit patrols in Somerset, less than 30 are alive today to recount their stories.

One thing is certain however. Had the German Invasion taken place, then there were courageous people in Shepton Mallet trained and armed and willing to resist."

Sources of Information

- Somerset versus Hitler – Secret Operations in the Mendips 1939 – 1945
- Don Brown 2001 (Countryside Books)
- With Britain in Mortal Danger – Britain's Most Secret Army of World War II
- John Warwicker 2002 (Cerberus Books)
- Public Record Office: Document WO 199/3390 – Auxiliary Units Nominal Rolls
- Wells Library: Kelly's Trade Directory for Somerset 1939
- Museum of the British Resistance Organisation, Parham, Suffolk
- Correspondence with Mr Don Brown, Uphill, Weston-super-Mare

Interviews:

Mr Francis Laver, West Pennard	February 2002
Mr Gerald Rodway, Shepton Mallet	9 March 2002
Mr Robin Dunford, Evercreech	2 May 2002
Mr Freddy Chapman	5 May 2002
Mr Archie Roberts, Shepton Mallet	16 May 2002
Mr Ted Edmondson, Bruton	26 May 2002

Mr Keith Padfield, Keysham	10 June 2002
Mr Fred Blinman, Shepton Mallet	13 November 2002
Mr AC Parfitt, Shepton Mallet	13 November 2002
Mr Stan Blacker, Shepton Mallet	13 November 2002
Mrs Calver, Milton Clevedon	1 December 2002
Mr Philip Baker, Australia	10 January 2003

26 July 1940

Shepton Mallet Rural District Council. Tenancy agreements against the keeping of Pigs, Poultry and Rabbits are now suspended under a new Regulation.

William Cave, a Brewery Foremen, fined £5 for 'abusive behaviour likely to interfere with the performance of their duties by His Majesty's Forces at a south west Police Court. He apparently shouted encouragement to a party of soldiers who tried to create a disturbance outside an institution. (Note. The very prominent position of this story in the paper suggests it was a Shepton story.)

Lighting Offences. Elizabeth Collins 6 Peter Street. Special Constable Corben said the light showed from a living room through the rear of the shop and was reflected on the opposite side of the road. When he knocked on the door the light went out. When he called out there was no reply. He shouted to Mrs Collins that she would be reported and there was no answer. When seen the following day Mrs Collins said "I am sorry because I don't want the Germans here" A fine of £2 was imposed.

Cricket. Shepton Mallet 163. Cranmore 36 P Hodges 5 for 20.
>   Note. Percy Hodges was one of the very few members of the Cricket Club who was not 'middle class' he was a local Butcher and a fine bowler. His daughter still lives in the town and is a member of the Local History Group.

Mr Eden, War Minister, announced in the House of Commons that the Local Defence Volunteers will in future be given the title of 'Home Guard'.

Advert. What do I do if I hear news that Germans are trying to land or have landed?
>   I remember that this is the moment to act like a soldier. I do not get panicky. I stay put.
>   I say to myself : Our chaps will deal with them. I do not say ' I must get out of here.' I
>   remember that fighting men must have clear roads. I do not go on to the road on bicycle,
>   in car or on foot. Whether I am at work or at home I just stay put.
>   Space provided by the Brewers Society, Issued by the Ministry of Information

Advert. ARP protect your windows with Cellulose Film. Demonstration and full particulars G W Biggin 60 Town Street and Mrs Vagg Garston Street, Shepton Mallet.

2 August 1940

Shepton Mallet Cricket Club. The balance of £3 proceeds from a recent enjoyable match with our Khaki visitors to the town has been handed over to the Shepton Mallet Knitting Party to provide wool for articles for soldiers.

Regal. Errol Flynn and Olivia de Havilland in 'Dodge City'.

Advert. Shepton Mallet Swimming Club. An Inter-Club contest will be held at the Swimming Pool on Monday August 5th at 7pm. versus the Visitors. Admission 6d Men in Uniform Free.

9 August 1940

Leslie John Allen, Charlton Road, Shepton Mallet. Claimed possession of a house, 35 Commercial Road, Shepton Mallet, from Mrs P T Ball, 35 Commercial Road. The house had been let to Mrs Ball's husband whilst he was in Mr Allen's employ but he had now been called up and the house was needed for another man.

16 August 1940

Shepton Mallet Urban District Council. The Council have had represented to them the danger arising from the indifference which some of the public show during periods of warning. If persons not necessarily engaged in Civil Defence work outside do not take cover promptly they are failing in their duty not only to themselves but to others. It should be understood that there is danger even miles away from the actual scene of action.

Public Shelters. Liberal Club, Manor House and Guesthouse, Bowlish going to have their cellars inspected for suitability. 'Public Paths such as Church Lane which run between substantial stone walls have much protection value'

Any other business. Mr Pullen said a number of ladies wanted to know if anything could be done in the town to raise a fund towards providing a Spitfire. Left to the Civil Defence Committee to deal with.

Letter from F J E Pullen, Percy Villa Waterloo Road, asking for old bits of carpet to warm the concrete floors of the depot where the first aid, rescue and decontamination parties are doing their tour of night duty. (Note. It is believed that this headquarters was in the cellar under the Co-op bakery which was in Monmouth House near the Crown Inn.)

Evacuated Children will gladly accept Old Comic Books, Tennis Balls and Indoor Games. Kindly send to Headmaster (West Ham) Kilver Street School.

Advert. Red Cross Agricultural Fund. Shepton Mallet NFU, Live and Dead Stock Sale.

23 August 1940

Shepton Mallet Rural District Council. Housing of Agricultural Armies. By a new regulation the Council is now responsible for housing if there is an influx of agricultural workers.

Regal. Jean Arthur and James Stewart in 'Mr Smith goes to Washington.'

To Home Guards. Don't forget that French, Polish and Czech airmen are flying with the Royal Air Force. A solitary Parachutist may be one of these and unable to speak English. If you see five or less they may be our own men.

6 September 1940

Trouble over air raid shelter. At Shepton Mallet Petty Sessions on Friday Richard Reakes of 2b Cornwall Road was summoned by John Bailey of 2a Cornwall Road for assault.

Reakes pleaded not guilty. The complainant said that on August 22nd an Air Raid Shelter was delivered at Mr Reakes house. He told Reakes he was going to have nothing to do with the shelter. Reakes, he then alleged, became abusive and said "You are too ___ lazy to do anything." An argument ensued about the shelter and he alleged that Reakes took off his coat and appeared in a threatening manner….. Bailey admitted that nothing but a few words passed between them. Reakes did not strike him.

At this stage the Chairman said there was no evidence of an assault having been committed and dismissed the case.

Note. It would seem most likely that the air raid shelter discussed was an Anderson shelter provided by the Council for council tenants, but not all tenants. Resident of the town John Newsome who was a child during the war in Shepton can remember that the council provided Anderson shelters for those in brick-built council houses but not for those in stone-built houses. It was thought that the walls were strong enough in the stone built houses and the residents just needed to hide underneath the stairs.

Failed to immobilize car. First cases bought in the district to be bought against motor drivers who failed to immobilize cars. Albert G Moon haulier of Coombe Lane. PC Weaver said he was at the Market Place and saw the defendants car. The windows were open and the doors were unlocked but the switch key had been removed. £1 fine.

Shepton Mallet Gas Company. 104th Meeting. C E Burnell Chairman of Directors with E F Henley, T Melhuish, W H Lintern and F W Delafield.

The Gas Works was in Cowl Street. Bob Woods was a child at the time and his father Mr H E Woods was the manager of the Works. From his history of the gas works some memories of the war years can be drawn.

"One point of note is the huge increase in demand for power that the influx of the army and others into the town led to. The Gas works which had provided for a depressed town of around 4,000 overnight had to start supplying a hive of activity of around 8,000. Particular problems were experienced in maintaining the blackout for the coal fired retort house during blackouts. On 16th October 1940 a German Dornier bomber crashed at Maesbury Ring just north of the town and there was a 'near miss at the Gas Works. In the hours of darkness there was a 100% blackout so the stokers in the retort house had to completely douse the red hot coke with numerous buckets of water before the coke truck could be taken 25 yards outside to the coke dump. It was not possible to store the coke in the retort house due to the obnoxious fumes and lack of space. However, it was never possible to remove all risk of a glow from the coke truck.

To control the removal of hot coke a member of the daytime Gas Works staff would act as a Fire Watcher especially during the periods when an air raid warning was sounded. The Fire Watcher outside the Retort House would only allow the stokers to bring the coke truck out when it was absolutely quiet and there was not a sound of an aircraft.

On the night of 16th October my father was on duty as the Fire Watcher and an air raid had been sounded. The stokers indicated that they had doused a coke truck ready to be taken to the coke heap. My father listened and all was quiet so he walked to open the retort house door. He was about six feet from the door when he suddenly heard the loud noise of a German aircraft flying low almost directly overhead. He didn't open the door for at least another 15 minutes!

The next day Dad and I cycled up to the crash site and saw at least four bombs visible in the wreckage. Dad said his heart nearly stopped when he saw the bombs as if the Germans had seen the glow from the coke trolley they may have dropped them on the Gas Works."

13 September 1940

The Empire and War. There was a large and representative attendance at the Senior Girls School, Waterloo Road to hear a lecture by Mr C M Maclinnes MA historian and author on The Empire and War

A worthy effort resulted in the collection of £5/10/- which has been handed to Mr Addleshaw, Commandant of the local VAD Red Cross by Mrs Mason. This handsome sum is the proceeds of the exhibition of Hitler's famous News Sheet, many of which were scattered about the country.

Letter from Mr F J E Pullen announcing the Spitfire Fund. A start of £12 had been made by Shepton Mallet and Cranmore Cricket clubs at a recent match. Miss Bishop of Bloomfield, Shepton Mallet will preside over a 'poppy day' style collection to be arranged.

Regal. Fred Astaire and Ginger Rogers in 'Follow the Fleet'.

20 September 1940

Cowl Street Chapel Harvest Thanksgiving service Sunday 6 o'clock. Cannards Grave Harvest. Next Sunday Services Holy Communion 9.30 Evensong 6.30, Monday Evensong 7pm followed by a sale of vegetables.

Methodist Church Services at its place of Worship. Sunday… the occasion of thanksgiving for the in-gathering of the harvest. There was a profusion of the choicest gifts of fruit, flowers and vegetables…. In the afternoon there was a children's fruit, flower and egg service which was well attended.
    John Burt Godfrey of Lower Downside Farm was summoned for showing lights, a fire in a field – gate and post being alight at 9.50pm.
    Mr Godfrey pleaded not guilty … said he had been to the field in the late afternoon and the fire was out. The gate had been unhinged with fire put out. There was nothing alight when the last man left the field.
    Mr Godfrey explained that it was the top of the gate and the top of the gate post that had caught fire "how did it catch?" he asked. He did not think it was caused by the fire in the field earlier that day. The case was dismissed as it was not proved as to how the fire started.

27 September 1940

Whist drive, Liberal Club in aid of the Spitfire Fund.

Congregational Church Harvest Supper 29th Sept.

Comforts Fund for local lads. Grand Dance to be held in the Drill Hall.

Waterloo Road Senior Girls School 'Spitfire Effort' Much enthusiasm has been shown by the girls of Waterloo Road Senior School in an effort to raise funds for the Spitfire Fund. Money has been raised by the sale of flowers, mascots, brooches and book markers made by the girls in their own time at home.

"It seems but a very short time ago that a rosy apple cheeked little fellow left school and joined the post office staff as messenger boy…. His antics on the office bicycle caused many a one to bless his acrobatic abilities… His irrepressible good cheer and bright happy disposition held good and his 'old Dad' now doing his bit in the Observer Corps is justly proud of him (as are we all) for Driver A N Sanson RASC has been awarded the Military Medal for Gallantry in the Field."

Regal. Gary Cooper and Ray Millard in 'Beau Geste'.

Advert. Red Cross Exhibition of Billiards and Snooker. Mr Claude Faulkner will give and exhibition at the Constitutional Club, Shepton Mallet on Friday 27th September at 7pm.

4 October 1940

Shepton Mallet Petty Sessions. Wyndham Laver Auctioneer fined for failing to clean poultry pens at his market.

Letter. HTM Hawley on the formation of an Evacuee Club in Shepton Mallet to promote entertainment and recreation of evacuees aged 14 and upwards. Meeting place the Scout Hut behind the Hare and Hounds Hotel.

11 October 1940

Women's Hockey Club urgently in need of new members. Please contact Miss D A Lintern 'The Lawns" Shepton Mallet.

Shepton Mallet Spitfire fund at £158/14s/2d. Contributions from Miss Martins Girls School 10/-, Pilton £17/19s/3d, Doulting £9/16s-9d, West End Inmates £3/4s/6d.

Shepton Mallet Urban District Council. Decontamination Squad. Arrangements made for men on 'stand by' to sleep on premises and it has been agreed that in these circumstances such men should not be required to start work until 9 o'clock the following morning.

ARP First Aid Post. The county council have intimated that instructions have been given for the strengthening of the premises used for this purpose at the Old Grammar School.

Fire Committee having to secure a lorry to transport 'canvas dams' which have been issued by the home office.

Miss Bishop elected to replace Mr W E Hayes who had died.

Regal. '21 Days' starring Vivien Leigh, Leslie Banks and Laurence Olivier.

18 October 1940

Shepton Mallet Town Football Club Annual General Meeting to be held at the Hut, Whitstone Park.

Shepton Mallet Rural District Council. A debate about the problems of billeting Evacuees.

Mr J Sperring complained that people were not being notified. Mr Lawless said it was better not to give notice in some instances. Case of a woman who stripped wallpaper off walls and said she had the decorators in so that she would not have to take refugees. In other cases householders had had relatives in from the villages to stay with them and fill up their houses when they knew billeting was being carried out.

Advert. Royal Air Force Recruiting Visit. Men who wish to volunteer for service in the Royal Air Force can be interviewed by a RAF officer at the Employment Exchange Shepton Mallet at 11 am and 2.30 pm on Saturday Oct 19th.

Men are especially wanted as Members of Aircraft Crews aged 18 – 32. Training as Wireless Operators (ground) aged 18 – 38 and Various Skilled Trades.

Electric '17' fund announce the Spitfire and Comforts Funds Dance in the Drill Hall Charlton Road, Monday October 28th. Final of local Foxtrot competition.

25 October 1940

Shepton Mallet Spitfire Fund up to £279.

Evacuee advertisement.

Shepton Mallet Town Football Club at their AGM agreed to carry on playing local friendlies. Mr S Shawe Chairman, Mr B White Hon Sec.

Advert for Poppy Day

1 November 1940

The Electric '17' club dance was attended by 458 people including many officers and other ranks of HM Forces and the scene on the floor was an animated and happy one, an unqualified success for the hard-working committee including the versatile and dapper little chairman himself Mr E T Jones.

The two bands played alternately to keep up a nonstop programme.

Regal. 'Top Hat' starring Fred Astaire and Ginger Rogers.

'The man they could not hang,' starring Boris Karloff.

8 November 1940

Shepton Mallet and District Spitfire Fund up to £405.

Mid Somerset Motors Ltd. Will clients in future kindly drive their cars and vehicles straight through into Cook's Paddock and also please remember that we are still giving the same Pre War Services in all points.

Plate Glass Window Smashed. One of the silliest accidents imaginable occurred in the High Street on Tuesday morning resulting in the smashing to smithereens of two costly plate glass windows of Messrs E Hobbs and Son.

A pony attached to a trap and momentarily unattended suddenly thought fit to stroll on, and proceeded at a walking pace to the crossroads where a good intentioned but misguided pedestrian shouted at the animal to stop it, as if heading off cattle. The pony – very well behaved – was given little or no option other than that of swinging round into the window, which it did with the result as stated. With the falling glass, even though cut, the pony still refused to be frightened, and one felt quite sorry for the plight in which it found itself.

British Legion. Annual General Meeting of the Women's Section at Bloomfield House by kind permission of Miss Bishop. Mrs Park Secretary, Mrs Frost Treasurer. The main activity for the year had been sending parcels to the forces.

Regal. 'Bulldog sees it through' starring Jack Buchanan.

Letter from Mr Pullen on the subject of getting elderly people to take up allotments as food sources become less available.

'Previous appeals have so far fallen on deaf ears, but I am sure our people will come forward to do all they can. We must break up the ground NOW and applicants should send in to the Town Clerk at once.'

Foot and Mouth Disease in Somerset. There are movement restrictions in place in parts of Devon, Dorset and Somerset.

Note. This must have been a busy time for the Shepton Mallet Veterinary Practice. Some information about the Vets at that time is available from an excellent unpublished history written by retired vet Lionel Stafford who although he only came to Shepton after the war based a lot of it on the memories of the practice founder Tom Patterson and his children, one of whom, Bill, has recently returned to the town.

The vets at that time operated out of a house in Compton Road and served a lot of the local farms. Treatment of horses was still as important as treatment of cattle. Tom Patterson had married Lilly Britten the daughter of local farmer Walter Britten who farmed Pitts Farm in West Shepton and also had a Butchers shop in town. He also had two sons one of whom, Arthur, qualified as a vet in Edinburgh in 1940 and came to join his brother in law during the war years.

Lionel Stafford remembers attending a veterinary Congress at Warwick after joining Shepton practice. A retired Ministry Vet saw his name tag and said "Ah, Shepton Mallet, Patterson and Britten, Foot and Mouth 1940." He had actually stayed with Arthur Britten's family whilst dealing with the foot and mouth outbreak in Shepton Mallet. Infected cattle were incinerated in the fields now occupied by the Ridgeway Estate.

15 November 1940

Armistice Day passed exceedingly quietly, there being little or no public observance. Privately, visits were made to the Cenotaph and wreaths laid.

Poppy appeal. Despite the rain and other appeals £105/ 0/ 2d was raised. Arranged by the British Legion Women's Section.

Remembrance Sunday. No service at the Cenotaph though various detachments assembled there prior to marching under their respective officers to the Parish Church. Town Council, British Legion, British Red Cross Society, Boy Scouts and others in uniform. At church they were joined by a splendid muster of the Home Guard. It was the first time that the latter had been seen on parade and they looked exceedingly smart in their uniform.

Meeting of the Shepton Mallet Branch of the National Farmers Union held at The Bell. H J Corp Chairman, A H Sealy Vice Chair. They had raised a splendid £543 for the Red Cross Agricultural Fund. (Note. This fund seems to have been the main beneficiary of fund raising activities by farmers as a body throughout the war and there are numerous records of sales and collections towards it.)

Shepton Mallet Urban District Council. Have issued notice to quit to three council houses in Cornwall Road where only one person is living. (Note. There was a perpetual housing crisis in Shepton Mallet throughout the war due to pressure of numbers.)
>More of the Council Hall is needed for evacuation work. Mr Pullen complained that it was being used for stores and there was now no room for meetings.
>Mr Hall – "is there no room in the basement stores?"
>Mr Pullen – "No it is full up of ARP supplies."

A committee formed looking at what action could be taken at the present time in the hope of securing establishment in Shepton Mallet of some industrial enterprise likely to be of benefit to the town after the war.

A letter was received from the Chamber of Trade, calling the Council's attention to unseemly behaviour in the streets of the town during the hours of blackout and asking if nothing could be done in the matter to correct the nuisances.

Regal. 'The Hunch Back of Notre Dame' starring Charles Laughton.

Shepton Mallet Rural District Council. Extra Staff needed to deal with evacuees. The number of evacuees in the combined Districts is now approximately 4000 and another 500 have been allocated.

Apologies were given by Ashwick and Oakhill who had given their Spitfire Fund Collections to Norton Radstock as they thought they had been left out of the Shepton Fund.

Advert. Bring your Boot and Shoe repairs to Bull Boot Shop, Whitstone Road, Shepton Mallet. Quick Dispatch

22 November 1940

Shepton Mallet Spitfire fund £567 following £72 from Cranmore.

British Legion Club Annual Meeting. Mr R G Byrt President, Mr Atkins Chairman, Mr W Perry Hon Secretary, Mr C B Rodway Hon Treasurer, Mr FJE Pullen Hon Secretary of Branch, Mr B Hall Hon Auditor. 180 Members. 141 ex service and serving and 39 Hon members. 23 members serving in H M Forces. They had sent a Christmas parcel to each serving member.

Editorial. Mr Winston Churchill will be 66 next week. He became Prime Minister on 10th of May 1940 at a moment when Britain was facing the greatest peril in her history.

Today Britain instead of facing Defeat is heading boldly for Victory, with her people united, her war effort steadily eclipsing that of her discomforted enemies.

Note. This piece then went on to list the famous quotations Churchill had made during the year. In retrospect it is interesting to see the impact Churchill had made so quickly. In reality it was at least another two years before the pendulum of war began to swing – but the resolve and belief appear to had been instilled.

Advert. Shepton Mallet Urban District Council. Air Raid Shelters. Tenders invited for the construction in Brickwork and Concrete roofs of six commercial and domestic shelters to accommodate 252 persons.

Notice from Somerset War Agricultural Committee. Damage by Rabbits and Rats. For a period of two months a reward of 1d per tail of all rats produced to the Committee Pest officers will be paid.

Advert. Lost Red Heifer (marked with a small white star on forehead and white patch on back leg) On Wednesday afternoon 15th November from Mendip Inn. Last seen going towards Shepton Mallet. Apply Mr M Gilson, Binegar Bottom, Gurney Slade.

29 November 1940

Advert. Today Red Cross Ball at the Drill Hall.

Shepton Spitfire fund at £602 thanks to £20 from the parish of Lamyatt.

Advert. Football Shepton Town Team v Army XI, Whitstone Park Sat 2.30pm in aid of Red Cross Fund.

Regal. 'Charlie's (Big Hearted) Aunt' starring Arthur Askey.

Notice to all farmers. Shepton Mallet market is closed until further notice owing to Foot and Mouth Restrictions. Wainwright, Laver and Crees Ltd.

Foot and Mouth In Somerset. Outbreaks of Foot and Mouth disease have been confirmed amongst cattle at Shepton Mallet. A 15 mile movement prohibition of cattle, sheep, pigs, goats and deer has been imposed.

Advert. Civil Defence Motor Cycle Messengers. Two experienced Motor Cycle Riders Required for Part Time Voluntary Duty as Motor Cycle Messengers at the Sub Control, Shepton Mallet. A licensed Motor Cycle will be provided.

6 December 1940

At the Bristol Assize on Monday Mrs Nancy Kate Reeves of the Cannards Grave Inn was granted a decree nisi by Justice MacNaughton against her husband Robert Theodore Reeves on the grounds of desertion. She asked his Lordship to expedite the decree as she wanted to marry a man in the RAF.

A verdict of 'death by misadventure' was returned by the coroner …. At an inquest at

Shepton Mallet Police Court on Gunner Russell Frederick Dunett, 24, who died at the Shepton Mallet District Hospital on Sunday after being involved in an accident. Evidence was given that Dunett was riding in a lorry at Cannards Grave. The driver took the wrong road and in an attempt to regain the proper road collided with a wall. The vehicle overturned and Dunett sustained head injuries. Dunetts home was at Lyce Road, Ipswich.

'Of interest to women' a series of Fashion and cookery tips for wartime economies.

Advert. Practical Gifts for Friends in the Forces and at home. Knitwear, Dress, Lingerie Length, Hosiery, Gloves, Umbrellas, Handkerchiefs, Scarves, Fancy Laces, Down Quilts, Thorne and Thorne.

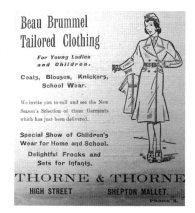

Thorne and Thorne advertisement.

13 December 1940

Advert. H Widdicombe. Gents Tailor, Hatter, Hosier etc. The Man's Shop for Xmas Gifts. Radiac Tunic Shirts. A large assortment of Ties and Scarves, Silk and Linen Handkerchiefs, Fancy Half Hose, Pullovers, Slipovers, Cardigans. 51-52 High Street Shepton Mallet.

The Convent School. Children of the Convent School will present a pantomime at the school on Wednesday and Thursday next week in aid of War Charities.

Ronald Welch, miner of Longbridge Shepton Mallet was fined 10/- for riding a pedal cycle without a rear light at Ashwick on Nov 12th and 15/- for a similar offence at Shepton Mallet two days later.

Gordon Kennedy electrician of 8 Market Place was summoned for displaying a light from a roofed building. He had forgotten to put the blackout shutters up. Fined one pound. (Note. 8 Market Place is still known as Kennedy House. It has been semi derelict for many years and is one of very few grade 2* listed buildings in Shepton Mallet.)

Mr C B Witcombe has had to write to the MP to get some action on repairing a shop window which has been smashed by a service lorry.

Shepton Mallet Urban District Council. Mr Bellchamber Clerk to both the Urban District Council and the Rural District Council is to retire. The Rural District Council has decided to have their own separate Clerk and Staff. This was much regretted by the Urban District Council especially at this time. They have so much in common: evacuation, fire services, registration and food control.

Mr Showering raised, in vigorous manner, the question of 'Blackout' or rather the apparent lack of it by the Military.

Regal. 'Sing as we go' starring Gracie Fields.

There was a large increase in the number of advertisements in the paper for Christmas.

These included.

- Thomas Laing, Tailor and Breeches Maker, 6 Town Street.
- Edwin F Henley's, Large selection of gifts.
- Harrison's, Drapers Outfitters, London House Shepton Mallet.
- Bowden's, Grocers and Provisions Merchant, 9 High Street
- Stephenson's of Shepton Mallet
- P C Vowles, Cycle and Radio Dealer 55 High Street, Shepton Mallet
- Ready Shortly, A Byrt and Sons, Household Almanac
- Usual poultry sales. Poultry, Turkey, Geese, Ducks, Produce and Rabbits. Wainwright, Laver and Crees.

20 December 1940

Nativity Play presented by the children of Ivy House School.

Regal. 'Road to Singapore' starring Bing Crosby, Dorothy Lamour and Bob Hope.

Advert. A Grand Christmas Dance will be held at the Drill Hall, Shepton Mallet. Les Phillips and his Band.

27 December 1940

Carols. Again on Christmas Eve carols were rendered in the main streets of the town by Salvationists – rendered extraordinarily well too. A collection was taken for local charities.

Christmas at the various institutions of the town including the hospitals were spent as gaily as circumstances would permit. There was no lack of Christmas fare and the respective Matrons and staff, true to tradition, did their best to ensure that those coming under their care derived the maximum amount of happiness.

The Christmastide generally passed off quietly in the town. Never the less for most people it was a happy day – a day at home by the fireside with new found friends to share ' just what happened to be going'. Both in the home and outside there was a manifest spirit of goodwill and comradeship which did much to allay the fears and anxieties of those absent from their own immediate circle.

Parish Church. .. despite the fact that there were no bells this year to usher in the glad tidings…

List of the Pianoforte successes obtained by the Pupils of Miss Betty Allen.

Advert. Red Cross Fund New Year Eve Ball at the Drill Hall Charlton Road.

Advert. Two lost Muscovy Ducks. Finder will be rewarded. Apply Curtis Summerleaze Shepton Mallet.

'This is Britain's Finest Hour' an article praising Churchill and the turn around since the beginning of the year.

Alford's shop.

The Old Rectory

Town Street.

Chapter 4

1941

- February, The 'Afrika Korps' under Rommel arrived in Libya and drove the British back to Eygpt.
- March – July the U-boat 'Battle of the Atlantic' reached its peak.
- May 24, The Bismark sinks HMS Hood. Three days later the Bismark herself is sunk after being disabled by torpedo bombers flown off HMS Ark Royal.
- June 22, Hitler launches the invasion of Russia.
- August 14, Roosevelt and Churchill announce the Atlantic Charter, a step towards Churchill's aim of involving the USA in the War,
- December, German advance floundering in the suburbs of Moscow.
- December 7, Japanese attack Pearl Harbour. The following day USA and Britain declare war on Japan. To fulfill treaty obligations Hitler declares war on USA.

3 January 1941

Post office. Report on the good work to get through the increased workload. 'But they were rewarded on Christmas Day by the knowledge that soon after mid day the work was done and that they were free to take a well earned rest.'

Hard Work in the Post Office. Colin Ryall interviews sprightly Nonogenarian Phyllis Pittard who reveals how hard work in the post office was during the War years.

For the first time I was to interview someone whom I had never met before. A mutual friend introduced me to Phyllis, at the house in the heart of Shepton Mallet, where she has lived for the past 45 years.

Being born in 1912 Phyllis has not only lived through the Second World War but through the first as well. I feared that I might find the lady reticent, vague or incoherent, but these fears proved entirely unfounded. Phyllis proved voluble and clear minded.

Phyllis had worked throughout the war in the Crown Post Office in the Market Place, living at that time in her birthplace 'at the top of Whitstone Road'. As well as working long hours she kept house for her bedridden mother and, after he had been bombed out of his home in Bath, her brother.

In going into the Post Office Phyllis was following in her father's footsteps, he had been a postman until enlisting in the WW I army. After training he was posted to India, but after only six months in Calcutta he succumbed to 'fever and a bad heart'. Phyllis' only memory of him is of on one occasion playing with the brass buttons of his Army uniform as she sat on his lap. 'I never saw him in his postman's uniform', Phyllis added ruefully.

At this time the P.O. had no motorised mail vans in Shepton, collections were made with motorbikes fitted with a box sidecar. Phyllis recalled that the horse and carriage operated by the Hare and Hounds ('one of the best hotels in Shepton') met the trains (in the hope of picking up customers for the hotel) and collected the incoming mail every day.

There were many more shops and pubs operating in Shepton than presently, as well as lining the High St., Town St. and Commercial Rd. shops could be found in Draycott, Tipcote Hill, Peter St., Board Cross and West Shepton, although it must have been a job for them all to make a living. Open all hours was the rule then, rather than the exception. Phyllis recalls the grocer she used staying open until 9pm. As very few of their customers had their own transport most stores offered a home delivery service. "Yes, they had boys, poor little boys used to struggle out on bikes." (A boy school leaver on a 'trade' bicycle fitted with an outsize basket over a small front wheel, or a tricycle with a very large box between the two front wheels.) " They were cheerful enough going back with a tip in their pocket, you'd hear them whistling the latest catch tune from the wireless."

There were also numerous roundsmen serving the town and more particularly the outlying districts. Like the shops the Post Office also kept long hours, opening from 8am until 7.30pm.

When asked how the war affected her Phyllis replied, "Oh my dear, the work, a lot of our men went, we had temporaries. Some of them were hopeless, they didn't know how to treat the public, they lost money on the counter and couldn't do counter work." Phyllis found her own workload increased dramatically.

"I did everything but drive a mail van, I did the teleprinter, telegrams, which are gone, wages, accounts, everything but drive the mail van! Every book had to be made up before you left."

Phyllis found herself working 60-hour weeks. Shepton P.O. was much more self-sufficient than today, having a far wider range of responsibilities than the present day sub-post office. As a Crown Post Office all the local Sub-Post Offices had to be serviced from Shepton. The P.O. still ran the telegraph service whereby a message telephoned or handed in would be delivered within an hour or so to the addressee anywhere in the UK. Messenger boys, school leavers too young for the services, took out the incoming telegrams. In wartime the recipients viewed the arrival of these telegram-boys with trepidation as they often heralded bad news; the telegram they brought was often the first notification from the War Office that someone was 'officially missing, feared dead'. This service was necessary as so few people were 'on the phone'. The telephone service was at this time also operated by the Post Office. The telephone exchange was sited in the High St, in the building now Challis Models & Hobbies. (The large clock marked 'Post Office' marks a previous site of the postal office.) Phyllis remembers that the telephone linesmen had a 'retiring room' (rest room) upstairs at the Market Place P.O. There was also a ladies' retiring room and a gent's retiring room for postal staff (separate of course!) and the Post Master's room.

Working routines were staid and old fashioned, leading live-wire Phyllis to fall foul of the Post Master when she suggested innovations. The whole P.O. atmosphere was 'starchy', formal and hierarchical, as was society in general.

"Stuffy and class conscious. A lot of stuck up nobodies. Ar! But the war changed all that, yes, at least it did that!," Phyl asserted, referring to some of the old time Sheptonians, revealing her own bolshie streak.

"I had rows with the Post Master, I nearly left. He was only a jumped up messenger boy anyway," Phyl claimed, "He's dead now," she added, not without a touch of self-satisfaction.

The war brought in some changes as the pressure of work meant that more flexible working practices had to be introduced. All permanent staff were also paid a wartime allowance. Phyl received 30/-(£1.50) per week on top of her flat pay of £2 10s (£2.50), plus overtime payment.

The increase in activity in the Post Office reflected the increase in the whole 'Peaceful and crime free' pre-war tempo of the town that Phyl remembers.

First to arrive as a result of the war were the evacuees. "We had no bombs in Shepton", Phyl told me, "so we had evacuees." Phyllis recalls some were housed together in Summerleaze House until they could be found long-term homes with families. The allowance paid per child taken in was paid weekly in cash at the P.O. counter. (Very few other than professional or business families had bank accounts, direct debit was unheard of.)

"Some kids were taken in as an act of benevolence, some for the 10/-(50p) allowance and the extra ration book," Phyl claimed, "if you took a bed wetter you got 12/-(60p)." (Separation from parents, loss of home life or past experiences of bombing or abuse disturbed many children, a few profoundly.) When the average wage was £3 it was understandable that the extra money could be a great incentive to the less well-off.

"Then the prison was re-opened as a British MP&DB (Military Prison & Detention Barracks). Pre-war it had been closed for several years with only a caretaker in residence." Phyllis remembers, "He was a betting man and would come into the P.O. to send a telegram putting his bets on." (This was long before betting shops were legal, off-course bookmaking was illegal. The creditworthy could open an account with a bookmaker to take their bets 'on account', Cash bets had to be placed surreptitiously with bookies runners, who could be found in most work places and pubs.)

The National Deposit re-located from London to Jardine's Mill (now Mulberry's). Many of the Society's employee's were young ladies, which was maybe why Shepton was so popular with the next influx to Shepton. These were the American service men (1942).

"But the Yanks absolutely….they loved it here. They did really, they really loved it. It shook the town up, that's what we want now, we want something to wake the town up," exclaimed Phyl.

"Of course the girls fell for the Yanks," Phyl recalls, "There were dances, know where the Drill Hall is? Well they had dances out there. I didn't go because of course I had my house. By that time my brother was bombed out. He was in lodging in Bath and that was bombed. He came home; there was nowhere else for him to go. He went up and down every day on the dear old S&D Railway, out Charlton. All gone now, its terrible!"

The Americans had their own camp at Townsend but even so some were billeted out in the town. Phyllis' neighbour had two billeted on her. Phyllis got on very well with them.

"They certainly enlivened the town" recalls Phyllis, referring to the 'Yanks', "The Regal was choc o'block every night. If I hadn't had a reserved seat I would never have got in," Phyl recalls. The cinema and the radio were Phyllis' sources of entertainment. "Today's stuff is not a patch on the old films and the radio programmes were wonderful," claims Phyl, "And we followed the news, of course."

"Going home in the blackout could be hazardous', Phyl recalls, 'It was all right in the summer, what with Double Summer Time but in the winter it was terrible. There were numerous accidents." Even though cars had to operate with partly obscured headlights, 'the blackout, you know', accidents would mostly have occurred to pedestrians as very few civilians had cars on the road. Many cars had been laid up 'for the duration' and petrol was severely rationed.

New Minister at the Baptist Church, Mr H T Turner from Edmonton London.

3 January 1941 (cont)

Silver wedding of Mr and Mrs Berkeley Hall. He came to the town twelve years ago as the right-hand man to Lawrence Gardner and Co accountants and by his sterling qualities he quickly won the goodwill of almost all. Mrs Hall is a valued member of the Shepton Mallet Nursing Association.

Two charming daughters Misses Pamela and Doreen. The former is now at home having been bombed out and the latter is on His Majesty's service.

10 January 1941

Good Service. For many long and weary months members of the various ARP services including the Auxiliary Fire Service and rescue squads have been practising weekday and Sunday alike to fit themselves to emergencies should they arise. Oft time the turn outs must have been wearisome and seemingly futile but still the men stuck in true Bulldog fashion and now many have good reason to be grateful to them for their untiring and unselfish services. On more than one occasion these services have recently been in action in the South West and have as confidently expected of them given a first class account of themselves.

Note. Stan Blacker who was a 16 year old at this time and a member of the rescue party remembers the trips they made. Twice to Weston-super-Mare and also to Bristol and Bath. It is most likely that this in particular refers to the work the ARP rescue party did on the Bourneville estate in Weston where they pulled 10 dead from

Gordon Vincent. A young Gordon proudly in his Auxiliary Fire Service uniform.

the rubble, one alive and one live dog. When you speak to Stan on the subject it is quite clear that the horrific images remain with him clearly over 60 years later. They had to go to Weston in the back of an open lorry which in the winter was extremely cold. Apparently they had to get the driver to stop at Ashwick so they could shake and slap some life back into their numbed bodies.

War Savings in Shepton Mallet Urban District. Since 1st January 1940 a grand total of £157,585 has been subscribed to the national effort. This is money for the purchase of National Savings Certificates, Defence Bonds and the increase in deposits in Savings Bank, monies paid into the Post Office and the three Banks in Shepton Mallet alone.

Shepton Mallet Spitfire find at £683.

Shepton Mallet Rural District Council appointed Mr Strickland as Clerk. (Note. Although nothing was printed, reading between the lines there seems to have been a fall out with the Urban District Council over some specific points.)

Letter from the Women's Land Army over the need for new recruits.

17 January 1941

Sunday school treat. Thanks to the exceeding kindness of the National Deposit Society and members of their staff who attended throughout, the children attending the Church of England Sunday Schools in the town were given a treat in the spacious dining hall at Kilver Street on Saturday afternoon. In all about 250 attended.
A bountiful tea was much enjoyed by the children who afterwards were highly delighted by a cinematograph show including films of Charlie Chaplin and Mickey Mouse.

Shepton Mallet Urban District Council. Establishment of a Communal Feeding Centre was under considerations and members of the WVS had kindly undertaken the necessary organization. Debate as to who was to be fed – was it just the evacuees?.

Mr A D Stockdale formerly Clerk to West Mercia Essex UDC was appointed Clerk to Shepton Mallet Urban District Council at a commencing salary of £400 per annum.

Regal. 'The invisible man returns" starring Sir Cedric Hardwick and Vincent Price.

Tribute to Amy Johnson who had died on January 5th after a crash off the Thames estuary while piloting a plane for the Air Transport Auxiliary.

24 January 1941

The London Gazetteer had reported that Lt Col J W Hyatt RAMC has been brought to notice in recognition of distinguished services in connection with operations in the field in March – June 1940. (Note. Dr Hyatt is one of the Shepton Doctors who are commemorated with roads named after them on the St Peters estate in West Shepton)

Lucy Godfrey prosecuted for selling large eggs at 4/- a doz. She claimed that she had been told that this was the right price but the price had been reduced to 3/6d a doz. The magistrate said the offence had been inadvertently committed – fined just costs of two guineas.

Worry expressed at people forgetting to carry their gas masks.

The paper was reporting the air offensive against Germany.

31 January 1941

The skittles competition organized by Messrs Showerings on behalf of the Lord Mayors Fund Bristol was played off on the luxurious alley at the Kings Arms and proved a great success.

A local branch of the British Youth Movement being set up for people of school leavers age.

Changing Shops. Housewives who would like to change their retailer may now do so providing they put their application to the local food office before the closing date of February 3rd. If they don't apply by this time they will not have another opportunity to do so for six months.

7 February 1941

Good luck Mr Eades who for some years past has conducted the Central Hairdressing Saloon, has reported for Military Duty this week. In his temporary absence Mr Helps will carry on the business.

Football. At its annual general meeting members of Shepton Mallet Town Football Club decided to carry on for the season playing friendly games only. It has now however been found impossible owing to the hearty response by our young men to the call of the colours. It has therefore been decided to suspend the activities of the club until further notice.

Shepton Mallet Petty Sessions. 14 Farmers in the district were summoned for failing to mark cattle, sheep and pigs moved on licence in accordance with the Foot and Mouth Disease Infected Area Restrictions.
   Many farmers pleaded ignorance of instructions printed on the back of movement orders. Each fined 4s.

Youth Movement. Letter from FJE Pullen (Note. Who else!) appealing for urgently needed leaders for classes such as singing, dramatic, engineering, dancing, light physical training for both sexes, horticulture and leaders for the six squads already formed ages 13 – 20. Headquarters, Market Hall, Townsend.
   The evacuees club that was already in existence was being merged with the Youth Movement.

Regal. "His Girl Friday" starring Cary Grant and Rosalind Russell.

14 February 1941

Shepton Mallet Urban District Council – Due to the pressure of space the Billeting Office was being moved to premises in Charlton Road.

The need for a ladder to use with every 'loaned' stirrup pump has been bought to the notice of the committee who recommended the purchase of 20 such ladders at 10/6d each.

More land has been made available for allotments. Mr Pullen said he was not in a position

Shepton Prison.

to give the number of allotments taken up but he believed that when a census was taken it would surprise them.

Debate on whether enough was being done to encourage fire spotters. Apparently some shopkeepers had failed to make provision,

Because of a shortage of transport and labour the Council decided to buy a 'Gritter' at £45/15/-.

ARP Circulars – 'The Committee has before them the usual batch of circulars from the Ministry of Home Security, the Fire Brigade Division of the Home Office and the Ministry of Health and have given appropriate directions in connection with those which appeared to call for action. (Note. What a beautiful piece of wording. Between the lines at both the Urban District and the Rural District Councils there appears to be an increasing scepticism of the huge number of directives being received and what they were expected to do with them.)

Sand for ARP. Approximately 56 tons of sand has been distributed to householders and 1210 sand bags sold.

Debate over the Fire Brigade's Armstrong Siddeley car which they disposed of because it was sluggish on cold mornings. Mr Witcombe asked upon whose authority is was decided to dispose of the car? Who had condemned it? It seemed to him a very trivial matter to get rid of such a car….from his own practical experience they were excellent cars – besides the winter was two thirds over.

Mr Pullen urged the Council to help the Youth Movement in little things. The chairman of the council had allowed the temporary loan of a piano. Miss Thorne said the piano was a valuable one worth over sixty pounds when new. She was rather worried.

Tragic Death of three soldiers. The inquest upon three soldiers who died subsequently upon being found in a serious condition after spending the night in a cell at a detention barracks of a west country town was conducted at Shepton Mallet on Thursday last when it was admitted that the men did not have sufficient space according to the regulations.

There were 413 men on military charges. The method had been Carbon Monoxide poisoning. There was a rank smell. Some of the cells had had windows broken but not this cell. Of the four men in the cell, three had died. There was a gas light that was turned down by a control in the corridor. At 6am a warder went along to relight the lights but there was no response from this cell. The room was a former bathroom which had been turned into a cell.

The inquest into this tragedy had to sit a number of times. Bob Wood remembers that one of the reasons was due to his father's illness at that time. He was the manager of the gas works and had to report as to whether there was any fault there. Bob can remember the whole inquest moving to a room in their home to interview his father. The reports include references to Taffe Finn, the prison Doctor. Apparently he was a well known local character who was often the worse for wear with alcohol.

The hearing on the 16th May gave the verdicts. There was conflicting evidence 'and after an all day sitting and a retirement of an hour the jury returned a verdict that the three soldiers died of Carbon Monoxide Poisoning, and that their death was due to misadventure. In a rider, the jury expressed the opinion that the Commandant of the Barracks, the Lieutenant and the Staff Sergeant were deserving severe censure because of negligence in allowing the occupation of the cell before a certificate had been granted by the War Office.'

Life in Shepton Mallet 'Glass House'

We have been extremely lucky to obtain the following fascinating record of what life was like for a British Military Prisoner during this period. Local History Group member Francis Disney has dedicated his retirement to researching the history of the prison and he has given us permission to use the following which the writer gave permission for him to use if they were of any use!

The memories of Mr. AA Risley as written to Mr. F Disney in three letters commencing Jan 85

"During the last war when the prison was in use as a detention barracks, I was an inmate from April to December 1941. Although that is a long time ago I very often think about it. In the evening's it was so still and quiet, so different from anything I had known before or since. So many memories, soldiers from every part of Great Britain and a few from the Empire.

During my time there I was firstly in C wing then A wing just a couple of cells away from the old condemned cell, and finishing my time in B wing. Although not in use for prisoners I believe there was another wing D wing which used to house the women prisoners when the prison was used for civilians and I heard during the war it contained Somerset House Records.

What I can remember was the Chapel. There was a plaque that contained the names of Prison Officers who had been killed in action during World War One.

Every second Wednesday afternoon instead of square bashing we attended a lecture in the chapel. Usually they were dry as dust, but we were sitting down for which we were grateful.

One afternoon however the form book went upside down. We filed into the chapel. The lecturer went to the pulpit. He was elderly, walked with a stoop and sported a Van Dyke beard. As soon as he started orating the fun began. He spoke in a high pitched voice and his arms waved about like TV's Magnus Pyke. We could not help giggling, and although the staff ordered quiet it was clear they were finding it as hard as us to stop laughing. It appeared the lecturer had spent most of his life in darkest Africa going from village to village and tribe to tribe. He regaled us with stories of dusky maidens walking about practically naked and how he had enjoyed their favours. He spoke of the strange customs and behavior of some tribes. But he brought the house down, or should I say Chapel, when he told of a tribe afflicted with a complaint called elephantitis, I think. It seems its effect was to produce lumps all over the body and to greatly enlarge anything that protruded such as nose or ears. He followed up with how he had seen tribesmen with home-made wheel barrows pushing them with their enlarged private parts inside them. This was too much, we fell about laughing, staff as well. When the lecturer stepped down we applauded whole heartedly. It was a couple of minutes before order was restored. That was a red letter day.

The other memory I have is a bit different. I still wonder how it ended. Although most of the inmates were soldiers there were a few RAF chaps. One I remember very well because when he arrived, on his tunic you could see where his sergeants stripes had been. But across his tunic were his Pilots wings. He had been reduced to the ranks and given 28 days detention for having airplane fuel in his car. It was reckoned if he had been commissioned he would have just had a ticking off and told not to be a naughty boy again. We were all a bit choked, this bloke was 'one of the few'. However he was given a red bands job and did no parades. No one begrudged him that. Rumour had it that in the night before his release his cell was unlocked, he was taken to the staff's mess and given a booze up. True or false I don't know. One thing is for sure, within a few days of his release his stripes were back on and he was up there doing the business. Whether he survived the war I cannot say. I sincerely hope so, a very brave chap.

In war time military prisons and barracks had only one purpose. That was to make life so intolerable that no one would wish to return. Rigid silence was enforced. Anyone caught communicating was put on report. Result punishment diet one and loss of remission. Only exception to this rule was a 10 minute period each day when men were lined up and allowed to speak to each other.

Alternatively, if you were not in a single cell you could talk to each other. If you were waiting to see any official for any reason you stood facing the wall with your face about six inches away. There was no such thing as going through stages or earning any kind of privileges so a soldier completing a two year sentence was in the same position as a man doing 14 days.

Smoking in 1941 was forbidden, although I believe it was later introduced under supervision, one cigarette in the morning and another in the afternoon. However this did not apply in my time although man's ingenuity made sure we got a puff now and then.

Food was poor, preparation left a lot to be desired and I dare suggest the cook sergeant had a good thing going for him " after all there was a war on"

Some soldiers for some unknown reasons came back for a second or third time. These were the ones who just did not care and just before being locked up at teatime they were given their tasks i.e. pieces of kitchen ware to be cleaned with bath brick which when mixed with water made a scouring powder. That plus elbow grease was expected to remove all grease and fat. Upon unlocking the following morning all second timer's would dash to C wing for their tasks to be examined. Usually a few second timers would finish up on report for unsatisfactory work, result PD one plus loss of remission.

Personal hygiene, bathing, haircutting etc was a joke. Haircutting consisted of putting the clippers as close to the skull as possible, we looked like lambs at shearing time. Funny how times change. Young men today spend a lot of money for the same result.

Shaving was done in the morning. Mirrors were outside the cells. One orderly went along the landing handing out the safety razors. Hopefully you were lathered up by the time he got to you. Before you knew it he was back for the razor. I think they changed the blades about one a year. Mind you the staff always looked very clean shaven.

Bathing took place once a week on a Friday under showers about 12 men at a time with domestic soap under lukewarm water winter or summer. Then came the order ' everybody out' accompanied by buckets of cold water from the ever helpful staff. I doubt if you had more than three minutes under the shower. You then doubled out naked on to the parade ground carrying your clothes to get dressed while the next bunch went into the showers, I should think the whole prison was bathed in less than two hours, we came out of our cells after dinner at 2 o'clock and banged up again at four o'clock, that was how it was.

Saturday morning we went into C wing for medical inspection. Not by an Army doctor but by a civilian Doctor, his speech always seemed slurred as though he had been hitting the bottle the night before. He would prod and grunt and if he pointed at your feet you were on report for dirty flesh. What else could be expected after drying and dressing in the open parade ground the night before. More bread and water and loss of remission. One thing always interested me at this parade. The fantastic tattoos of some of the regulars who had served overseas had were works of art. One chap had a cobra's head on his chest, it twined all round his body and across his buttocks. Where the tail went modesty forbids me to mention. Trouble with Tattoos is that they are as easily identifiable as finger prints.

So much for everyday routine, we were locked up Saturday dinner time until breakfast Sunday morning. If you shared a cell it was not too bad, you could have a jaw. On your own it was a case of finding yourself something to do, polishing, cleaning, something like that. By the way, no mattresses, you slept on three bed boards between two trestles. The spaces between the bed boards were a nuisance but you got used to them like everything else. Sunday's church parade was compulsory. The first time I went in I thought this looks just like old paintings of the chapel in Newgate Prison. The Parson always ended his sermon by telling us on release to go out and 'fight the good fight'. No point in me telling him that as an Eastender I had fought the good fight and a few bad ones at the now defunct Mile End Arena. 6X2's One pound. Had to get the 'old girls' money somehow.

Most of the inmates did their best to get through their sentence and avoid trouble, myself included. However there is always the odd one. Such was Teddy W. From the outskirts of North London. Blonde with blue eyes and absolutely without fear. He despised the staff and told them in a voice that could be heard some distance away. This resulted in the loss of all his remission. What further infuriated the staff was that he called them all Sid. On one occasion he told the commandant that if they could not win the war without his assistance they might as well 'turn it in'. At the same time he proved his fitness during PT training. He would go over the vaulting horse head first, hands behind his back and always land on his feet. He came in a hard man and went out the same way. Years later he was headlines in the News of the World when he was sentenced to 8 years penal servitude for an offence in which a policeman was seriously injured. Last I heard of him he was living in a caravan in Hertfordshire.

Another character was Georgie M. from Edmonton, by profession a safe blower. For a time I shared a cell with him. He deliberately got solitary. As, he remarked to me, if you make a living breaking in – breaking out is not impossible. A few mornings later at role call all hell was let loose. Too late, our George was long gone. In later years he escaped from Wandsworth and Chelmsford, always posting his prison clothing back so as not to be subsequently charged with stealing prison property. However with the Prison Amendment Act of 1948 Escapees only suspended the sentence, but that would not worry George. Last I heard of him he was running a stall in Hackney market – I wonder if he sold locks and security devices, after all he was a bit of an expert.

There were two kinds of military Provost Staff Corps. The older ones were those who had served their time with the colours and had joined the prison service recalled at the out break of war and sent to serve with the MPSC. These older ones you could live with, give them no hassle, do as you're told and things went smoothly. The other kind were different again, all young like most of the inmates, all conscripts they were jack the lads. They went looking for trouble, sometimes they got more than they bargained for. They used to have a sweeps stake each day to see who could get the most on report. No wonder flare ups occurred from time to time. This caused bad feelings among the old regulars and we the inmates often became the pig in the middle. On Dec 31st 1941 I walked out of Shepton Mallet a free man after serving a one year's sentence. Fifty years on I can recall most of it, yet somehow I don't seem to remember what happened last week. I reckon the war years were eventful and the memories will always be there.

14 February 1941 (cont)

First Aid Classes. Staff of the National Deposit Friendly Society have arranged a course of

St John's Ambulance lectures on First Aid and Home Nursing. They invite members of the public who are interested in qualifying to attend.

Births Deaths and Marriages. In loving memory of our dear son Charlie Stock who lost his life at sea. Always remembered by his loving Mother, Father and Brothers. (Note. There is still no direct mention of war casualities at this time.)

21 February 1941

Annual Brewster Sessions. Only one member of the public had been convicted of drunkenness during the year. In the district there were 38 ale houses, 17 on-beer houses, 6 off beer houses, 2 licenced grocers and 3 wine and spirit merchants.

The Spotlights. Councilors F J E Pullen and W A Price and others are sponsoring a concert program at the Regal on Sunday evening in aid of the local 'Spitfire Find' So far the fund has been 'hard going'. Sunday's concert will enable many who otherwise could not afford it to support the fund.

Frank Cox a soldier was summoned for using obscene language.

28 February 1941

A meeting will be given in the Liberal Club by Mr D Edwards of the Ministry of Information on 'Hitler and the Nazi Spite.'

Spotlight entertainment at the Regal for the Spitfire Fund had proved very popular with 'every available seat occupied'. At the interval a tableaux, representative of the services Regular and Auxiliary was 'put on.' A short and appropriate address was given by Councilor F J E Pullin who was the originator of the fund locally.

Regal. 'Old Mother Riley Joins Up' starring Kitty Mcshane and Arthur Lucas.

Farms at War. Every unit should be self contained, plough more land, use more fertiliser, grow more feeding stuffs for stock and make more silage.

7 March 1941

Thorne and Thorne. The 17th anniversary was celebrated on the 4th of March of the Misses Thorne taking over the old established Drapery and Ladies and Children's Outfitters from Messrs Golder and Co. Celebrated with staff past and present at 'Holmcroft' (between Whitstone School and the Leisure Centre).

A concert was given in the Convent School by

Plough Now – advice to farmers.

the famous musician Louis Godovsky supported by accomplished local musician Miss Nora Byrt.

Albert Nightingale dairyman of Town Street Shepton Mallet was summoned for permitting a person under the age of 17 to drive a motor vehicle. He claimed that he thought they could drive at 16.

Shepton Mallet Rural District Council. In the six months August to January 30 tons of paper had been collected which had been sold for £81.

14 March 1941

Advert. Allen and Foster Ltd are pleased to inform allotment holders and gardeners that they have now received a consignment of general fertiliser and sulphate of ammonia.

Shepton Mallet Urban District Council. Agreed that under present circumstances the construction of a footpath in Compton Road must stand over.

Piano. It has been decided that in future the piano shall only be moved at the discretion of the Chairman and Mr Hall (Vice chairman).

L Mills. Application for the release of L Mills from the Army is being made on the grounds of his being needed in connection with Youth Movement activities in the Town.

Fire Watcher. The hours of the paid Fire Watchers at the Council Offices will be 7.30 pm – 7 am until further notice.

Armstrong Siddeley Car. It has been decided to keep the Armstrong Siddeley car (for the Fire Service) for the time being, the Vauxhall car not coming up to standard.

Regal. 'Behind the Door.' starring Boris Karloff.

Advert. Umbrellas!! Supplies of new goods restricted to 25%. Let us recondition and re-cover your old umbrella and make it like new. Re-covers from 5/6d. Rapid Service – Excellent Workmanship. Thorne and Thorne, High Street, Shepton Mallet.

Advert. 'Champagne of Somerset'. Showerings Ltd are now bottling this seasons Sweet Sparkling Cyder. You can taste that exquisite fresh apple flavour in this Cyder because unlike most Cyder a large proportion of the natural sugar in the Somerset apple is retained in the finished product.

Dances advertised in Pylle Hall and the Memorial Hall Cranmore.

Advert. Wanted a Sexton for Shepton Mallet Parish Church. Salary approximately £60 per annum with emoluments. Applicants must be a communicant. Apply Churchwardens, Shepton Mallet.

21 March 1941

A great attraction is booked by the local detachments of the British Red Cross Society for the Drill Hall on Wednesday April 2nd in the engagement of Joe Loss and his famous Broadcasting Dance Band. It is a great 'pull off' and tickets are already eagerly being sought. There is little doubt that the evening will be a memorable one.

Shepton Mallet District Hospital Annual Meeting. Expenditure exceeds income. Mr C Burnell President, Mr W A Corben Secretary, Mr S G Lemon Hon Tres, Berkeley Hall auditor. Amongst others present Sir Richard and Lady Paget, Mr and Mrs Belchamber, Dr Taffe Finn, Mrs Spencer, Mrs Wainwright, Messrs C Penhulm, Ingleton Rowe, H Matthews and W W Gilson.

Hospital Figures	1940	1939
Numbers of in Patients (inc accidents)	348	305
Total Number of Days in Hospital	5586	5205
Average Days per Case	16.05	17.06
Daily Average	15.3	14.2

170 males 178 females
216 cured, 89 relieved, 21 died, 21 other causes.
7 remained at the end of the year.
The number of operations during the year was 235 against 146 last year.
Out patients 926.

Number of Massage and Electrical Treatments	2867
X Rays	231
Films taken	360
Electrical Exercises	8
Sunlight	80

Number of Private patients 40 against 25 last year.

Chairman's report. They were sorry about the debt but it was difficult during the war to raise extra money. He alluded to a suggestion for reorganization of hospital services on a regional basis by the Ministry of Health after the war and thought it probable that some assistance would then be forthcoming to preserve and maintain the work of the Voluntary Hospitals. (Note. Sixty years on it seems almost incomprehensible that Shepton Mallet at that time was organizing, funding and running its own hospital. One expects the cost of bureaucracy were considerable lower as a percentage than the NHS has ever achieved.)

Shepton Mallet and District Hospital League (of Friends) 10th AGM held in Council Hall. Membership 4071 an increase of 131 during the year. Contributions Two Thousand two hundred and sixty six pounds.

Regal. 'Elizabeth and Essex' starring Bette Davis and Errol Flynn.

Cricket Club AGM reported that so many people had joined up that they were not sure what sort of a side they would put out. (Note. The cricket club shortly after this teamed up with Cranmore Cricket club and for the duration of the war played as Shepton Mallet and Cranmore United Cricket Club. Finding a team seemed nearly as hard then as it does for the same clubs today, as someone who plays for both knows!)

Letter. Day of Prayer. Mr E A Norman Chairman of the Urban District Council asking local organizations to attend the Morning Service 11o'clock March 23rd.

28 March 1941

Spitfire fund at £737. £43 from the Spotlight Concert.

4 April 1941

Scouts Annual Meeting. Scoutmaster Cyril Amor gave at report. 80 boys are attending weekly lectures, instructional classes etc. They have done much useful work including filling of sand bags, collection of waste paper – six tons and the formation of a messenger service. Mr Amor is devoting five nights a week to scout work.

Evacuee George Bartlett has many memories of being in the scouts.

"I was a member of the 1st Shepton Mallet Scouts and we met where the Co-op is now situated. Two very dingy rooms but we had a lot of fun and made lots of friends. Paper collection, jam jar collection, string collection in fact we collected anything which accelerated the war effort. I remember going on general camping holidays, setting off with our bags and baggage singing any songs we knew. One camping holiday was on the Cheddar Hills. We were camping on a farm. It rained and rained accompanied by thunder and lightning. We used to draw our water from stand pipes and we were getting tremendous shocks from static electricity! The camp fires in the evening, lots of games and suppers which were drummed up from all sorts of left overs. Finally the good old sing song with tunes such as 'We're riding along on the crest of a wave'."

Shepton Mallet Rural District Council. Two steam rollers are at present employed on patching and resurfacing. Work during the month was carried out on Norton Down Road, Ilchester Road near the New Inn Lydford and on Frome Road near the turning to Downhead. The white lines throughout the district have now been repainted.

Letter from Ernest H Froud Hon Sec, Grammar School Shepton Mallet points out the official recognition of the ATC and asks all boys 16 and over to join.

John Jeeves, a soldier, was charged with stealing 5d from a till in a shop adjoining Smith's Garage in Pylle. Jeeves was remanded under military control until the following Friday.

11 April 1941

Egg week. Eggs are urgently needed for the Shepton Mallet District Hospital and arrangements have been made for an Egg Week from 14th – 19th April. Any quantity will be welcomed by the Matron at the hospital during this period.

Presentation to Mr H Belchamber prior to the Shepton Mallet Urban District Council meeting. He had been connected with the council for 30 years and the clerk for 10. War had taken its toll and broken his health. The gift was an oak bureau.

Dig for Victory. Land on the west side of Barren Down Lane is in a neglected state. A letter sent to War Agricultural Committee

The Bowling and Croquet Club have offered land formally used as Croquet Green for allotments. The committee have accepted. (Note. This land is still being used as allotments today.)

Shelters. Domestic Communal Shelters. Lowest tender for six communal shelters had been accepted: £753.

Shepton Mallet Police Court. A case against John Richard Dixon, a soldier, accused of indecently assaulting a female under the age of 16 was dismissed.

> The tone of the report suggested that the soldier had on a number of occasions been playing with children under 12 and had mentioned the lavatories. Mr Ames defending said it was an unlikely story made up by the children. The case was dismissed as the Army said the soldier was on fatigues duty at the time of the alleged offence.

Advert. Shepton Mallet Urban District Council. At the request of the Ministry of Food a community feeding centre will be opened at the Market Hall Townsend Tuesday April the 15th. Run by members of the WVS. Meals served daily 6d and 8d from 12.30pm – 1.45pm. The centre will be open to all who wish to take advantage of it.

Regal. 'Virginia City' starring Errol Flynn, Randolph Scott and Miriam Hopkins.

25 April 1941

AGM of the Bowls and croquet and Tennis Club. Secretaries report by Mr Witt showed that interest in the club was, in spite of all the difficulties caused by the war, on the whole well maintained. Mr L S Witt was presented with a chiming clock. He had to resign prior to being called up for military service.

2 May 1941

Advert. Shepton Mallet Gents Hairdressers will be raising their prices on and after Monday next. Haircutting will be 8d and shaving 4d.

Advert. A dance will be held in aid of the Shepton Mallet Home Guard and Red Cross (13th and 18th Detachments) on Monday night at the Drill Hall for 400 people. Hal Fox and his Ambassadors and the Avalon Dance Bands.

Tragic Death of Four Soldiers. Premature explosion at a Demonstration. (The position of this piece in the paper suggests it was very local probably on the firing ranges on Beacon Hill above the town.) The deaths of four soldiers was described to the coroner for South East Somerset. The officer commanding the regiment stated that he ordered a demonstration of a mortar platoon coming into action. The battalion was lined up as spectators in a semi circle about 25 yards from the mortar. The detachment nearest the mortar commenced to fire and the first round was normal. The second round appeared to have exploded immediately on leaving the muzzle of the mortar, although he was not watching it at the time he heard the explosion and looking around at the battalion he saw men on the ground and smoke clearing from the mortar. He then found that a number of officers and other ranks had been hit.

> The medical officer of the regiment said one soldier was dead on admission to hospital, two died the same day and one died the following day. He thought it likely that there would be at least one more death. The cause of the death in each case was due to shrapnel wounds.

9 May 1941

People were still being fined for blackout offences. Mrs Nancy Kate Reeves Cannards Grave Inn. In a room where a light was not working in the morning so no blackout was put up. Someone must have fixed the light without her knowing. Fined 15/- as a second offence.

Kenneth Emery roadman of 33 Victoria Grove was fined 10/- for displaying light from a fire.

Advert.
For sale. Bean Sticks. Tutton, Basket Shop, Church Lane Shepton Mallet.
For Sale. Tandem Four pounds. Butler, Market Place, Shepton Mallet.

Silage campaign. Ministry Van touring the west. A mobile exhibition van demonstrating the national silage campaign has started a tour of the market towns of Wiltshire and Somerset. Includes models, illustrations, sound equipment. The van will broadcast a message from the Ministry of Agriculture.

16 May 1941

Shepton Mallet Urban District Council. Pigs. The War Agricultural Executive Committee point out that pig keeping by the council will not be an economic proposition. The matter has been considered and the surveyor instructed to enquire the price of Boilers for Sterilising Swill.

Air Raid Distress Fund. This committee has met and decided to make an advance to an applicant.

Fire Brigade. The Mid Somerset Motors Co has offered the council a 28 HP 8 cylinder Hudson Car in exchange for an allowance of £60 on the Armstrong Siddeley car and a cheque for forty pounds.

Civil Defence. The committee further reported that the Regional Technical Advisor had not approved the revised scheme for Communal Domestic Shelters but had instructed that a further revised scheme should be submitted.

Chairman Mr Norman announced that War Weapons Week was to be held Saturday 7th June – Saturday 14th June aiming to raise £40,000. This was being dealt with through the National Savings Movement. Mr Lemon is Chairman of the committee.

Mr Witcombe. ' I think we are rather late in the day for a war weapons week. I think people have given their utmost or they should have done by now. It is very late to start a scheme now.

Tribute was paid to the WVS running the Communal Feeding Centre which had made a good start. It reflects credit on the town and the whole neighbourhood.

Advert. Tizer were advertising about the need for people to return their bottles.

Domestic Fruit Preservation Scheme 1941. To the inhabitants of Shepton Mallet Urban District Council. Will all fruit growers who wish to sell their surplus fruit in aid of the above scheme send their estimates of the quantity they wish to dispose of to Shepton Mallet

Garden Fruit Committee. Box F Journal Office. Gooseberries, Strawberries, Raspberries, Blackcurrants and Rhubarb.

28 May 1941

Advert. Shepton Mallet War Weapons Week. June 7th – 14th. Three ways you can help. Talk about it. Work for it. Subscribe to it.

Complaints over conversion of a neglected and dandelion covered plot situated in Collett Avenue. When turned into a small allotment the whole of the rubbish, sods and all have been banked around the area presenting a most deplorable sight in a residential area. The proper thing, of course, would have been to burn it by degrees and not to have piled it up mud wall fashion, (Note. Collett Avenue would be considered one of the more exclusive residential parts of Shepton Mallet!)

War Weapons Week. How much things cost. Battleship £8 million, Aircraft Carrier £3 million, Cruiser, £2 million, Submarine £350,000. Torpedo £2,000, Air Force Bomber £20,000, Fighter £5,000, Barrage Balloon £700, Army Tank £15,000, Heavy Machine Gun, £350, Smaller Machine Gun, £100, every AA shell, £4.

Letter from FJE Pullen suggesting that the Spitfire Fund's £800 be added to the War Weapons Week Total. (Note. Seems to have been a good way out of what had become a bit of an embarrassment.)

30 May 1941

Shepton Mallet and District Homing Society 84 mile race.

Bumper crowd at Regal Sunday concert by Al Lever and his band from the Winter Gardens Weston-super-Mare in aid of the Red Cross. So full was the Cinema that many were unable to gain admission.

Regal. "Gas Bags" with the Crazy Gang and Moore Merriot.

Editorial on the sinking of the Battle Cruiser HMS Hood and the relentless search by the Navy for the Bismark.

Advert. Beacon Leisure Park. Dances over the Whit weekend.

6 June 1941

War Weapons Week to have an indicator in the Market Place where the previous days receipts will be chalked up at 10am.

13 June 1941

War Weapons Week – amount raised so far £64,444. The crowds turned out in their thousands for the opening ceremony and watched a procession through the streets of Military and Civil Defence units. Home Guard, Auxiliary Police, Fire Brigade, Auxiliary Fire Services, ARP Wardens, Red Cross Detachments men and women, Rescue Squad, Cubs, Scouts and Guides. They marched to the east side of the lake in Collett Park. At the saluting base – the band stand - Sir Frederick Berryman, President of War Weapons Week, R A Hobhouse

RDC E H Norman UDC, Mr B Hall, Mr S G Lemon Chairman of War Weapons Week committee, Major V D S Williams, A W Chidgley, E E Poles, Miss F A Berryman. Regional Commissioner Major General Lindsey CBCMG DSO arrived in Mufti. His arrival must have been welcomed by the processionists who had been standing for an hour. Unfortunately the loud speaker system failed.

At 5 pm the indicator unveiled £26,659 raised. Later in the evening a composite band under Mr R Marsh rendered an excellent programme in the Market Place. It was the first time a band had been heard playing in the Market Place on a Saturday evening for many a long dreary month.

20th June 1941

Shepton Mallet and District War Weapons Week Objective Quadrupled. Amount raised £163,111/13/5d.

Two oranges in a sale at Wainwright Laver and Crees raised nearly £150!!

Summary of the money

- 2.5% National War Bonds   £35,500
- 3% Saving Bonds   £27,270
- 3% Defence Bonds   £42,725
- National Savings Certificates   £50,880
- National Savings Stamps   £1,225/17/1
- PO Savings Bank Deposits   £8,310/16/4

Shepton Man's Silly Act. Henry William James Godden a tiler of 77 Garston Street pleaded guilty to retaining in his possession an article dropped by enemy aircraft.

He dropped an incendiary device in the Hare and Hounds Hotel causing damage to the floor and two doors. PWR Trott said he was passing the Hare and Hounds Hotel when he heard a woman shout 'fire' and saw a doorway illuminated by white fire and smoke coming out.

The defendant had found the device while working in Bristol. He had shown it to his employer R Showering who told him to take it to the police. He took it home and forgot about it. His wife nagged him to get rid of it. He put it in his pocket to take to the Police Station, He called in at the Hotel on his way and after showing it to some friends, placed it on a seat while he had a game of darts. About closing time his wife came in and asked if he had still got it. He told her it was all right as it was a 'dud'. He picked it up but it fell from his hand and exploded. He was very sorry for what had happened and was willing to pay for the damage. He was fined £1 and 5s costs for retaining the bomb.

Note. I featured this story in the Shepton Mallet Magazine during the researching of this book. About a month after it appeared I received a phone call from a Professor Barry Godden in Canterbury Kent. He was intrigued where I had got the story as he thought it was only known inside the family. Henry Godden had been his father. There are still a number of Goddens living locally.

Regal. 'Tom Brown's Schooldays' starring Sir Cedric Hardwicke and Freddie Bartholomew.

Editorial on the War Weapons Week. 'The week's effort was a great achievement and reflects credit upon all, not least of whom are the small investors'.

Editorial comment also on how efficiently Messrs Standerwick of Bridgwater had put up Council Houses at Westfield for Shepton Mallet Urban District Council- all done cheaply because of the speed. In marked contrast has been the erection of a brick wall in the district during the current week – one brick today and another tomorrow style. – no wonder the rate payers grouse.

27 June 1941

Soldiers to help farmers at harvest. Farmers who need help should apply to the CO and providing the duties do not interfere with Army training a number of men will be released for work.

War-time haymaking, a young Nelson Butt on the waggon.

4 July 1941

The Evercreech Platoon Home Guard held a fairly successful dance in the village hall on Friday. Starting a small fund to cover the small things the War Office forgot to provide.

The Regal Circus. Cook's Paddock Shepton Mallet. Monday – Tuesday 7th and 8th July twice daily.

Editorial. At Shepton Mallet Petty Sessions on Friday the much tried and overwrought caretaker of Collett Park Mr T Rowsell appeared to answer a charge of assault in respect of a lad. He pleaded guilty and on hearing the evidence the justices in their wisdom, dismissed the case on the payment of costs.

For 14 years Mr Rowsell has been the park keeper and he has cared and tended it to almost perfection and its well kept and beautiful appearance has oft times been commented upon by visitors to the town. At times Mr Rowsell must almost have died of a broken heart for seats have been overturned, wire baskets uprooted and trees damaged all with no subsequent prosecutions to act as a healthy deterrent.

It must have been to him, under the circumstances, a burning irony to find himself before local justices for having in a moment of desperation stood a young man 'on his head' in the lake.

There is to be no rationing of beer and spirits, a parliamentary question was answered. 'The Cabinet has come to the conclusion that it is in the public interest that the production of light beers should continue at the present amount.

11 July 1941

Shepton Mallet Urban District Council – Allotments – notices are being posted warning owners of dogs of the penalty if their animals are found straying on the various allotments.

The Council discussed the case of the park keeper and supported the idea that the public should be more supportive in providing information allowing them to prosecute vandals. Berkeley Hall commented that people held back from things that led to official action.

18 July 1941

Shepton Mallet Hospitals. W/E July 13th. Admitted 11 Discharged 5 Outpatients 85. The matron acknowledges with many thanks the following gifts – Mrs Matthews, lettuce and onions, Mr C Moon rhubarb, Miss Burnell gooseberries and rhubarb, Miss Coles peas and cabbage.

Advert. Public Air-Raid Shelters. Persons willing to act as voluntary Shelter Marshalls at any of the below mentioned shelters should please communicate with me at once.

Collett Park, Charlton Cross Roads, Highfield 'Park Road', 'Bunch of Grapes' public house, A Hobbs shop, High Street, signed A D Stockdale Clerk to the Council.

25 July 1941

Scholastic Success. Two more children of the West Ham evacuated school at Kilver Street have gained scholarships. This makes a total of nine successes at this school.

Sunday School Outing. Wesleyan Sunday School, took place an Wednesday. 50 adults (Parents, Teachers and Friends) and 85 children went by rail.

Shepton Mallet Rural District Council. Salvage. The committee have, at a moderate rental, secured premises at Milbrook Farm Downside for the storage and separation of salvageable materials.

Regal. 'Old Bill and Son' starring Morland Graham and John Mills.

1 August 1941

Report on Garden Fete: The fixture was keenly anticipated by all, who had on former occasions been privileged to attend similar functions, to enjoy the pretty grounds so perfectly kept, to converse with the kindly host and members of his family, (C R Wainwright at Summerleaze house) to patronize the heavily laden stalls and to participate in the various sideshows.

Many prominent citizens were present including Sir Richard and Lady Paget.

Shepton Mallet Petty Sessions. Arthur E Curnish, Station Road, North Woolwich was summoned by his wife Rosetta Curnish now residing at Town Lane Shepton Mallet who applied for a maintenance order in respect of herself and child. Curnish said his wife and children were evacuated to Shepton in September and he sent his wife £1 a month until December when certain information came to his knowledge. Since then he had sent only 10/- which was forwarded each week to his daughter who was staying with his wife. This was a daughter by a previous marriage. When he heard his wife was going to have another baby he stopped her allowance and although he had been employed he had not drawn an allowance in respect of his wife and her baby.

Regal. Edward G Robinson, Ann Southern and Humphrey Bogart in 'Brother Orchid'.

Advert. Shepton Mallet Rural District Council advising on the sale of special steel helmets for workers in Commercial Premises, Small Factories and Agricultural Workers. Sold to employers at the request of the Government.

Advert. Headmasters of Sexey's and Kings School, Bruton asking farmers to get in touch with needs for schoolboy labour as they had organized 'harvest camps'. 1,000 boys available in the county. 6d an hour at 16, 5d an hour below that age.

8 August 1941

Sir Frederick Berryman's strong warning to boys. "You have committed a very serious offence. In these times when all the world is engaged in war works to have police and railway officials wasting time preventing you doing what may do very serious damage to the railway network in times like these, this is a state of affairs this court will not tolerate. You will each be fined 15/- if you undertake not to repeat the offence in the of future. Shepton Mallet Juvenile Court addressed to five Shepton lads between 12 and 16 when they admitted trespassing on the railway. They had been seen picking up stones from the permanent way and throwing them in the direction of the Park. The Police had recently had complaints of stones thrown through the window of a train at this point.

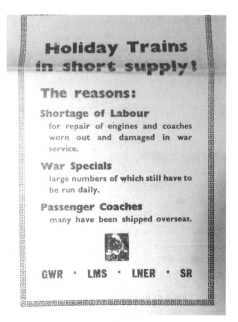

Train shortage.

Bank Holiday Crowds at Sea Side Towns. Not as large as in pre war days but it seems many had ignored the Government's 'stay put' injunctions. Lots of people travelling by train. 13,500 to Weston-super-Mare, 3,600 to Severn Beach and 700 to Portishead.

Advert. West End House, Shepton Mallet. Sale of the Hospital Growing Crop of Wheat. Standing on about 2 acres of land situated near the above adjoining the Old Wells Road. Wainwright, Laver and Crees.

15 August 1941

Hearty Congratulations. The many friends in the Town and District of Miss Doreen Hall will offer their hearty congratulations upon her promotion to 2nd Subaltern in the ATS. She is the first young lady in the town to receive a commission. Miss Hall is now on leave and expecting to be posted any day. (daughter of Berkeley Hall)

Home Guard Shooting Competition. At the Red Cross Fete held at Westcombe House on August 6th the Home Guard of the Shepton Mallet Company competed in a shooting competition at which Field Marshal Lord Birchwood was an interested and keen spectator.
> Every Platoon in the company entered a team. The eliminating stages under the direction of the platoon commanders were keenly contested during the short training. The Evercreech team were the winners whilst the East Pennard team were runners up. Captain Milsom was the Range Officer and carried out his duties in a very able manner. The officers present were Major Luff, Capt Franks, and Lieutenants Bennett, Horler, Martin, Norgrove, Napier and Livingstone.

Shepton Mallet Urban District Council. A bit of a contretemps over filling a vacancy by co-option. It had been agreed to offer it to the WVS to put someone forward. However, the WVS had replied that 'most of them are, however, fully engaged in war work and there seems no great desire on the part of the other part to accept this office.' Mr Chidgley was co-opted – he had done excellent work in War Week and was in the ARP organizers office.

Spitfire Fund at £823. Mr Pullen asked the council for help with winding up the fund. He found that since the advent of War Savings had come about, it had knocked the Spitfire fund all to pieces and the best thing to do was to close it.
> He felt let down by the council reporting that the Rural District Council had more than doubled the town collection and compared Shepton unfavourably with the effort in Wells. He was sorry too that the spirit of giving had given place to saving.

A costly mistake. Alice Marsh, 13 Town Street, Shepton Mallet was fined £1 for selling fish above the agreed price. She claimed that when asked the price of fish she was referring to haddock not cod. Mr C W Harris prosecuting for the Shepton Mallet Food Office said that this case should be regarded as far more important than the sums involved would justify, for fish was obtained at great cost of fishermen's lives. It was shocking that a commodity obtained at such a price should be exploited for the profit of a private trader.

Advert. Harrison's 'Calling up sale.' Harrison's, London House, Shepton Mallet.

Editorial of the WVS co-option issue. A letter from Miss Berrymen said they had suggested these people were too busy. Few towns were better served by their women folk than

Shepton Mallet; and it redounds to their common sense to know and admit their limitations.

22 August 1941

Dig for Victory Show – Most Successful. Opening ceremony by Mr C E Burnell, F J E Pullen President, E J Hardwidge Chairman, Geoffrey Budd Vice Chairman, Mr Grimshaw Hon. Sec. A good show put on.

Regal. 'Torrid Zone' starring James Cagney, Ann Sheridan and Pat O'Brien.

29 August 1941

Big Blaze in Paul Street. Sheptonians and others were given a first class thrill on Saturday afternoon when the Old Cinema in Paul Street and adjoining premises in High Street very nearly went up in smoke.

Fire had broken out in the oil department of Messrs E Hobley and Son Ironmonger. Within four minutes the brigade under the command of Arthur Hobbs were on the scene. It was a tight spot to get to and oil and water don't mix. Foam composition was applied but proved ineffective due to continuously bursting barrels. The spread of fire was so rapid that within 20 minutes the roof of the Old Cinema ante room fell in. Wells fire brigade arrived and set about combating the fire from the Constitutional Club side running the hose through the passage of the Central Motor Co.

It looked as if it would spread to the dwelling house of Mrs Hobley and innumerable willing hands including Boy Scouts applied themselves with a will to removing the furniture from the upstairs rooms to a place of safety. Fortunately it was contained in time but considerable damage was done.

The previous time there had been a major fire in the town centre was 1916 when the 'Spirit Vaults' had caught.

Petty sessions. Kate Dennett, Middle Ham Farm prosecuted for making cheese without a licence. She admitted cheese was found on the farm but it was for use in the farm house and not for being sold. Chairman of the Board decided an offence had been committed.

Advert for 'Salvage for Victory'. A great drive for paper Material and Bones. September 1st – 13th.

Editorial on the fire. The Auxiliary Fire Brigade, although not called officially, stood in and lent a hand when and where they could. The Shepton Mallet Water Works Company was , through its secretary (Geoffrey Budd) alive to the situation and at once shut off the mains to the outlying districts to enable full pressure to be brought to bear in the conflagration.

5 September 1941

National Deposit Friendly Society. Highly successful dance held at their offices on Wednesday the proceeds of which were donated to the Boy Scouts. Billy Lukins Tor Dance Band.

Messrs E Hobley & Sons plate glass window smashed yet again. A huge caravan on turning from Paul Street into High Street crashed into the second series of panes.

Regal. Tommy Trinder and Claude Hulbert in 'Sailors Three' plus 'No No Nanette' starring

Anna Neagle and Roland Young.

12 September 1941

Sunday had been a day of Prayer. The Church was full and the parade included Serving men, Home Guardsmen, full contingents of the councilors, Boy Scouts and Girl Guides making a splendid muster.

Shepton Mallet Urban District Council. Civil Defence. No names have been received for Shelter Marshals. 500 sandbags have been rot proofed and are ready for distribution.

Letter from ARP Commandant W A Price appealing yet again for more men for casualty services. Volunteers urgently needed for first aid parties. 12 hour night turns 3 times a week. Now including women in the appeal or girls as long as not already in the Women's Branch of the Red Cross as they were already needed there.

19 September 1941

Prisoners of War Red Cross Fund. Cricket match between Shepton Mallet and Cranmore United and Wells Public Schools. At the Grammar School Admission 6d.

Shepton Mallet Rural District Council. Concern at Damage done by evacuees during the Summer Holidays. 'Evacuee children had caused much damage and annoyance to local residents. As their school teachers had been on holiday there had been no-one in charge of them. Mr J P Luff said he had seen one child standing on a roof taking off tiles and throwing them at other children.

Editorial. Evacuees. No-where in the county has probably given a more spontaneous welcome to these lads and lasses. The common grouse both in the Urban and Rural Districts however is the lack of subsequent authoritive supervision following school hours.

Letter asking if anyone knows the names of any Shepton prisoners of war. The only names had were Corpl Mason, Lance Corpl Denning and Sergeant J Stead. They wanted to make sure all were getting Red Cross Parcels from funds received.

26 October 1941

Salvage. The Girl Guides have collected a magnificent 15 tons of waste paper.

Seeing for themselves. Cadets of the Shepton Mallet Flight Air Training Corp recently spent a very entertaining, instructional and enjoyable afternoon at a Royal Naval

Save Gas advertisement.

Air Station.....each was shown around the 'drome by a young naval officer of Narvik fame. Skua, Fulmer, Hurricanes etc were inspected, the Cadets settling themselves in the cockpits and thus learning something of the pilot's task.

The Somerset Challenge Cup, originally presented by Sir Ernest Jardine to the Shepton Mallet Sports Society has after a long period of use been brought back into commission. At an auction in aid of the Shepton Mallet Nursing Association, it was sold for £9 to Shepton Mallet Motor Cycle Club.

There were three letters criticizing the previous week's stance taken on evacuees pointing out the small amount of damage, that there is supervision and that some of the damage is done by locals. It was 'too easy to blame it on the evacuees.'

Regal. 'Spare a Copper' starring George Formby.

3 October 1941

Flying Officer C W Holbourn RAF awarded MBE. Son-in-Law of residents Mr & Mrs W Crosby.

A vegetable show was held at Shepton Mallet on Saturday open to all employees of the CWS Bacon Factory. The first of its kind held for the benefit of employees but it is hoped that it will be the forerunner of many such in the future. Entrance Fees were given to the Red Cross and a good proportion of the exhibits were given to the local hospital.

Report on Mid-Somerset Agricultural Society annual meeting. Had problems doing the educational work of hedging and thatching but its importance was stressed. The County Agricultural Inspector had recently commented on how he could always tell when he was in the Mid-Somerset Agricultural Society area by the high standards.

Advert. Shepton Mallet Urban District Council Emergency Powers. Requisition of unnecessary railings. A Survey is being carried out of all iron or steel railings, posts chains, bollards, gates, stiles etc in the Urban District Council area with a view to removal and collection for use in the national war effort. Exceptions. i) Railings which should be maintained for safety reasons ii) Railings necessary to prevent cattle etc from straying. iii) Railings of special artistic merit or of historic interest.

10 October 1941

Thomas T Gane, boarding house keeper, 'Lynfield' Cranmore was fined 15/- for displaying a light from a building.

National Rose Hip Week. Letter from Cyril Amor 1st Shepton Mallet Scout Group asking for local people to assist the scouts and cubs to collect hips to provide the Hospitals, Children and Invalids with Vitamin 'C'. He also appealed for old scout uniforms as he was finding supply difficult.

Regal. "The Ghost of St Michaels" starring Will Hay and Claude Hulbert.

Billiards. Shepton Mallet Liberal Club v Shepton Mallet Constitutional Club. Snooker Shepton Mallet British Legion v National Deposit Friendly Society.

17 October 1941

Skittles Tournament. The Red Cross penny a week fund Skittles Cup, presented by Messrs Showering draw: The Red Cross v Showerings. British Legion v Rural District Council. The Police v Fire Brigade. Pilton Home Guard v Garstonians. Special Police v MPSG(prison guards). United Bank v Post Office. The Assistance Board v The Crown Inn. The Air Ministry v The Navy. National Deposit Friendly Society v Home Guard. Urban District Council v Observer Corp. The matches will be played at the Kings Arms.

Shepton Mallet Urban District Council. Debate on whether to buy a new snow plough for £40. The Surveyor, "The old plough is about 30 years old and was originally pulled by three horses. Last year it was attached to Mr Oatley's lorry and it then had to be loaded with ballast to keep it down. Three or four men were also required on the guide rope to look after it. I do consider it essential to have a snow plough."
   (Note. Mr Oatley's lorry seems to have been much in demand. Stan Blacker informs
   me that it was also the transport for the ARP rescue party.)

21 October 1941

Leonard Creed Westbrook Farm Evercreech fined 10/- for failing to notify a change of ownership of a motor car. Chairman asked the press to give publicity to the fact that such an action was necessary.

Regal. 'Major Barbara' with Wendy Hillier, Robert Morley, Rex Harrison, Emlyn Williams and Dame Sybil Thorndyke.

31 October 1941

Much Impressed. Friends and Members of the Baptist Church were privileged to visit the ARP Headquarters on Saturday. Pastor H T Turner said 'that he would not only like to congratulate all the workers of the ARP who are doing their work so ungrudgingly to this Parish, but to thank them. If only, he said, all inhabitants realized the great care taken to ensure safety for themselves and their homes, every moment night and day, they too would join whole heartedly in his vote of thanks and if called upon would enlist in this happy band of voluntary workers.

7 November 1941

Soldier fined at Shepton Mallet. Expensive 'bit of fun'. A soldier William Drewitt pleaded guilty at Shepton Mallet Police Court to obstructing the highway by laying a wooden gate thereon.
   A resident saw soldiers in the village throwing stones at a tin shed, smash a window of
   a telephone kiosk and unhinge a gate and lay it in the road. A car came up the road and
   drove on to the gate and had to reverse off before it could be moved.
   "We went down to this village on a Saturday night to have a bit of fun and got a bit
   merry. We thought the villagers would take it in good part. I remember unhinging the
   gate and I put it in the road for a joke. The others started running away and I followed
   them and left the gate in the road. We had been drinking cider." He was fined £1 plus
   costs.

Bravo. Miss Doreen Feltham of Oakhill who was formally manageress of Miss Parfit's hairdressing saloon in High Street and Miss Olive Carter also formerly employed in business in the town, now members of the Women's Land Army Corps came in for high commendation by the Ministry of Agriculture when he recently visited Somerset. Together these two girls whose ages are 24 and 21 have done most of the work on a 740 acre farm recently taken over by the Somerset War Agricultural Committee. Up to date they have tackled single handedly all the disc harrowing and drilling of 400 acres at Steanbow Pilton. Both girls were trained by the Woman's Land Army before being put on the land which was in a poor state of cultivation but is now fertile and productive again.

(Note. There would seem to be an element of exaggeration and perhaps propaganda here. In fact Steanbow was the area farm for the training of the Women's Land Army.)

Regal. 'The Ghost Train.' Starring Arthur Askey and Stinker Murdoch.

14 November 1941

Remembrance Sunday at Shepton Mallet. Members of the various services of the Crown attended an intercessory service conducted by Mr F J E Pullen. The huge gathering reverently joined in the response 'We will remember them' for Ron Hayter, Charlie Denning, Fred Manby, Jack Stead, Hubert Mason and Jack Walshe. 'They shall not grow old as we that are left grow old." The last Post and Reveille were sounded by Mr Henry Tucker and the procession moved off to the church.

(Note. Some of these names were definitely prisoners of war. I am not sure if some were also from the role of honour as the wording would imply.)

Shepton Mallet Urban District Council. An application received for the use of the Market Hall one night a week for country dancing lessons.

War Damage. Orders have been issued to local builders for the necessary first aid and repairs to be carried out to houses damaged through enemy action.

Discussion over the removal of railings in front of peoples' homes as only 25s a ton offered for the metal. Surely the government did not mean to deface peoples homes for 10/-. "If the railings are taken it is as if damage is done by a bomb."

Residents had a right to object in writing stating the reason.

Mr Norman, Chairman, had unilaterally closed the Market Hall (for dances) because of complaints of 'rowdies.' Mr Pullen strongly objected to the fact that it had not been put on the Council agenda – taken into committee.

Edmund Harold Norman, Chairman of Shepton Mallet UDC.

An Old Gunner and His Wife. Colin Ryall Interviews a couple with many memories of Shepton In Wartime.

Contributors: Mr Ernest & Mrs Kathleen Hodges (Mrs Hodges died on 27th April 2004 during final preparation of this book) .

Born a year before the Great War Ernest was trained as a compositor on the Shepton Mallet Journal, printed and published from premises in Commercial Rd, Shepton Mallet. ('Only 8 pages pre-war') .

For 7 years prior to WW II he was a 'Territorial', that is, a part time soldier. His was a Royal Artillery Unit (374 Battery) equipped with 18 pounder field guns of WW I vintage, based at the Drill Hall, off Charlton Rd.

"I joined when they brought in the 30cwt Morris lorries to pull the guns, but, if you please, we were mounted on horses," Ernest recollected, "cos I was in the signal section and we were mounted on horses." The horses came from local farms. "One of my horses came from Swain's Farm, Charlton," Ern recalled.

Ernest joined for the bounty, £5 per year and the 'generous' expenses paid. ('Three days at 2/6 per day to go to Taunton, when the trip only took one day.') For these were hard times, Ern can remember Welsh miners marching through Kilver St. and the householders giving them tea and sandwiches. "They were looking for work, any that were lucky dropped out, the rest marched on. They were mostly unlucky in Shepton, Shepton had it's own unemployed."

Ernest left the Territorial's a year before the war but volunteered immediately after war broke out. So after only a year of marriage he was soon posted away, arriving in East Africa he was lucky to be diverted to India rather than ending up in ill-fated Singapore.

"Oh! You'd be surprised!" was Kath's lively response when asked what she got up to while Ernest was away, "but best not to go into that."

"Well I had to go to work of course, had evacuees. One of them was a little devil, but still, we still hear from them." Kath added. Asked how she managed with the rationing Kath commented, "We managed alright, didn't we, it was a case of having to." Then Kath took a job at the Co-op, then a grocer's, clothes and furniture shop. (Then at the bottom of Town Street, demolished in the 70's to make way for Batch Road.)

"Many lines only came 'loose' then," Kath recalls, "sugar, tea, butter all had to be weighed and wrapped to order, bacon and ham (when available) sliced to the customers liking."

Meat, butter, cheese, eggs, sugar, sweets and in particular imported goods such as tea, chocolate, fruit, both fresh oranges and dried fruit were strictly rationed. Bananas and many 'fancy' products disappeared entirely e.g. there were no cakes or buns at the bakers.

Because of its high sugar content, 'Jam was rationed to 1lb(454gms) a month'. Bread and jam were part of the staple diet. However potatoes, greengroceries, bread, offal and offal products were not rationed except by cost, but supplies fluctuated. It was a case of queuing for this and queuing for that and taking what you could get, which was seldom as much or of the quality you would have liked. Regulars were looked after and for the favoured few items would be put back and kept 'under the counter'.

Kath recalls that despite retail price control some families were so hard up they could not afford to buy all the meagre rations they were entitled to, their surplus 'coupons' went to cover extra purchases by the better off.

Both to save expense and to supplement rations men were exhorted to 'Dig for Victory'. Allotments were popular but with so many men away working an allotment was too much for hard-pressed young mothers to take on. Healthy appetites were sated with 'stodge', spuds, suet puddings or bread and dripping. Children had to suffer the wartime austerity, there were no toys in the shops, sweets severely rationed and comics scarce, ice cream and lemonade disappeared ('Coke' was unheard of). Toys and dolls were home made or second hand. There was a good deal of swapping and trading, produce or 'coupons' in return for labour or childcare. Hard pressed mothers were delighted with gifts of second-hand children's clothes and toys, there were a great many 'hand-me-downs'. 'Make do and mend' was the order of the day.

"Oh, yes we were alright like that." Kath reflected.

However in wartime there was a strong sense of 'Share, and share alike'.

For a bride the family would rally round with 'coupons' for the dress (or more often dress material) for bride's and bride's maids' dresses and 'points' for, or gifts of, sugar and dried fruit for the wedding cake!

Beer, spirits and tobacco products weren't rationed but were in short supply, sometimes it would be a case of 'No Fags Today' or 'No Beer Today'. New stocks were not displayed but kept under the counter so there could be no argument when a customer was told, 'Sorry, we're out.' Retailers and publicans looked after their regulars and doled them out a portion of their normal purchases, hard luck for strangers! For those with money and few scruples there was always the black market.

Despite the severe shortage of newsprint the Shepton Mallet Journal was printed throughout the war. Ernest returned to find his old job open to him, as promised before he left for the war, and life for Ernest and Kath reverted to much like their pre-war existence.

Superficially it would seem the war had little lasting effect on Ernest & Kath but for Ern he traveled further and gained wider experience than he could ever have expected. He made lifelong friendships with wartime comrades. For Kath, she had to learn to cope on her own 'for the duration' and care for dependant children.

For both of them the war was one of the big events of their lives although Kath finds, as the alarms and excursions of war fade into the dim and distant past, "Doesn't seem as though it happened now, after all these years."

21 November 1941

Regal. 'Love on the Dole' starring Deborah Kerr.

Advert. Messer's R G Harrison of London House, due to service call up, is transferring business to Mr A S F Painter of London. Men's Cloths and Outfitting department will be suspended until the end of the war. The Drapery, Children's and household depts, will operate as previously. A selective selection of Ladies and Children's dress, lingerie and woolen piece goods will be introduced.

18 November 1941

After a lapse of some time the annual pound day on behalf of Shepton Mallet Hospital was reinstated this year and held on Friday. Despite the war and its many restrictions, the call met with a most gratifying response and exceeded all expectations.

Baptist Church. Both services on Sunday were under the complete control of members of the Armed Forces. Pastor H T Turner suggests that such gatherings should appeal to residents of Shepton Mallet. "These men are prepared to give their experiences as regards Christianity and should be encouraged."

Regal. 'Rookies' starring Bud Abbot and Lou Costello.

5 December 1941

For King and Country. Mrs Hayter, 4 Catsash who for many years has been a loyal and regular member of the Women's Section of the Shepton Mallet Branch, British Legion received official intimation on Monday that her son Percy, popularly known as 'Ronnie' died of wounds at Malines 12 July 1940 whilst a prisoner of war. Mrs Hayter returns thanks for the many kind expressions of sympathy she has received.

Mid-Somerset Show secretary Gordon Perry had received subscription of £2 from Vice – Admiral Sir James Somerville. A great man who can, despite the pressures of state that lay heavily upon him, remember the little things.

Shepton Mallet Urban and Rural Local Savings Committee Warship Week Target of £120,000. Date set for the last week in March next year. The target is the cost of a 'Corvette (light destroyer) fully commissioned.

Advert. Red Cross aid to Russia – a dance will be held in the Jubilee Hall Evercreech. Band of the 88th Co, Royal Engineers.

12 December 1941

A warning. The Chief Constable of Somerset desires to again draw attention of the general public to the activities of a man who calls at private houses ostensibly for the purpose of repairing electrical cleaners of a certain well known brand and when left alone steals, particularly from bedrooms.

Shepton Mallet Urban District Council. Questions on the removal of railings on the roundabout at Townsend, painting white lines to divert traffic and a disputed suggestion that the beech tree may have to be taken down.

Mr Norman's action in closing the Market Hall had been supported. A Caretaker was now in position and new terms drawn up for all hirers. It reopened for social activities on 26th

November.

Christmas activities for evacuee children. The clerk said that a cinema show and entertainment had been arranged for the morning and afternoon of 23rd December. Sweets and Chocolate would also be distributed and half of these had been obtained.

Regal. 'Vivacious Lady' starring Ginger Rogers and James Stewart.

Evacuee Hostel. Springfield Evercreech. Estimates have been submitted to the Minister of Health for works of adaptation and equipment required at Springfield Evercreech. The Rural District council wants to transfer the hostel for evacuees there from Croscombe.

Working group member and former evacuee George Bartlett spent some time living in this Hostel which was closer to Stoney Stratton than Evercreech. He has memories of walking to Shepton and back to school and the adventures they had.

"I suppose we all look back on sunny days when we were young, and there were plenty of those – the big local war effort parades, the Church parades as a Scout, the feeling of pride for your Country and thinking you were the smartest scout on parade!! We even did our bit by growing vegetables in our local School garden. The long walk to and from school amounting to probably six miles a day. Of course the roads were much safer in those days, as traffic was almost non existent. In fact we often cadged a ride on the local railway cart and the local milk deliverer with her pony and trap.

I can remember snowy winters. The sledging on the meadows. One winter during the war a great freeze and there were very large icicles hanging on the trees, telephone lines and our favorite place was the local viaduct where icicles would form from the draining pipes under the arches. To aim at these with a stone and bring one down, you were a hero for the day. To finish these few recollections of our school days was punishment at school. To be caned was one thing, but to be called to the front in assembly and knowing you were to be caned. The humiliating part was to have to walk the whole length of the assembly hall, go to the cupboard, collect the cane and receive it to each hand. Fellow school mates will recall our Headmaster, Mr Poles."

19 December 1941

Treat for Old Folks. Residents of Shepton Mallet over the age of 55 (!) are cordially invited to a Cinema show and tea on Christmas Eve, This is being provided free through the generosity of a local businessman.

Fined £10 for receiving. At a West Country Police Court on Friday, Reginald Churchill, brick burner, Springwell Cottage, Evercreech was fined £10 for receiving a quantity of Army foodstuffs knowing them to be stolen. Leonard Frank Hurst 21, soldier, was fined £2 for stealing army foodstuffs valued at £1/0/1d. The defence of both was that they had had too much to drink at a dance.

26 December 1941

Crazy whist drive. A merry evening was spent at a crazy whist drive held in the Church Room at Cannards Grave on Thursday.

Margaret Gilles, spinster of Easton Cottage Pylle applied for an affiliation order against John Jeeves a soldier. Jeeves who was stated to have received conduct money to pay his fare and enable him to attend court admitted paternity and stated that his wife was now instituting divorce proceedings against him. He was ordered to pay 10/- a week until the child attains 16 years of age.

Note. It was particularly noticeable that there was not as many Christmas advertisements as in previous years. John Newsome provides a few memories of what war time Christmasses were like.

"I spent my wartime Christmasses with my grandparents at Wellow either by bus and walk from Peasedown or by train. My Christmas stocking contained a few small toys, an apple and a lump of coal wrapped in paper. We used to make our own decorations for the tree, it was amazing the candles instead of lights didn't catch the decorations alight. We all used to sit around the piano and sing carols and play charades. The only time we ever had poultry was at Christmas when we had a cockerel – a real treat."

The Public Record Office in the cells at Shepton Mallet Prison.

Chapter 5

1942

- January 15, Singapore falls to Japanese. 60,000 British troops captured.
- January 26, First American forces arrive in the UK
- May 30, Cologne was the target for the RAF's first thousand-bomber raid.
- October 23 – November 4, Montgomery defeats Rommel at El Alamein, the beginning of the end for the Axis forces in North Africa.

2 January 1942

Christmas Tree at the Parish Church. The Christmas Tree appeared to be bigger and better than ever before and despite the times there was a magnificent array of presents, together with a gratifying sum of monetary gifts. The Christmas Tree was the Rector's own scheme and he was richly rewarded for its introduction by the genuine warmth and practical support accorded it.

A splendid innovation for the parish was inaugurated at the Parish Church on Sunday when for the first time in its long history a Christmas Carol Service was held.

Children Entertained. Thanks to the generosity of a local gentlemen 1,000 school children were given a free show at the Regal Cinema last week for which they were all truly grateful. As they left each child received presents including sweets and a three-penny bit. These were provided by the local authorities.

Distinguished Flying Medal awarded to Sergeant R Norman Luff known to a wide circle of friends in the town. Before the war he was associated with Wainwright, Laver and Crees. He is a keen and reliable observer who has navigated his aircraft successfully to various targets throughout Germany and Enemy Occupied Territory. He is particularly cool when over the target area and his bombing proficiency has set a high standard for his colleagues.
   We understand that Sergt Luff has since been granted his commission.

Shepton Mallet Youth Movement. 'Many of the folks around Shepton Mallet doubtless heard us singing Christmas Carols in the week before Christmas and we thought we should tell you that our collection amounted to £5 which we have handed over to the Shepton Mallet War Charities Committee to be used to aid Russia.

9 January 1942

Advert. Quarrymen Protect your Feet. J E Hooper, Market Place, Shepton Mallet has just received a quota of Quarry Boots with steel toe caps.

Boy Scouts annual party. The Market Hall on New Years Eve was the scene of festivity when local and evacuee Scouts and Cubs gathered for their annual Christmas Party. After a 'sumptuous' feast, games were played. The 'do' finished in the usual way with a sing song.

Advert. A Byrt and Son's Household Almanack, a handy little booklet with gardening notes and Diary Complete. A few copies left, secure now 3d.

Somerset War Agriculture Executive Committee. Instruction to threshing machine proprietors to give priority to wheat.

16 January 1942

Shepton Mallet Urban District Council. Traffic Roundabout. The County surveyor intimates that he cannot agree to the proposed construction of a traffic roundabout at Coronation Plot at the junction of Compton Road as the radii of the curves are too short.

Allotments. It is resolved that the whole of the field adjoining the Charlton Inn with the exception of the tennis courts be taken over for allotment purposes.

Salvage. A salvage committee formed. Members of WVS, representatives of Boy Scouts and Girl Guides with Mr B Hall. In the three months to the end of November they had collected.

> Paper and Cardboard 22 ton 5 cwt, Scrap Metal 16 ton 8cwt, Tins 6 ton 1 cwt, Bones 1 ton 4 cwt, Rags 1 ton 7 cwt, Glass Jars 60 dozen, glass bottles 64 dozen, batteries 13 dozen.

Regal. 'Angels over Broadway,' starring Douglas Fairbanks and Rita Hayworth.

23 January 1942

National article about Italian prisoners of war. Most farmers saying their conduct and work was good. From 2nd January an experiment taking place with 'good conduct' prisoners being allowed to live on farms. (Note. A look at the phone book today will show how many Italians eventually settled in this area.

Advert. Lost Elkhound Dog. Information Hill, The Chestnuts, Evercreech.

30 January 1942

On the front page the paper leads with a National story – only time in entire war. Article on Churchill calling for a vote of confidence to gag concerted criticism of him. He had got flak for being away in America – paper thinks he was a hero for undertaking such a journey. He said "if you don't like me kick me out." Prepared to have his say and stand or fall by it. 'Guts' for which at this time the country may be truly grateful.

> It was the socialists and liberals who were more supportive of Churchill. Conservative 'back stairs intrigue.'

Member of Emborough Home Guard, 2nd Lieutenant Austin Foxwell was killed when hit by a car in the blackout.

Urban and District Warship week.. The committee had received intimation from the Admiralty that if the financial objective were reached it has been agree to name the ship HMS 'Mendip'. The ship will be a destroyer of the Hunt class. (Note. All vessels of this class were named after hunts.)

Regal. 'The Prime Minister' with John Gielgud and Diana Wynyard.

Somerset War Agricultural Executive Committee. Wood Pigeons. Need to reduce numbers urgently. Asking for people to shoot them.

6 February 1942

Advert. Violin Teaching. Madame Simeon (Diploma of the Schola Cantorum, Paris) visits Shepton Mallet weekly.

Ancient Order of Druids 74th Annual Dinner. Bell Hotel Shepton Mallet. Gone was the turkey and the roast joints together with the glorious baked potatoes and steaming brussel sprouts with a host of other good things which in pre war days were served up so lavishly.

Never the less the dinner was quite one of the best ever. Mine host Mr & Mrs Compton who, after the manner of producing rabbits out of a hat, served up a most delectable cold spread.

Chamber of Commerce and the Delivery of Goods. Outlined a joint plan from the Ministry of Transport, the Ministry of Food and the Board of Trade to rationalize all deliveries by retailers whether by motor vehicle, electric vehicles, horses and vans, hand trucks or bicycles. To achieve savings in fuel and manpower.

Quite considerable objection by traders who seemed to think the plan was unworkable. Mr Addleshaw (local Solicitor) said that the Government did not care two hoots how the trader or he himself fared. There was a war on.
The plan abolished all deliveries under a mile – a revolution.

Editorial. The editorial felt the delivery ban would be a good thing as people had got podgy from being able to phone up and get a 2d packet of safety pins delivered or three eggs value a penny ha'penny. It would do people good to get exercise.

13 February 1942

Advert. Bakers of the Town announce that as from Saturday 21st February bread will only be delivered three times a week viz Tuesday, Thursday and Saturday and they appeal for the sympathetic co-operation of the public in this wartime measure.

Mr & Mrs D Lockey of 20 Cornwall Road have received intimation that their sailor boy, Jack, is missing and presumed dead. (Brother of long serving Councillor Colin Lockey)

The Red Cross Skittles Tournament has been won by the Rural District Highways team. They beat the MPSC (Military Prison Service Corp?) in the final. Other semi-finalists were the Royal Observer Corp and Pilton Home Guard.

There had been a series of letters in the paper over scrap. Mr Pullen started it with a jibe at Wells over an old Russian military gun from the Crimea. 'Ivor Good Memory' from Wells retaliated by criticizing scrap lying around at Darshill and bickering about a fountain in Shepton Mallet Market Square – mainly stone, scrap metal worth 1/-.

This week 'Scrappy Memory' wrote "When Ivor can show 200 tons of scrap 'delivered up' as the owners of Darshill have done it will be time enough to talk of sacrifice, in the meantime my good friend, cling to your gun – even if you can not stick to them."

20 February 1942

Licensees in Shepton Mallet District congratulated that no persons had been convicted of drunkenness during the year.

Firemen Crash. Three firemen were injured on Saturday night when the Shepton Mallet Fire Engine and trailer pump crashed into Greylake Bridge on the main Wells to Taunton Road. Two of the men were taken by ambulance to Bridgwater Hospital and detained. They are Cyril Richardson 41 of Zion Hill, who sustained head injuries and Cornelius Blinman 45 of Cornwall Road with an injury to his shoulder. Serious as the accident was, it was a mercy that all escaped with their lives.

Letter. Dear Sir – May we be allowed through your column to tell your readers that the knitting party known as 'Mrs Bennett's Knitting Party' can no longer continue to make garments for Shepton Mallet members of H M Forces because of rationing of wool… yours faithfully Mrs Bennett's Knitting Party.

Regal. "Here comes the Navy' James Cagney and Pat O'Brien.

(Note. In general there are very few entertainments of any sort being advertised at this time.)

27 February 1942

Constitutional Club. Annual General Meeting – in good financial state. The Games Committee reports that for the first two years of the war there had been little or no activity but they found it too dull so they had revived Snooker and Billiards Cups this year and were forming a skittles league.

6 March 1942

Reported Missing. Flight Lieutenant E J Durston RAF ardent sportsman and keen player of the Shepton Mallet Rugby Football Club. Also Flight Sergeant Bower son of Mr & Mrs C J Bower.

Shepton Mallet Rural District Council. Two steam rollers have been employed during the past month strengthening and resurfacing in the parishes of Downhead and Stratton on the Fosse.

Somerset clergyman promises not to drive car again. George Henry Mitchell, Clerk in Holy Orders of Eldemere, Old Wells Road, Shepton Mallet gave an undertaking to magistrates. Mr Mitchell was driving a vehicle towards his house at a point where the road was only 12 feet wide collided with a milk float driven by Henry Robert Allen farmer of Hitchen Lane. The shafts of the float were broken and the pony bolted dragging Mr Allen 30 or 40 yards. Mrs Allen, who was a passenger in the float was thrown out and sustained concussion.

    It was alleged the defendant kept to the middle of the road although Mr Allen waved at him to draw to the near side.

    Cross examined as to his age, Mr Mitchell said he was 75 on the day after the accident. He was driving carefully and thought he could pass the pony and float safely. He did not pull in to the nearside as there was a ditch full of water on that side he wished to avoid.

Shepton Mallet Rural District Council. Row over the council buying a new Bedford 5 ton lorry in Dorset and not from local traders. Vauxhall had written to say this was unusual. The council said the terms offered by Messer's Hockey Waterloo Road were not as good – especially for trade-in of the old Ford Lorry. (One senses that there was some anti-town feeling on the RDC since at this meeting they also rejected proposals for a Joint Evacuation Committee with the Urban District Council.)

Editorial on lorry asked why all motor traders had signed a letter of objection except for Mr Hockey – was it as he had the contract to service the council's heavy lorry. Those signing: L Allen - The Mid Somerset Motor Co, E M Catley - Wells Road Garage, F Hodder - The Central Garage, A Williams - The Charlton Garage, R Whitehead - Motor Engineers, Evercreech.

13 March 1942

Two cases of theft by evacuee boys in Shepton Mallet Juvenile Court. A 10 year-old had stolen a Diamond Jubilee Shilling from his billet. It had great sentimental value as it had been given to the householder when he was in parade with the Old Volunteers.

    13 year old boy had stolen cigarettes and a postal order. He had taken them out of a parcel that he was on his way to post.

The Baptist Church followed up it's 'all soldiers' services with an 'all ladies' one. "The ladies did extremely well with their part singing….this weekend has proved beyond doubt how magnificently our ladies can take the lead. Their courage, in spite of war and all that it means to them, has shown Shepton Mallet their unquenching faith in their Heavenly Father."

Regal. 'King Solomon's Mines' starring Paul Robson, Anna Lee and Cedric Hardwicke.

Shepton Mallet Urban District Council. Council Houses. Resolved that 2 Westfield be offered to Mr A C Moores of 'Bunch of Grapes' and that the next house to be offered to Mrs Woods of Garston Street.

Note. Ken Moores, one of the history group members and whose idea this project was, was the son of A C Moores and a boy at the time. Before the War they had lived in one of the semi detached houses by the prison but this had been commandeered. Accommodation was in very short supply in Shepton and for over two years they had had to occupy rooms at the "Bunch of Grapes' Public House in the Market Place before eventually getting this council house. Ken can remember the 'Bunch of Grapes' well especially during the air raids when they all went down the cellars and had a feast and sing song.

Cellar Bunch of Grapes.

Citizens Advice Bureau required. Committee set up to run it: E H Norman (Council), F J E Pullen (British Legion) Miss C A R Bishop (British Legion Women's Section), C Bailey (Soldiers Sailors and Airman's Families Association), C W Read (Public Assistance Officer) representative's of Methodist Church, Unitarian Church, Congregational Church, Baptist Church, Church of England, Roman Catholic Church, Salvation Army, Ministry of Labour, WVS and Mr H Belchamber.

Bus Shelters. Resolved that Messer's Chidgley, Hardwidge and Lintern consider the provision of a bus shelter near the War Memorial.

Ambulance. Mr Cyril Richardson has been released from whole-time service with the National Fire Service in order to be available for driving the Ambulance.

Mr Lintern spoke of the problems of getting enough volunteers for the ARP Fire Guard Service.

20 March 1942

Cases in court relating to Christmas Poultry Sales. Apparently a form had to be filled in relating to birds sold by auction for laying, rearing or resale. Mr Laver of Wainwright, Laver and Crees said they had not known of the regulations until a few moments before the sale. As they had no copies of the form they had got customers to sign a declaration and informed them.

> Clerk Lionel Edwards confirmed that he had received instructions to see that purchasers signed that the purchase was for stock purposes. Wainwright, Laver and Crees were found guilty on 11 cases fined 10/- for each.
> Mr Albert Drew was fined on a similar offence. He bought a bird in a sale but later resold it to a Mrs Tilly at cost price. Mrs Tilly was also fined for not completing the form!

Shepton Mallet Youth Movement squad section 'Eccentric Sale" in the Council Hall for Red Cross Fund. They had made lots of toys and collected lots of items. A few of the more wonderful articles were auctioned by Mr Wyndam Laver who in his humorous way got a good value for the goods.

Three letters promoting Warship Week. A model of H M S Mendip will be brought to the opening. 'A full programme of events has been published and copies enough printed to go around' It is in booklet form and carries with it a forward by Vice-Admiral Sir James Sommerville KCB KBE DSO RN.

27 March 1942

Shepton Mallet Urban and Rural Districts Warship Week. Target £120,000 Amount raised to date £82,509.

> 'Friday evening whilst the finishing touches were being applied to the embellishments of the Market Cross and Square, traders were equally heavily engaged in finally arranging their shop windows. Messrs Henley – the 'official window' not in the shop competition – displayed a model of the warship, plaque and messages of goodwill, festooned in Red White and Blue.'

The procession was headed by an officer and ratings of HMS Mendip followed by a huge model of the ship, naval ratings on either side. Detachments of the Royal Engineers, Royal Army Service Corps, Royal Army Ordinance Corps, Pioneers and Home Guard. ATC all looking equally smart and spick and span. Somewhere in the middle was sandwiched a massive tank of the Guards Armoured Division, illustrative of the offensive power of the modern army. Down the street it came and in some mysterious manner slithered from High Street, round the corner into Paul Street and on to Collett Park.

Warship Week logo.

The fine Naval and Military Display was impressively supported by members of the Civil Defence Units, ARP Wardens, the Town and visiting Fire Brigades, detachments of the British Red Cross (male and female) looking very business like and ready for emergencies. A word to the lads and lasses of the Boy Scouts, Cubs and Girl Guides.

Advert. Coal. Do not blame your coal merchant if he is unable to supply you with your usual quality coal. He is doing his best under very difficult circumstances. Issued by Mid Somerset Coal Merchants Association. W H Feaver Sec.

3 April 1942

Shepton Mallet Urban and Rural Districts Warship Week 'HMS Mendip Saved' Amount raised £199,150/2/10d.

'There is an old proverb which says it is the unexpected that happens' Who could have expected to beat the War Weapons Week total of £163,911, to be honest very few, Surely few Towns and Districts of this size have done better. Following a somewhat slow and cautious beginning by the Executive Committee the tempo, under the wise and gracious guidance of Col V D S Williams OBE, began to increase and this, thanks to the Publicity Committee, was spread abroad and gradually fanned into unbending enthusiasm. Collecting Boxes. During the week a series of collecting boxes, ingeniously made in the shape of a warship, were placed in various establishments. 'Downside £9 Mr Whitcombe £8/8/3d, British Legion Club £6/7/7d Horseshoe Inn, Constitutional Club, Hare and Hounds, Nettlebridge Inn, King William, Charlton Inn, Railway Inn, Bell Inn, Mr Henly's Drapers, Bunch of Grapes, The George, The Vaults, Red Lion, The Black Swan, Manor House Ditcheat, Brewers Arms, Somerset Garage.

Street group collectors had raised between them £1,868.

HMS Mendip

Warship Week represented the start of a long relationship between the town and the Ship and the crew. This was kept alive into the 1980s largely by the efforts of then town councilor Mabs Holland. A few details of the ship and its history are of interest.

- Class Hunt Type1 Escort Destroyer. Pennant Number L60 (Later reclassified as a frigate L160.

- Builder: Swann Hunter. Wallsend
- Laid Down 1939, Launched 9 April 1940
- Displacement 1,000 tons
- Length overall 280 ft, beam 29ft
- Armament 4 x 4in guns, 2 x 20mm Anti Aircraft
- Machinery 2x Parsons Turbines 19,000 HP, 2 Shafts, 2 x 3 drum type boilers
- Maximum Speed 27.5 knots
- Complement 146

Later History. May 1948 Sold/loaned to Chinese Nationalist Army (named 'Lin Fu). May 1949 Returns to Royal Navy Hong Kong. Nov 1949 Transferred to Egyptian Navy, Oct 1956 Captured by Israeli Navy during battle of Haifa. 1972 deleted from records, presumed scrapped.

Shepton Mallet Rural District Council. A Letter from the Chairman of the London County Council concerned at the drift back, of children to London and asking for help to discourage it. W W Gilson alleged that parents came down to see their children and often took them back although the children did not want to go. Miss Bethell alleged that some mothers took their children back to the evacuation areas so they could get priority by having a child under 14 living with them.

Regal. 'Footsteps in the Dark' starring Errol Flynn and Brenda Marshall plus 'Atlantic Fury' starring Michael Redgrave and Valerie Hobson.

HMS Mendip.

10 April 1942

Warship Week grand total £200,939.

Boy Scouts. Eastertide weather was not very conducive to camp life yet 17 members of the 1st Shepton Mallet Scouts made the best of it at Washingpool Farm where they encamped by kind permission of Mr A E Whitehead. During the weekend they made a special waste paper drive and collected over half a ton.

Is your journey necessary for the Railways. Important to keep lines clear for Tanks, Coal, munitions and equipment for the Army, Navy and Air Force. Because the number of engines was stretched they were reducing passenger trains. 'First things first and essential supplies must have primary place.'

17 April 1942

Unlawful possession of Army Blankets. A plea to be allowed to pay a fine as he had an invalid wife was made by Henry Edward Walsh (55) labourer of Longbridge Shepton Mallet when he was sentenced to two months imprisonment at Shepton Mallet Police Court on Friday for being in unlawful possession of four army blankets.

> His appeal was declined by Sir Francis Berryman who said he should have thought of the consequences. Walsh told the court he had been given the blankets by a soldier who he had not seen before or since. Inspector Sealy proved eight previous convictions against Walsh.

Regal. 'Strawberry Blonde' starring James Cagney and Rita Hayworth.

Shepton Mallet Urban District Council 'Cow Keeper' Your committee recommend that an application by Mr Marshall of Kilver Street for registration as a cow keeper be permitted.

Early Memories of the Bombings

Local History Group member John Maidment has memories of Shepton Mallet during the war mainly around the Kilver Street area. As he was only five when the war began he suggests that his memories of incidents are patchy.

"My father volunteered and joined the RAF before the war started, this left my mother to bring up two young boys and run a home. Like many others at this time she was a very resourceful woman and could turn her hand to most things. Through air raids, power cuts, extreme cold, frozen pipes and shortage of food mother coped with it all.

During the height of the war when Bristol and Bath were being bombed so severely, she made a 'safe area' in the hall, the strongest part of the house for us to shelter in. The dining table was moved into the hall along with mattress and bedding. Sandwiches were made and hot drinks in a vacuum flask in case the electricity went off. The bombers very often flew over our house on their way to and back from these raids. Our home was of course blacked out, and on no account was a light to be shown. So very often we only had candle light to see by when we heard the bombers going overhead and waited for the siren to sound the 'all clear.'

During the day, my brother and I would very often visit the Somerset and Dorset Railway. The station could be very busy during the war and a good place to spot those unusual locomotives at the head of long ambulance and armament trains.

The army convoys that passed our home were also of great interest to us boys, including big units pulling low loaders with tanks on. The American army soldiers on occasion threw us ration tins, these contained chocolate and biscuits – a welcome prize for small children always looking for something to eat.

I remember that during one such convoy a tank transporter ran away while coming down Kilver Street hill. It eventually stopped when it hit the corner of a house in Town Lane. The damaged vehicles were dragged up to the Charlton crossroads which at that time had a petrol station and a flat area where the American army sorted out the chaos.

The petrol station was also used as a stopping point by the American army's doughnut van, this bought American style doughnuts for the boys and girls who seemed to come from everywhere once it arrived.

Mother not only found time to look after us, the garden in which she grew fruit and vegetables and cater for granny who lived down the road but she also took up a position of clerk in the National Deposit Friendly Society. On top of this she found time to be hospitable to 'WRENS' who came for a long soak in the bath, some home cooking and a break from their service jobs."

24 April 1942

"Spring is here" The Cuckoo has been heard several times during the week but the first time was on Sunday evening.

1 May 1942

'Illegal use of Ration Book, Shepton Mallet Woman fined. Mrs Mabel Green of 18 Darshill was using the ration book of an evacuee who was billeted on her for two weeks while he was in Pylle Sick Bay. £1 fine and £1/1/- costs.

Clothing ration card – belonging to E. H. Norman, Chairman of Shepton Mallet UDC.

Shepton Mallet becomes a prescribed area for Fire Prevention. From 1st May extra obligations on occupiers of all business premises to be able to take prompt action to put out fires caused by enemy action and on the Urban District Council to detect and deal with fires elsewhere e.g. churches and dwelling houses.

8 May 1942

Mr E Hobley and family welcomed home son Frank Hobley Chief Ordinance Artificer on well deserved furlough. He joined the Navy in 1919 and has since seen continuous service. Last week he attended Buckingham Palace and was decorated by His Majesty the King with the British Empire Medal in recognition of his services in connection with the sinking of the Bismark.

15 May 1942

Shepton Mallet Urban District Council. Air Raid Siren. Your committee have received complaint concerning the inadequacy of the present air raid warning systems and the clerk has been asked to urge the provision of an additional siren at the Bacon Factory.

Stirrup Pumps. The clerk. "50 pumps are on order and when they arrive we shall have 90, something like one pump for every eight or nine houses."

A lot of discussion on the fire guards and how the scheme was working. Some fire guards complaining of inadequate instructions of their responsibilities. Mr Pullen had been to a lecture and thought there was a little weakness in the scheme – a lack of water! Suggesting residents slide buckets of water onto the street as soon as trouble threatens.

22 May 1942

Letter. Unnecessary travel. Dear Sir, Travelling from Shepton Mallet to Wells everyday by bus, one is amazed at the number of people, mostly women and children making unnecessary journeys….If you really must go to 'have a look at the shops'….In any case before you go ask yourself 'Is my journey really necessary?' H J Pullen 23 Compton Road.

Regal. "Good morning Boys,' starring Will Hay and his boys.

Cricket. Shepton Mallet and Cranmore 41 v Doulting 41

Applications are invited for the appointment of full time Fire Guard Staff Officers. Preference given to applicants with administrative experience in a Civil Defence organization.

29 May 1942

Shepton Mallet Rural District Council. Scheme to reduce transport requirement for meat pies for rural residents and workers. To be made at Co-op Bacon Factory and to be distributed by bakers and grocers in the district to retail as part of ordinary business. Scheme approved by the Ministry of Food. (Note. What on earth was this all about?)

5 June 1942

Advert. Thorne and Thorne announce that they are now in a position to accept a limited number of down quilts for recovering and refilling and suggest that anyone requiring this service before the autumn should take advantage of the opportunity as they may not be in a position to make this offer later.

Formation of Rabbit Club. A representative gathering assembled in the Council Hall Monday under the Chairmanship of Mr Wells the local Food Officer supported by Mr F J Speed and Mr H G Viner with a view to the formation of a rabbit club.

Editorial. Report of the two colossal air raids carried out by the Royal Air Force over Germany thus fulfilling the promise of the Prime Minister two weeks ago.

Advert. Men old at 40. Be as young as you were at 25 Oystrax Brand Tonic Tablets contain revitalisers, rejuvenators, invigorators. First Dose starts new life, vigour, vital force.

Sweet rationing to start on July 27th. Government helping sweet shops build up stocks which they are not allowed to sell until rationing commences.

12 June 1942

United Nations Day. Letter from Mr E H Norman. Dear Sir, At the wish of HM Government and President Roosevelt, Sunday next the 14th June is to be observed as United Nations Day.

Shepton Mallet Urban District Council. Mr Pullen asking what is going to happen to 64 Town Street the former business premises of the late Mr James Alford, the narrowest part of the street.

The editorial says 'Bad as it is, it is difficult to see how 'looping' is going to affect any great improvement… from the Market Place to the bottom of Town Street there is a clear line of vision and why it is necessary for two large vehicles to get jammed in the narrowest part of the street is beyond comprehension. The question is largely one of patience and common sense.

19 June 1942

Presentation of Certificates to Air Cadets. A very interesting ceremony took place in front of the Council Hall on United Nations Sunday. After Church, marching in fine RAF style, Cadets of the Mendip Squadron Air Cadets Training Corps came smartly to the 'Halt' in front of Sir Frederick Berryman……stood waiting to inspect the cadets and to present Proficiency Certificates and Proficiency Stars to Cadets who were successful in a recent Central Trade Test Board Examination.

Regal. 'One night in the tropics' starring Bud Abbott and Lou Costello.

'Baedeker Raids' 1337 killed in April and May. Bombings of Bath, Exeter, Norwich and York as well as less densely elsewhere.

Advert. The RAF wants flying men (17 – 33 years of Age) and WAAFs. Volunteer now. A Royal Air Force Officer will attend to interview Volunteers at the Council Hall, Market Place, Shepton Mallet, Wednesday June 24th.

26 June 1942

Girls Training Corps. Meeting of those interested in the formation of a Girl's Training Corps will be held in the Council Hall on Friday July 10th. Mr E H Norman Chairman of Shepton Mallet Urban District Council will be in the chair.

Shepton Mallet Rural District Council. A letter was received from the Urban District Council inviting the appointment of a representative to serve on the Town Development Committee which was considering improvements which might be affected after the war. Amongst the suggestions was one that a public hall should be provided in the town where plays, concerts and music festivals might be held.

Mr Matthews said he thought the proposal was one that didn't interest the rural areas to any great extent.

3 July 1942

Evacuee Outing. A party of evacuee mothers and children numbering 30 had a most enjoyable outing last week when they spent an afternoon sightseeing at Cheddar and concluded with a strawberry tea. The visitors were much interested in the caves and appeared to enjoy every minute.

Letter. From Geoffrey Budd, secretary to Shepton Mallet Waterworks Company asking members of the public to identify to him all wells and springs in case Shepton became isolated from its normal source of water supply in the event of invasion.

Making the most of 'Stay at Home' Holidays by a Medical Officer. Pointing out need to refresh, 'forget worries'. Suggests, instead of eating at home, taking a few meals at the British Restaurant. Recommends watching a days cricket.

10 July 1942

War Charities fete at Summerleaze. The Band of the Royal Marines proved a great attraction at the War Charities Fete held in the charming grounds of Summerleaze by Kind Permission of Mr C R Wainwright on Wednesday afternoon. War Committees Charity Chairman Mr S G Lemon with magnificent help from Miss A Tucker and Miss D Lintern worked hard to ensure success. Opened by Lord St Audries now a familiar and popular figure in Shepton Mallet.

> C R Wainwright remembered a visit to Fairfield the St Audries family seat where his great-grandfather had presented him with 10/- to buy his first cricket bat.

Every week at this time the paper was running a series of 'Rabbit Notes' on the breeding of rabbits for meat. Interesting hints on matters such as when to wean and how many more rabbits were being raised in Germany.

The papers seem even more full of self-help articles, poultry rations, car pooling, using a weapon. Plus there was the continuous coverage to encourage and advise farmers.

Shepton Mallet District Council. Collett Park. The offer of 30/- received from Mr Vagg to cut and remove grass in the park has been accepted, this being the only tender received.

> A Discovery. Mr Pullen said that he was now in his tenth year of being a councillor, and he knew at times he had been rather a nuisance. If he had upset them he was sorry but he now felt in the light of a discovery he had made, that he had been right in the things he had advocated and was vindicated.
> He had found a book of the council dating back to 1918 which contained evidence of the council maintaining highways and byways which had been repaired and maintained by the council, including those for which he had regularly campaigned but which the Council had repeatedly turned down, Quarr, Hitchen Lane, Martins Hill etc etc.
> The Chairman was most interested and said the Council would look into it after the war.
> Mr Pullen. 'War or no war I do want to push Hitchen Lane and ask that as much as possible can be done there now.
> Mr Hall. 'I suggest that you let the clerk have the book.'
> Mr Pullen. 'I would not lose that for £50.' (laughter)

Town Development Committee represented by Mr Price. Factory Sites. The committee have given instructions for further enquiries to be made with regard to the proposed development of factory sites.

Advert. What do I do? Putting out scraps for pig and poultry food.

24 July 1942

A Girls Training Corps is to be formed in Shepton Mallet at an early date. Application forms are now in the hands of the Commandant (Mrs D Lawless) and officers Miss Hunt and Mrs Rawlinson. The unit is open to all girls 16 – 18 years.

Regimental Sports a thrilling programme. The local Royal Army Service Corps contingent held a sporting meeting on Saturday on the field adjoining the bus terminus at Townsend.
Includes High Jump, Long Jump, Egg and Spoon, Veterans Race, 100 yard open race, Potato race, Three legged race. Later in the evening dance was held in the Market Hall at which the unit Dance Band made a very capable debut.

31 July 1942

Oakhill Airman's Funeral. Much esteem and sympathy were evident at the funeral on Saturday at Oakhill Parish Church of Sergeant Pilot John Reeves eldest son of Mr & Mrs Arthur Reeves of the Post Office Oakhill.
Note. John Reeves was killed in a training flight accident. A number of local people still remember him. His plane went into a dive and never pulled out. No complete explanation was ever found. He was the elder brother of Michael Reeves who for very many years was a prominent local cricketer, accountant, and was involved with J H Haskins and Sons. He died in June 2004. Their father ran the Oakhill Post Office which was also the telephone exchange. On one occasion a German bomber crashed at Stoke St Michael and the crew had jettisoned before it crashed. One injured airman found himself by the lonely Beacon Country Club on Beacon Hill. There was only a female caretaker inside when the German knocked on the door. Mr Reeves senior got a panicky phone call at the Post Office from the terrified woman asking to help. He got the Home Guard out to round up the German.
Being the telephone exchange meant being on duty 24 hours a day: nothing automated then. This was all right until the arrival of the Americans who didn't seem to know when the middle of the night was. He quite frequently got woken up at 3 o'clock in the morning to put a call through. As there was nothing else to do he used to listen in to the calls and found some of them most interesting. One night was particularly active. There had been an incident when a soldier assaulted a woman in Wells and the Military Police had to round him up.

14 August 1942

Tragic Death of Capt J W Hillier. News of the tragic death on Sunday of Capt. J W Hillier Home Guard of the Cottage Oakhill created a profound sensation not only at Oakhill but throughout the district. The circumstances attending his death make his passing the more pathetic for at the time he was fulfilling his duties as an officer of the Home Guard and was actually giving instructions in the firing of an anti-tank grenade. Suddenly something that will probably never be explained went wrong, there was a violent explosion and Capt Hillier fell mortally wounded. It was probably a faulty grenade.

28 August 1942

Dig for Victory Show. Shepton Mallet and District Allotments and Gardeners Association. As we confidently forecast last week the second annual 'Dig for Victory Show held on Saturday…..proved a huge success and the organization has all the essentials of doing really big things in the future. The venue, the spacious Market Hall, situated in the repository sale yard and generously placed at the disposal of the Association by Messrs Wainwright, Laver and Crees was ideal.

Mr C E Burnell congratulated the exhibitors on staging such a wonderful lot of vegetables and said he was pleased to hear they had a record number of entries.

At the conclusion of the show Mr Wyndham Laver in his usual happy vein kindly sold the produce the proceeds of which went to the Red Cross.

By kind permission the Association kindly allowed the newly founded Shepton Mallet and District Rabbit Club to hold a show 'alongside….. Eighty eight entries, comprising most of the well know varieties.

A letter from Mr W A Price asking for contributions towards a new children's paddling pool to be built in the park.

Controversy. Dear Sir. Owing to the controversy and difference of opinion concerning the final awarding of the first prize in Class 19 (collection of potatoes) in the recent allotment show, I should like the committee or persons responsible for the disqualification of my exhibit to answer the following query through the Press to the satisfaction of numerous members and myself. –

An half hour AFTER the prize had been awarded and the show opened one potato was found to have mysteriously disappeared and my entry was disqualified. Surely this is contradictory to rule number 6 of the schedule which clearly states that the Judges decision is final.

Yours faithfully a keen exhibitor. A J Foot, 2a Cornwall Road, Shepton Mallet.

4 September 1942

Advert. Just arrived: 'Test Times' Utility Boots for Agricultural Workers, 26/9d pair. Guaranteed. S Millard, High Street, Shepton Mallet.

Maximum retail prices for pheasants and partridges have been fixed by the Ministry of Food and came in to force on Sunday.

Note. Food shortages where obviously getting quite severe by this time, the rations provided only a bare diet. Being in a country area there were many ways of supplementing your diet..

Mrs Prince says she found trying to live on rations terrible – a little bit of butter, little bit of cheese, one egg to make sandwiches for three, 2oz of this, 2oz of that. Makes you wonder how they ever survived.

One time she dried elderberries for currants very slowly dried in oven. Husband Sid, a quarry worker, had a 'currant bun' in his lunch box and his workmates wanted to know where the currants had come from!

Nothing was wasted, sour milk was whipped and whipped into soft cheese. Bacon with maggots washed and cleaned with vinegar before cooking. No 'sell by' dates then!

Ken Norman when working in Leaver Bros can also remember being told to soak a joint of bacon he found with maggots in a bucket of vinegar – and that was before it was even sold!

Shepton Mallet Magistrates Court. Two people were fined for falsely obtaining free milk for children under five. Income had to be les than £2 a week per couple plus 6/- a week for each dependent. In both cases the wife had signed the form. In one case the defence was that she had not known how much her husband's income was, only what he gave her for housekeeping.

Case in Stratton-on-the-Fosse where Mrs Dorothy Bennett was found guilty of letting a cottage at an excessive rent. Had put furniture in the cottage and charged 12/- for cottage and 13/- for the furniture. The court said the furniture was not worth that much and fixed that the total rent for cottage and furniture should be 10/-. She was told to repay the difference although the tenant had been perfectly happy with the previous rent and had offered to pay more.

Editorial. Entering the 4th year of the War. Let us make a new year resolution as we step boldly into this fourth year of the battle for civilization. Let us resolve that we shall no longer think of ourselves as individuals, that we shall no longer consider our own comfort, career or convenience. Let us do only what the national cause demands.

11 September 1942

CWS Bacon Factory. The second annual vegetable show conducted under the auspices of the CWS Bacon Factory was held in Shepton Mallet on Saturday.

Shepton Mallet Urban District Council. Recommended provision of additional street lamps at Cenotaph, Commercial Road (Catley's), Leg Square, Town Street (York House).` (Note. Quite why they were discussing this during days of blackout is not clear.)

Bus Shelter Station Way. Mr C W Wainwright is prepared to grant an easement to the Council for the erection of a 'Bus Shelter in his Shrubbery adjoining the G W R Approach Road.

18 September 1942

Letter from R A Hobhouse Chairman of Shepton Mallet Rural District Council and E H Norman Chairman of Shepton Mallet Urban District Council. The Ministry of Supply has just made a new salvage order relating to rubber which emphasizes the urgency for saving every available ounce of rubber. 90% of the natural rubber resources of the world are now in enemy hands.

25 September 1942

The Shepton Mallet Snooker League AGM at the Bell.

2 October 1942

Fire Guard Instruction. An opportunity for all to learn something of the new incendiary bombs now being dropped by the enemy will occur on Sunday 11th October when free instruction is to be given to all persons over 14 years of age who care to attend at the Regal Cinema.

Used up Surplus Petrol. Nancy Hobday, The Priory, Ditcheat was summoned for using an unlicensed motor car. The road fund licence had expired but the owner said she had been told she could use up surplus fuel left in the tank. A fine of 10/- was imposed.

Note. Petrol use was cut down for civilians from the start of the war. All the famous brands of petrol disappeared and it was all called Pool Petrol. It was moved in tankers painted grey with the word 'Pool' on the side. All Petrol depots were guarded – especially airforce petrol dumps.

Notice ENYD wishes to thank all her clients for their kind patronage, and begs to inform them that owing to war conditions the Business of Ladies Hairdressing will be closed from October 3rd for the duration.

Shepton Mallet Chamber of Commerce. Closing hours for the winter months. Mon Tues 5.30pm, Wed 1.00pm, Thurs 5.30pm, Fri, Sat 6pm. It is hoped that all traders of the town will observe these hours and thereby assist in saving light and fuel.

Rubber shortage. Don't delay, get in touch with H R Trimnell, salvaged rubber dispersal storage. Cannards Grave, Shepton Mallet. Certified by the Ministry of Supply.

Fire watch. Edith Wallace née Brooks fire watching to the rear of Leaver Bros. – now Dredge and Male.

9 October 1942

Death of Mr Silas Davis aged 93 years. The town has lost one of its most esteemed and picturesque characters. He loved to talk of bygone times and to tell of some thrill encountered upon his rounds during his 40 year meritous service as a rural postman. His daily round was from the Town Post Office to Pylle, East Pennard and Wraxall returning to East Pennard and Pylle Post Office and Shepton Mallet – 17 miles. It is estimated that during his service he walked 246,000 miles.

Debate in the paper about the slovenly rate of work being done by the labourers building the two camps in the town – particularly on the south side of the station. It appears that the labourers were forced to work there – the under aged, over aged and infirm with little experience of building and it would seem with totally inadequate supervision. Obviously the men objected to the criticism and there were examples given of how hard Shepton Mallet men do work.

Regal. 'Turned out nice again' starring George Formby.

16 October 1942

Ministry of Fuel and Power Announcement. Household fuel assessment form. Every household has to fill in a form. Non-Industrial Premises including Shops, Offices, Cinemas, Dance Halls also have to complete one. T P Jordan. Local Fuel Overseer.

> Shepton Mallet Urban District Council Fire Guards. Business Premises Block System – there are now 10 teams on duty every night. This is less than 50% of the number required according to minimum standards but no increase is possible unless compulsory enrolment is brought into force.
>
> Business premises own teams. National Deposit 5 teams. The CWS Bacon Factory 2 teams, Messrs Showering 1 Team. Each team consists of 3 people.

Emergency Information Officer. A letter received from the Ministry of Information submitting the name Mr J H Addleshaw for appointment to the voluntary position of Emergency Information Officer. His duties will include the organization of services for conveying to the general public in times of emergency instructions on behalf of the Local Government Authority or the Invasion Committee.

Shepton Mallet Rural District Council. Col J A Garton wrote to the effect that since he had now been away for two and a half years on Military Service he thought it his duty to resign from the council. The Chairman felt they had no option but to accept the resignation and then write to ask Col Garton to reconsider the matter. He said Col Garton has done a lot of useful work for the Council and we do not want to lose him.

Shepton Mallet Baden Powell Week.

- Sunday – Parade Service, Parish Church.
- Monday – The Gang Show (sound film) Council Hall
- Tuesday – Variety Concert, Market Hall
- Wednesday – Whist Drive Council Hall
- Thursday – Social, Market Hall

- Friday – Dance with the heats of the Old Fashioned Waltz Competition, Market Hall
- Saturday – Football Match, Whitstone Park.
- Saturday - Hockey match Grammar School Ground. Between teams representative of Shepton Mallet Youth Organisations.
- Wednesday 28th – Dance with finals of the Old Fashioned Waltz Competition, Market Hall.

Bombed Out in Shepton Mallet

Although around 200 bombs and incendiary devices fell in Shepton Mallet during the War, very little damage was done. I was delighted to receive a phone call from the only family who were actually 'bombed out of their house'.

Lionel Pearse. Now of Hill Farm East Pennard. Interviewed August 2003

Lionel was born at Bullimore Farm on the east side of Shepton Mallet. Up what used to be called Bullimore Lane but is now Frog Lane.

Just short of the farm there was a railway bridge on the GWR line. Next to this there was a farm building then the farmhouse on the far side of the barn.

In October 1942 he would have been about 10. He went to bed about eight o'clock in the evening but hadn't long been asleep when a plane went over and dropped a land mine. The parachute of this land mine caught in the telephone wires along the top of the railway embankment and it dropped right on top of the railway bridge which the explosion totally destroyed. It also wrecked the big high wagon shed, the roof of which caved in onto a tractor and an old car.

The blast blew all the windows out of the back of the farmhouse and the lights went out. Lionel's father said they couldn't stay there so they left in their night clothes. Obviously they couldn't get under the railway bridge so they climbed over the embankment. They found an ash tree which had been hit by the blast with its twigs still glowing and where the debris had fallen through the roof of the old car it had landed on the horn which was 'blaring' into the night.

They went down the lane to Charlton House the home of Brewery owner and prominent local citizen Mr Charles Burnell. They stayed at Charlton House for ten weeks while the railway bridge was being rebuilt and the farmhouse repaired.

The bombing was not allowed to affect normal life. The next morning, Lionel wearing borrowed clothes went to school as usual, travelling by train to Cole on the Somerset and Dorset line and then to Sexey's School in Bruton.

The railway engineers put in a temporary railway bridge made of wood while they rebuilt the masonry. A large railway crane came and lifted the temporary bridge out. Took about six weeks he thinks. The navies came in by train and went home by train. Lionel paled up with the navies and sat and had lunch with them. Bread, cheese, raw onion and Oxo cube in hot water. He says that they were a rough lot but the steam crane driver let him work the taps.

Local builders Melhuish and Saunders did the rebuilding of the farm house and buildings.

In the meantime, the Pearces stayed with Mr Charles Burnell at Charlton House. Very much upstairs downstairs and they ate with the servants. Mr Burnell was the head of the Charlton Brewery. Before the war the Burnells had a Chauffeur, four or five domestic staff and half a dozen gardeners. Mr Burnell lived with his two sisters Kate and he thinks Edith. None of them married. When they wanted to go out, the chauffeur had to take the car around the front of the house (pre war) at a certain time. The women wore veils and the car had smoked glass in the window. The sisters did a lot of charity work around Shepton Mallet and all the surplus vegetables from the gardens were sent to the local hospitals.

Whilst he was staying at Charlton House, Lionel can remember spending many evenings peeling walnuts.

23 October 1942

Letter from E H Norman. Chairman of the Shepton Mallet Hospitality Committee for American Troops asking householders to be willing to allow American troops to spend periods of leave in English Houses. An opportunity to understand both the American and English point of view.

Shepton Mallet Youth's Service Movement. First Annual General Meeting took place in the Council Hall on Friday and was attended by representatives of the ATC, GTC, Scouts, Junior Red Cross and St John's Organisation.

Regal. 'Pimpernel Smith' starring Leslie Howard and Francis Sullivan,

31 October 1942

Home Guardsman Fined. At the Petty Sessions on Friday Albert Watts of Waterloo Road was summoned for absenting himself from parade as a Home Guardsman on the 19th of July last. In his defence he said he was working away all week and on Sundays went around with the papers for his father. He was fined £5 with £1/1/6d costs.

Austerity Poppies for 1942. Of the 40 million emblems to be sold only 4 million will be of the more attractive silk type. Even these will be smaller than usual in some cases having only one layer of petals instead of two. The wire stalk is giving place to an ingeniously contrived cardboard stalk while the well known metal centre is being replaced by a printed paper centre.

6 November 1942

A welcome. During the past fortnight a cordial welcome has been extended to Mr Berry's successor, Mr G F Coles, as station master at the Somerset and Dorset Railway Charlton Road Station.

A Red Letter Day. Liberals Jubilee. Wearing the uniform of airborne troops, Capt J Brown, prospective Liberal Candidate for the Wells Division, was given an enthusiastic reception when he unexpectedly walked in to the jubilee celebrations of the Women's Liberal

Association at the Liberal Club on Wednesday.

Editorial. Shepton Mallet Rural District Council on sending out the rating demands for the current half year….on the lip of the outside envelope was stamped a request: in the interest of economy, that it be returned, inside the blue (return) envelope when the rate was paid. Of twenty seven blue envelopes received to date only fifteen rate payers had acceded to the request …..really extraordinary.

13 November 1942

Remembrance Sunday – One of the best parade services of recent years organized by the local branch of the British Legion.

By happy thought our 'American Friends' were given the place of honour, and the first wreath was laid by Lieut Whitson.

Led by the Royal Navy, the parade moved off to the Church in the following order: RAOC, RASC, Pioneer Corps, British Legion (Men), British Legion (Women), Home Guard, British Red Cross (Men), British Red Cross (Women), British Red Cross (Juniors) St John's Ambulance, Civil Defence Units, National Fire Service, Somerset Constabulary, Air Training Corps, Girls Training Corps, Boy Scouts, Girl Guides.

Boys Destructive Time in Car Park. Shepton Mallet Schoolboys in Trouble. Destruction caused by a gang of Shepton Mallet school boys in a private car park was told to the local Juvenile Court on Friday when 14 boys whose ages ranged from 10 – 14 years were accused of doing damage to certain properties and vehicles, the property of Mid Somerset Motor and Carriage Co of Shepton Mallet….

The cases against the four boys who pleaded not guilty were dismissed but the other ten boys were placed on probation for 12 months.

It was only because they had had good school reports that they were being dealt with so leniently. Sir Frederick Berryman warned them as to what would happen if they got into trouble again.

Shepton Mallet Rural District Council. A proposal to close the sick bay for evacuees at Pylle, and substitute a more suitable house at Shepton Mallet was debated.

Note. This mention of the sick bay at Pylle answered the one mystery I had in the following wonderful contributions I received from Mrs Jean Chapman, née Hughes. She had been visiting Shepton in the summer of 2003 looking to see is she could find the locations of her war time experiences. Thanks to excellent help from the staff of our Tourist Information Centre she was able to find the location of the farm she stayed in. The TIC also gave her my number and a subscription form for this book. Mrs Chapman phoned and I asked her if she would please write down some of her experiences. Some months later the following arrived along with a note apologizing for the delay but she had been learning how to use the computer to type it. I am extremely thankful that she did!

Memories of Shepton Mallet 1941-42

"My very first memory of Somerset was as an evacuee child of six, walking up the drive of a large house, with my mother and her best friend Queenie; whose large family – the

Tidemans – had also been evacuated to Shepton Mallet. We had left Manor Park in the East End of London when the bombing of the area had become so severe.

The house we had been invited to live in was Barrendown Farm owned by the Rugg family. We were made welcome and given two rooms at the top left of the house, overlooking the front lawn and the lane alongside the property. Here, apart from missing my father so much, I was to spend the happiest summer of my childhood.

At first I was very nervous of the strange sounds and even of the silence but I soon began to enjoy the peace and security of living in the country – a far cry from sirens, noise, fear and many hours spent in a damp air-raid shelter.

Barrendown was a busy dairy farm and Mum, along with others, worked in the outhouse washing the returned milk bottles. The women wore scarves around their heads and were bent over a huge lead sink, up to their elbows in bubbles. The whole place smelt of sickly warm milk and was very noisy, as they had to talk loudly over the din of bottles being dropped upside down into metal crates to drain. There was a good supply of cardboard milk bottle tops which, when the middles were pushed out, we would wind with raffia to make shopping bags and table mats, or with wool to make pom-poms.

The milking-shed fascinated me as until that time I had no idea where milk came from. One day, as I watched Mr Rugg and his helpers milking the cows, he asked me if I liked milk. When I told him that I didn't, he replied, 'It's lovely when it's warm,' and promptly sprayed me from head to toe – straight from the cow! I remember them laughing as I ran out. Mum wasn't very amused, as she had to leave her work to clean me up and I got a good telling off for being in there.

I also remember kindly Stan the milk delivery man, who sometimes took me on his rounds with him. He drove a three wheeled van and to make me laugh, he would turn it full circle several times in front of the dairy, before we went up the drive and through the iron gates on our way.

Another kind person, a maid from the farm whose name I can't recall, took me to Weston-super-Mare for the day. It was my first visit to the seaside and I was very excited. However, on arriving there I was so disappointed to find that we weren't allowed on the beach. It was covered with rows and rows of barbed wire and we could only look down on it from the road above. The word 'invasion' was mentioned and I was promised another visit when the war was over, but of course it never happened.

Apart from a neighbour's cat, I had never been in contact with animals. One day in the driveway, I suddenly came face to face with a herd of goats. Their horizontal slit eyes were on a level with mine and they scared the wits out of me! The shrill sound of the cock crowing also alarmed me and when I was told it was a huge bird that might chase and peck you, I dreaded meeting that too. I did like the cows and their big 'velvet' eyes.

Having only lived in an upstairs flat with no garden, I really loved the grounds around the farmhouse. I especially liked sitting on the large round lawn in front of the house, reading or drawing in the shade of a huge tree or laying back on the grass looking up at the shafts of sunlight through the leaves and branches. The lawn was covered with daisies, which I thought looked wonderful but Mrs Rugg complained that they were just weeds and she would gladly pay a penny for every one I could pick. I quickly set to work on them, thinking she would be pleased and I would earn my first pocket money, not realizing of course that she was joking. Apparently they found me a couple of hours later, exhausted on the lawn, having barely made an impression on the daisies.

Another 'lawn' memory is of sitting there happily one day when an air-raid siren sounded. I looked up and around but there were no airplanes or noise and nobody calling out or rushing around. I had been 'trained' to run into the nearest air raid shelter in London but as there wasn't one and all was quiet, I felt perfectly safe and started reading my book again.

Suddenly, Mrs Rugg dashed out of the house shouting 'silly girl!' She grabbed my arm and rushed me indoors into a small dark cupboard under the stairs where I was crushed against her large bosom barely able to breathe. I was more frightened then than I had ever been in a shelter during a bombing raid and couldn't understand her panic. When Mum finally found us, she tried to explain to Mrs Rugg what we had been used to after the siren, compared to being there, and why I wasn't stupid – just unafraid. I realized then how very different the war was for people fortunate to live in the country. They were so safe and yet seemed more terrified of the thought of being bombed than those who had been.

Alongside the farmhouse a steep narrow lane led up to the school and the fields above. (It felt steeper recently – sixty years on!). I enjoyed going to school. In the class we used small cream shells as counters but writing materials were in short supply. We didn't waste a scrap of paper and pencils had to be used until it was a stub that could barely be held before teacher would give you a new one, and woe-betide anyone who lost it!

It was a lovely summer and sometimes we would have lessons and games in the field behind the classrooms. One poor girl had been told by her mother that she must keep her liberty bodice on – even in the hottest weather! She was so uncomfortable but couldn't be persuaded by the teacher to remove it, so she sat in the shade as we played.

In the highest field behind the school, I remember watching folk of all ages harvesting. Men pitch-forking hay high up on to the carts and corn was bound into bundles by women and boys and stacked in threes – wigwam style. I believe these were called stooks and we younger children would dive into them one after the other, having the time of our lives! Everybody worked so hard, day after day until the light faded. Even the smallest of us helped by raking up loose straws and for that we were given a share of the workers' lunch and praised for our efforts – which made us feel very important.

In Leg Square where I lived there was talk of a 'glasshouse' nearby and at first I thought it must be a crystal palace like the one in London I'd been told about. I was surprised to learn later that it was only a prison behind the huge stone wall and the soldiers with red hats were army policemen. We were told to stay away from that area but I couldn't understand why, because the wall seemed to be a mile high.

All the roads around us were flanked by stone walls and being small for my age I was very frustrated that I couldn't see over them whereas my friends could. In the square was a building with a tall chimney. I presume it was a bakery because we got to know that if we hovered around the gateway after 4.30pm, (I remember the time well) someone would appear with a few cakes or biscuits for us to share. We sensed it was all a bit secret because we never told our mothers. There weren't many treats to be had during the food shortages and we weren't going to risk being told not to accept them!

Mum loved going to the local dances and it was the only time I remember seeing her really happy. Life must have been difficult for her as she was still only in her twenties and must have missed her friends and family in London very much. I remember her singing 'You are my sunshine' and 'The sailor with the navy blue eyes'. After one particular dance she worried me by staying in bed all day. She told me later that she had been persuaded to try the local cider not realizing how potent it was and had spent all night watching the ceiling go up and down feeling very ill. She vowed never to drink cider again – and she didn't!

For some unknown reason, we left the comfort of the farmhouse where I had been so happy, to share a home with another family. The terraced cottage we moved into was in Garston Street and I remember it for very different reasons. It was dark and cold inside with a flagstone floor and just a water standpipe in the corner – not even a sink. When you turned the tap on, the cold water hit the ground with such force that it sprayed all over you. I was afraid of it and hated it.

The front door opened straight onto the lane. Opposite were narrow steep gardens with a deep gully across the top. There was a stream below and we would 'dare' each other to crawl across the log that straddled it. I nearly fell into the water more than once but it was fun to us and we didn't realize the danger we were in.

An old lady lived in one of the cottages. She dressed all in black and walked very stooped over her stick, which she would wave angrily at us children and threaten to hit us if we stole the gooseberries from her garden. We were all too scared of her to even think of it because we were sure she was a witch., but I was always polite to her.

As I was sitting on the doorstep in the sunshine one morning, she appeared as from nowhere and to my horror, took hold of my hand and led me up into her garden where she picked and gave me some of her precious gooseberries, saying that I was a good girl – not like the others. I remember the gooseberries were pink and hairy – and delicious.

That winter I and two other children in the cottage became ill and we were taken to a hospital of some kind, which I think was called Peel (Pylle) Sick Bay. I seemed to be there for quite some time feeling very miserable and abandoned. Eventually my mother collected me and we went to live in Bristol – which was being bombed at the time! However, after a few months we made yet another move, this time to Fleet in Hampshire where my father was stationed at the time. We never went back to London and sadly lost touch with most of our family.

Last August, thanks to the superb efforts of the staff in Shepton's Tourist Information Office, I found my way to Barrendown Farm again. It is now two homes but I was pleased to see that it looks exactly as it did all those years ago. It was quite an emotive moment standing in the shade of 'my' lovely old tree once again (it is an ancient Tulip tree) and looking at the farmhouse, with so many memories coming back.

The war tore families apart and they were traumatic times, which is why I remember them so well but the one good thing that came out of it for me personally, was the wonderful year spent in Somerset. I wish we could have stayed or returned there as I believe many evacuee families did, but at least it left me with warm memories and a lasting love of the countryside.

Haymaking, gooseberries and the smell of warm milk will always remind me of Shepton Mallet!" Jean Chapman, (née) Hughes. Nov 2003

20 November 1942

National Savings Movement. Workers in the National Savings Movement attended in gratifying numbers at the Council Hall on Monday evening to meet the deputy commissioner – Mr R H C Hammond – who gave a most excellent and helpful address. Col V D S Williams presided and was supported by Mr Phillips the newly appointed Assistant Commissioner for the Shepton Mallet District.

Regal. 'The Night has Eyes.' starring James Mason and Joyce Howard.

Editorial. Sunday was 'Civil Defence' Sunday. A day especially set aside by H M the King to pay tribute to the glorious deeds members of the various Civil Defence Services…..
> All over the country similar parades were being held. Why? It may well be asked was there no such observation in Shepton Mallet? Can it be that the 'City Fathers' who have hitherto set such a fine example … did not approve or was there genuine feeling on behalf of some that two successive Sunday parades was really after all too much of a good thing?
> Be that as it may. The neglect was a pretty poor tribute of gratitude.

27 November 1942

A Mother's Neglect. Conditions under which a mother and five children lived in one room were described in Shepton Mallet Police Court on Friday when Blanche Baker 1 Great Gardens, Shepton Mallet was bound over for three years for neglecting her children in a manner likely to cause neglect.
> The husband was now in the army and the defendant and five children lived in one large room in which they ate, lived and slept in their clothes. Panes of glass were out of the windows and there were no proper coverings for the children's beds. As a result of the husband overstaying his leave, his family allowance had been stopped.
> The children were removed to an institution and now showed a remarkable improvement. Defendant handed in a written statement and said it was her husband's fault she had lost her home and pleaded to be allowed to keep her baby.

Advert. Father Christmas requests the pleasure of the company of Mr & Mrs Everyman and family at a Christmas Fair 3pm to 6pm Saturday December 5th in the Council Hall when all your Christmas gift problems will be solved. Admission 6d Children 3d Music Teas etc.

4 December 1942

National Young Life Campaign. Another well attended and successful rally has been held in connection with the National Young Life Campaign Shepton Mallet Group this time in the Baptist Church. The speaker was Mr Roy Hessian NYLC Staff Evangelist Midland Counties who gave a most instructive and searching message based on the parable of the ten virgins.

'Post Earlier than Ever' this Xmas. Public can help to cope with the rush. This Christmas the Post Office will have to face one of the hardest tasks it has ever had. Still more of its skilled staff have left for service with the forces.....

11 December 1942

Sweets for Christmas. At a meeting of the local Chamber of Trade on Tuesday mention was made of the extreme shortage of sweets in the town and it was unanimously resolved to make fitting representation to the proper quarter to ensure adequate supply for the children during Christmastide.

Shepton Mallet Urban District Council. The Community Feeding Centre found it had been making a loss which came on the rates. They agreed to put up their prices from 6d to 9d for dinner and sweets from 2d to 3d.

Editorial questions the purpose of the restaurant. 'The whole thing is of course just too ludicrous....why on earth it is necessary for over worked housewives of the town to give their time to provide cheap lunches to people who can well afford to pay for it, or could provide it for themselves in their own homes if it were not too much trouble is a question which seems to defy any reasonable answer....

    Presumably the kitchen was originally intended to help those who through no fault of their own were in distress (bombed out in the blitz)

    (Note. The British Restaurant in fact carried on until very near the end of the war. It's role seems to have been providing meals for those who were working long hours, often away from home, doing 'essential work.')

18 December 1942

Christmas Greeting. The editor received on Wednesday a Christmas greeting from a Sheptonian now serving his country in the Middle East Forces. It runs as follows 'May I convey, through the courtesy of your firm, my heartiest wishes to you and all the inhabitants of dear old Shepton. God Bless them all from an Old Sheptonian (E B Dredge).

Nativity Play at Ivy House School. The pupils of Ivy House School presented on Friday afternoon a nativity play to their parents and friends at the school. The performance included the singing of many well-known carols and the dialogue was spoken by the pupils of Miss Hutching the elocution teacher. The whole performance was received with appreciation and a collection for the Red Cross Prisoners Fund amounted to £3/10s.

Regal. 'Let the people sing' starring Alistair Sim and Fred Emney.

Editorial. 'Provision merchants in the town and district are being almost badgered to death in the demands made upon them for Christmas puddings. The sordid truth is of course that there are none. One resident told us last week that he had had seven puddings in his establishment with which to supply 700 would-be customers.

Similarly with toys, there are none, but why worry. The war news has been better during the past month than at any time since 1939.

25 December 1942 (published 23rd)

'Greetings from H M S Mendip'. 'A Christmas Card to 'All our friends of Shepton Mallet to wish them health, joy, peace, success and all that makes true happiness' has been received by Mr Chidley from the Chief and Petty Officers Mess, H M S Mendip.

Evacuees Christmas Party. – The mothers of an evacuees club have held a small Christmas party for their children. It was very successful and thoroughly enjoyed by every mother and child. A lovely tea and a present from Father Christmas was provided.

Shepton Mallet petty Sessions. For driving a horse and cart on the highway at 10.55pm without the necessary lights Frank Bolton, dealer, West Pennard was fined £1.

Regal. 'The 39 Steps' starring Robert Donat and Madeline Carroll.

Editorial. The Government has announced that on Christmas Day church bells may be rung. The ban imposed on ringing except as a warning of enemy attack is therefore waived to cover any period between 9am and noon on December 25th.

Fete ticket.

Chapter 6

1943

- January, Russians destroy the Sixth German Army at Stalingrad and go on offensive.
- January 14 – 24, Casablanca Conference, Churchill and Roosevelt announce that the Allies will demand nothing less than the unconditional surrender from aggressor nations.
- May 13, German and Italian forces surrender in North Africa.
- July 9, Allied forces land on Sicily.
- September, Italy surrendered to the Allies and in October declared war on Germany.
- Autumn, 37 U-boats sunk resulting in Admiral Doenitzy suspending U-boat operations.

1st January 1943

Christmas at the Hospital, the West End Institution and the Joint isolation Unit was observed in much the same manner as in former years commencing with carols in the morning followed by 'Christmas Dinner', relaxation and visitors in the afternoon. At each institution the Matron and their respective staff did their best to ensure as happy a time as possible to those committed to their care.

Carolling. About thirty members of the Youth Service Movement delighted the local residents with their carol singing…. when they made an appeal for Aid to China. £5 will be sent to the Chinese.

The Christmastide of 1942 will long be remembered not only for its austerity but also for its essentially stay put character in which hundreds of thousands of people cheerfully made the very best of things just where they found themselves.

Home Guard enjoyed an evening off. It was something really refreshing to see the members of the Shepton Mallet Company Home Guard not only off duty for once but assembled together in happy conviviality at the Drill Hall, the occasion of an old time 'smoker' on Wednesday night. In they came from Evercreech, Ditcheat, Croscombe, Cranmore, East Pennard and Pilton plus a full contingent of the local boys.
    A warm welcome was given to 'our American Friends' who contributed in song to an excellent and varied programme…..A marvellous evening concluded with the lusty singing of the National Anthem.

8 January 1943

Workers Educational Authority (WEA) Shepton Mallet Branch. A course of six fortnightly lectures on International Affairs will begin at the Senior Girls School on Friday January 15th.

Shepton Mallet Rural District Council. …the Salvage Department of the Ministry of Supply had written stating that of the 402 rural districts in the country sending in salvage returns, the Shepton Mallet Rural District council was placed twelfth for the month of September. Congratulations were offered to all on this magnificent response.

Shepton Mallet Urban District Council, Collett Park. Your committee are much disturbed at the recent increase in wanton damage in Collett Park and recommend that a reward of £5 be offered to any person giving information leading to the conviction of the person or persons responsible for such damage.

The fire hut in Cooks Paddock is now in operation and eight supplementary instructors for the Urban Districts have been trained and received certificates.

Letter on the debate on Local Government. It had been suggested that no local government should be responsible for less than 10,000 people. FJE Pullen (of course) objected, claiming that this was a threat to local democracy. The editorial referred to the proposed changes as 'alarming in their scope' (Note. Although there were some changes in specific responsibilities it was the early 1970s before changes in the structure of local government were made. It is interesting that from this point of the war, there is a fair amount of discussion about how things needed to be developed after the war.)

Cannard's Grave Children. A letter was received from Mrs Mary Williams asking the Council if nothing could be done in the way of arranging transport to convey the small children of Cannard's Grave to school at Shepton Mallet. Many of them, she said, were ill shod and had no mackintoshes, and got wet through before arriving at school and often-time on returning home later in the day.

22 January 1943

Shortage of Batteries. The shortage of bicycle lamp batteries was alluded to at the Police court on Friday when James Grimshaw 14 of Kent Shepton Mallet was ordered to pay 4/- costs for riding a bicycle without a lamp… Batteries he said were unobtainable in the town.

29 January 1943

Shepton Mallet to build a tank. Great Scrap Metal Week planned. The people of Shepton Mallet are going to try to put a tank into action to help the great victory offensive. A great drive is to be made during the week January 30th – February 6th for scrap metal with the aim of collecting 16 tons, enough to build a Valentine Tank.
> The depots for scrap metal will be as follows: Town Street, Charlton Cross Roads, Corner of Kilver Street and Town Lane, Waterloo Road School, Kilver Street School, Playing fields Westfield, Board Cross, Compton Road and Garston Street.

Regal. 'Bride came COD' starring Bette Davis and James Cagney.

Next week the local ATC will celebrate its 'second birthday' and readers will generally join in wishing them 'many happy returns.' The lads under S/L A E Showering and P/O Fraud have acquitted themselves well and afford a fine example of how much good can come from proper use of spare time – Sundays not excepted. Congratulations all round.

Salvage campaign advertisement.

5 February 1943

Regal. 'Great Guns' starring Laurel and Hardy and 'Keep Fit' starring George Formby.

12 February 1943

Advert. A R Bowden & Son. Coffee Merchants, 9 High Street, wish to announce they can now supply any member of the public with their freshly roasted coffee. Easy instructions for making coffee can be procurred at their establishment free of charge.

Enjoyable smoker. As only befitting, having regard to the anxious days in which we live, the local lodge of the Ancient Order of Druids, cut out for this year their annual banquet……
Instead they organised a smoker and this was held at their headquarters at the Bell Hotel.

19 February 1943

Aid to Russian Fund. All who were kind enough to help the LCC Senior Girls at the Grammar School in the effort to raise money for the Aid to Russia Fund will be pleased to know that a cheque for £4/5/2 has been sent to Mrs Churchill.

Gifts in Abundance. The Shepton Mallet Red Cross Unit 2026 has received from the American Junior Red Cross a large number of gifts and sweets for the evacuees and other children of the town.

Letter appealing for material for 'fly tying (fishing flies) to be sent to Prisoners of War – materials required include complete bird wings of woodcock, crows, starling, waterhen. grouse, partridge, jay and mallard.

26 February 1943

The Park. Just a word or two of congratulations and encouragement to Mr Rowsell who once again has the beautiful Collett Park in excellent trim. During the past three years his had been a most unenviable task and at times he must have felt overwhelmed with the seemingly uselessness of trying to keep in order. Whatever his feelings he persevered and the result is not only pleasing to us all but must afford him no small measure of satisfaction.

Constitutional Club Meeting. Col Boles the local MP gave a talk on 'let's get on with the war'. He spoke of the Beveridge Report saying the Government was widely in favour but asked before passing it in its entirety to be allowed to examine it and consider ways and means. (Note. The Beveridge Report was a paper which set out the basis of the post war welfare state.)

5 March 1943

Black and White Menaces. Two dogs, the one black and the other white, who spend much of their time in annoying pedestrians at Townsend will one day probably learn by hard experience that their 'playfulness' can be equally painfully countered. There is nothing so irritating or discomforting to the average pedestrian than to be chased by a yapping snarling dog whose chief aim apparently is either a trouser leg or skirt – besides it is so unseemly.

Shepton Mallet Rural District Council. Mr R Britten of Shute Farm, Downhead has let a piece of land to a firm of Quarry Owners Messrs Perry's of Yeovil for stone quarrying operations. The land is closely adjoined by seven cottages, a Methodist Chapel and another farm, some cottages being not more than 20 – 30 yards distant.

Downhead Parish Council making complaint couldn't do anything about it as the County Council had given approval.

12 March 1943

Shepton Mallet Urban District Council. E H Norman absent due to the sudden death of his brother William Golledge Norman, the manager of the Westminster Bank in Somerton. Berkeley Hall presided.

A Great Sportsman. Congratulations to Mr Rupert Modford on his latest achievement; always a good sportsman whether in the saddle or with the gun. With the fishing rod too he is no mean angler, but surely his latest catches must have surprised even himself. Last week when fishing in the Brewery Pond at Charlton he had a really good 'bite' and following successful play – though not perhaps very lively – he hooked and landed with rare agility and courage a fully grown girls Raleigh Cycle. The machine has since been claimed by Anthony Evans Gould of Wells.

A quiet wedding of much local interest was solemnised at the Parish Church on Saturday between Mr Frederick J Baker son of Mr and Mrs J H Baker of Shepton Mallet and Miss Constance M Aspden second daughter of Mr and Mrs E H Aspden of East Barnett Herts. The bride has been a member of staff of the National Deposit Friendly Society for a number of years.

Regal. 'How Green was my Valley.' starring Walter Pidgeon and Maureen O'Hara.

19 March 1943

Shepton Mallet Petty Sessions. Sunday Cinema Show. The bench granted permission for the Regal Cinema to open on Sundays for the showing of Training films to members of the forces and civil defence personnel. It was stated that no charge will be made for admission.

Editorial. The Somerset County Educational Committee have arranged for a number of one day schools to be held at Frome, Keynsham, Shepton Mallet….on Friday March 26th in order to impress on all concerned the urgent need for study of the problems of household economy and to emphasise the fact that this is a national effort.

26 March 1943

(The editorial was giving quite detailed accounts of the army progress in Tunisia. An obvious change from previous information policy.)

The Annual General Meeting of the Shepton Mallet Hospital was held on Wednesday when the committee presented a highly satisfactory report of a years work most excellently achieved under ever increasingly difficult conditions.

2 April 1943

Football. The Shepton Mallet ATC team to meet Westover Old Boys at Bridgwater on Saturday in the semi final of the Somerset Minor Cup is as follows. R Oatley, Davis, Shave, Vagg, Hutchings, Rossiter, Plumbley, West, Sparkes (Capt), Reeves, Chapel.

Editorial. The Annual General meeting of the Shepton Mallet and District Hospital League was held on Tuesday when the committee's report…. Was a record of another excellent years work…. The amount the league has paid to the District Hospital during the year is approximately £1,300 and of a truth did Mr Berkeley Hall say that had it not been for the foundation of the Hospital League twelve years ago the hospital would not have been able to exist.

Mr Burnell, President of the Hospital, generously acknowledged the assistance of the League and spoke of the difficulty of making financial ends meet.

9 April 1943

Football. Somerset Minor Cup. Thrilling Semi-final….. match drawn. The replay which takes place at Whitstone Park tomorrow (Saturday) at 3.15pm should prove to be a smashing game with plenty of thrills.

Special Sunday Evening Concert. – The 'All Star Variety Concert' in aid of the local Red Cross detachment, held by kind permission of Mr Truman Dickens in the Regal Cinema and under the able management of Mr P G Warwick on Sunday evening proved an unqualified success. The crowded house was richly rewarded.

Advert. Wainwright, Laver and Crees Ltd. Sale this Friday at 12.45 Shepton Mallet Horse Repository. 45 horses of all description. Entries include Heavy and Halfway Horses, Harness Cobs, Ponies, Hacks and unbroken horses. Vehicles, harnesses and sundries.

There was an article in the paper about how important the horse had become again on smaller arable farms after it had seemed to be gone for ever.

Advert. Save Tractor fuel wherever possible 'to speed the tanks'. This advert also recommended the use of horses.

Advert. The St Johns Ambulance Amateur Dramatic Society presents two short plays. 'In the Blackout' by Gertrude Jennings and 'Gossips Glory' by T D Morris, at Jardine's Mill (by kind permission of Commander Langdon- Griffith.

16 April 1943

Shepton Mallet Petty Sessions. A number of cases of people using motor cars without a road fund licence, including Thomas David Evans, quarry manager, The White House Dean and Herbert Wilfred Clothier, farmer, Lower Farm, Milton Clevedon.

The news of the sudden death of Mr A J Ross came as a profound shock to his many friends in Shepton Mallet and Pilton and caused a painful sensation amongst his colleagues of the Royal Observer Corp. Mr Ross was an enthusiastic member of the ROC to which within a few days of three years he had been enrolled as a member. He was a ready favourite and generally popular…. As one would expect of a man of his calibre and of one who saw active service throughout the last war he was a first class observer…. One had only to say to him – 'Ross 7pm – 11pm tonight' and the reply was always the same, 'Yes, all right, I will be there', and he was.

23 April 1943

Football. Somerset Minor Cup. Local Corps ATC splendid win in second replay at Weston-super-Mare…'and ran out successful winners by 5 goals to 1 after a hard game.'

The final takes place next Saturday on the Weston Super Mare Rugby Ground two minutes from the Great Western Station. Kick off 3.30pm. They…. will field the same team except for Vagg who is being called up to colours. Maggs will take his place.

Editorial. During the week workmen have been busily engaged in the removal of iron railings in the town, and on all sides one hears strong utterances of protest. These protests are two fold – an out-and-out objection to the removal of certain railings at any price and a strong objection to the manner in which the 'holding masonry' is being damaged in the process of removal.

In regard to the first there can be little real sympathy….agreed it will in many instances cause not only much inconvenience … all will agree that when only sons are dutifully sacrificing their lives… the giving up of railings, however precious, is by comparison a small thing.

30 April 1943

A Happy Reunion. Home from Italy. Almost two years to the day after he was captured in Libya L/Cp S H Youngman only son of Mr & Mrs H P Youngman of Bowlish House Shepton Mallet has been repatriated under the recent exchange of British and Italian Prisoners of War. He arrived home fit and well on Tuesday and his family experienced the happiest Easter of their lives.

Having served in the RAMC (Royal Army Medical Corp) with the Third Light Field Ambulance unit he was included amongst the protected personnel of which there were more than 100 repatriated on this occasion.

Note. The return of a soldier from overseas was news. However at this time many soldiers were still based in England and would visit home on 48 hour passes. Stan Blacker has given me a story of a less official temporary leave which a soldier got away with. Prior to the War Jim Blinman had been an 'outrider' (salesman) for Showerings. When based at Knook Camp near Warminster he was taking part in a military training exercise. A few of them were sent out to hide themselves and the rest had 72 hours to locate and capture them. Soon after leaving the base a Showerings lorry went past and the driver recognising Jim stopped and offered him a lift. Jim accepted and came back to Shepton for a nice spot of leave before another Showerings lorry gave him a lift back. On arrival back at camp, he was summoned by his commanding officer – and congratulated on avoiding capture!

Football. Cup comes to Shepton Mallet. The 1182 ATC (Shepton Mallet) did well on Saturday at Weston-super–Mare when they beat Langford Rovers in the final of the Somerset Minor Cup by 7 goals to 2 after a very fast exciting game.

The cup was presented to Sparkes the 1182 Captain by Mr Dunford of the Somerset County Football Association who congratulated both teams on the game.

The ATC team was as follows: Oatley, Penny, Davis, Maggs, Sparkes (Capt),Shawe, Lineman, West, Hutching, Reeves, Chappell.

GTC. A very interesting and instructive talk on 'The Beveridge Plan' was given to the cadets last Thursday evening when Mr H Scott-Stokes, Mayor of Glastonbury and Street, was the speaker. Mr Stokes being a director of Clark & Son and Morland Ltd was able to explain to the Cadets the benefits both employers and employees would obtain if the scheme were generally adopted.

Note. Mrs E Jones remembers the Girl Cadet Corp. Both she and her sister where involved in it. One of the features was the camps they went on to Blue Anchor Bay. Quite a distance under war time conditions.

Easter Camp. Shepton Mallet Scouts together with Cheddar Scouts spent four days under canvas at Washingpool Farm by kind permission of Mr Weatherhead and in spite of the weather a very happy time was spent.

Girls Training Corps at Blue Anchor.

7 May 1943

Good News. Mr & Mrs Whittle of 10 Westfield received notification on Monday from the War Office that Pte J Gardiner Suffolk Regiment is a prisoner of war in a Japanese camp at Malai. Pte Gardiner of whom nothing had been heard for some 16 months will be remembered by local sportsmen for his interest in the town's Football Club for which he acted as linesman.

14 May 1943

Wings for Victory Week. Preview of Week. Mr Chidgey Hon Sec of the Shepton Mallet and District Wings for Victory Week. "Will you kindly allow me to appeal to the traders and shopkeepers of the town to comply with the request…to close shops…1.30pm – 4.30pm on Saturday…so that employees may all take part in the procession and opening ceremony."

Shepton Mallet Nursing Association – A splendid record. Congratulations on nearly 50 years of successful and very useful work were offered to the Shepton Mallet District Nursing Association by Mr C E Burnell when he presided at the 49th Annual Meeting…in the Council Hall on Monday.

Summary of work done in year. Town District (including Croscombe) 2 Nurses. Cases. Midwifery 49, sick nursing 195, County Council Inspections 26, Infants visited 360. Number of visits: Midwifery and sick nursing 3503, Casual 516, County Council Work 1206. Total visits 5225.

Doulting District. 1 Nurse. Cases: Midwifery 9, Sick nursing 98, County Council Inspection 4, Infants visited 81. Visits. Midwifery and sick nursing 1171, casual 189, County Council work 661, Total visits 2021.

21 May 1943

Wings for Victory Week. Target £150,000, raised so far £96,236. Towards the end of last week enthusiasm began to rise; shop windows assumed a festive and competitive appearance and the streets slowly but gradually became festooned and by the Saturday, with the increasingly good news from North Africa and the rise of mercury (good weather) tense excitement prevailed. The finishing touches to the arrangements were completed with the fixing of the indicator in the Market Place and the erection and adorning of the saluting base in the park.

The procession. Headed by a band of the Highland Light Infantry Regiment it marched with a rare swing down over the Great Western Railway Bridge into the High Street and thence to the park via Paul Street and Collett Avenue. It would be difficult to adequately describe the impressive scene such a display made upon hundreds of spectators who witnessed it. The Royal Navy contingent was magnificent and as it passed by, led by a gallant officer with drawn sword and with the men at the slope with fixed bayonets, a thrill of pride instinctively rushed through our veins.

In order of March: Highland Light Infantry Band, Royal Navy, WRNS, RASC, Pioneer Corps, Home Guard, RAF, 4th Somerset Home Guard Band, WAAFs, ATS, VAD, Red Cross LD, Red Cross Cadets, GTC, 2nd South Gloucestershire Boys Band, National Fire Service, 30th Order of St Johns, Air Training Corp. Girl Guides, Boy Scouts, Land Army, Army Cadet Training Corp, Police.

On arriving at the Park the salute was taken by Air Vice Marshall Sir Alfred Iredall KBE CB.

Speaking of the object of the 'Wings for Victory' Week Campaign Sir Frederick Berryman asked if they could support a finer object – The Royal Air Force. He said 'it was difficult to find words to adequately express appreciation of the courage, self-sacrifice and duty shown throughout by that gallant force. Recent events in the Middle East filled them with joyful anticipation and made them feel that their efforts there will be crowned with complete success.

Regal. Elsie and Doris Waters in 'Gert and Daisy's weekend'

28 May 1943

Wings for Victory Week. Target £150,000. Total raised £190,000. 'Bearing in mind that Shepton Mallet before the war had been classed as a distressed area people were amazed at the setting of a target of £150,000; but there is a long history of generosity in the town.'

It was sheer bad luck that the boxing tournament to have been held at the Drill Hall, had to be cancelled, due in part to the healthy way in which the pugilists had set about each other the previous night.

Shepton Mallet Rural District Council. Before commencing the business of the agenda Major Shore referred to the tragic disaster that occurred at Downside Abbey on the previous Saturday when nine boys of the school were killed when a plane crashed in the Cricket Field…..Major Shore said he did not know if they, as a Council, could do anything to try and prevent planes flying over houses and playing fields so low as they do… He was glad to see that questions had already been raised in Parliament.

Note. This was probably the biggest single tragedy of the war in this area, the more so in that there was no enemy involvement. On a peaceful sunny afternoon the boys at Downside School were playing cricket on the playing fields at the school when a Hurricane of the Fleet Air Arm at Yeovilton on a training flight for no apparent reason crashed into the cricket field. Ploughing across it in its wake it killed nine boys, the young New Zealand Pilot and seriously injuring eleven others.

The sense of shock was profound and a memorial was erected to the dead.

4 June 1943

The Curfew. For the first time since the ban was placed upon the ringing of church bells – now lifted- the curfew was rung on Monday night thus renewing the old and ancient custom.

Splendid News. The many friends of Miss Laura Dowling – the marvellous little hostess of the Crown Inn will rejoice with her in the splendid news…..her brother, Mr Eddy Dowling, is alive and a prisoner of War in Japanese hands. No word or any news had been received for over a year…

Vera Mary Game, the Old Grammar School Shepton Mallet pleaded guilty to causing light to be displayed from her residence and also to wasting electricity. 10/- for the blackout, 5/- for the wasting electricity. – she had forgotten to turn the light out!

Regal. 'Women Aren't Angels' starring Robertson Hare, Alfred Drayton.

Editorial. Evidence that the Downside School authorities had previously complained of low flying was given at the resumed inquest on Tuesday, on nine boys who were killed when a Fleet Air Arm plane crashed on the playing field on May 15th.
The jury returned a verdict of accidental death…The foreman added that there was no evidence to show what caused the plane to crash.

Advert. Shepton Mallet Urban District Council. Book recovery and salvage drive. During the period 29th May to 12th June a book recovery and salvage drive is being held throughout the Urban District of Shepton Mallet. The object of the drive is to obtain books for the following purposes.

a)   For distribution to HM Forces
b)   To meet the needs of war damaged libraries
c)   To meet the needs of Museums
d)   For distribution to Children's Hospitals
e)   For repulping.

Target 8,000 Books.

11 June 1943

Prisoner of War Fund. A Crib Tournament and Dart competition came to a very successful conclusion last week at the Charlton Inn when a large number of the players met at a smoking concert and prizes received by the winners were kindly handed back in aid of the Red Cross Fund (Prisoner of War Fund) which benefited by £8.

Shepton Mallet Urban District Council. Arising on the question of salvage the Chairman said they had received a letter from Mr Hales, Manager of the Bacon Factory respecting the waste collection in the bins for pig swill.
'With reference to the weekly consignments of pig food we have recently found quite a

large quantity of newspaper, coal ashes, bones, rhubarb leaves, pieces of glass….Do you not think an appeal through the local press might be made to obviate this trouble?'

18 June 1943

For the third successive year the Shepton Mallet War Charities Fund Committee, by kind permission of Mr C R Wainwright held its fete in 'the beautiful grounds of Summerleaze'. It was a happy thought in these 'stay at home days' that prompted the committee to hold this years fete on Whit Monday thereby providing an out-of-doors programme for the Bank Holiday.

Soldier Fined. Joseph Chapman, a soldier, was summoned for insulting behaviour with the intent to insult two young females.
    Evidence was given by a 25 year old Pilton young lady and a 32 year old Shepton Mallet school teacher who said they saw the soldier acting indecently. He was fined £2.

Cricket. Shepton Mallet and Cranmore 50 (Reeves 5 for1) Doutling 46 (Achilles 9 for 10)

25 June 1943

Home Guardsman Honoured. In the King's Birthday Honours List appears the name of Sergeant Edward Fry who received a certificate for good service. Sergeant Fry is the armourer Sergeant of the Shepton Mallet Company. The honour was well merited, and its award gives great satisfaction, not only to the local company but to the many friends of Mr Fry.

Shepton Mallet Rural District Council. Erection of Road Signs. The surveyor reports that, subject to the approval of the Military and the Police, certain signs throughout the district are now being erected. The surveyor said they were not putting all signs back, only those on through traffic routes.

Regal. 'To the shores of Tripoli' starring Randolph Scott, John Payne and Maureen O'Hara.

2 July 1943

Home Guard Dance. The support accorded to the Home Guard Dance on Monday night from 9pm – 1 am surprised all expectations and the large company clamoured for an extension to 2am which was granted. The Equatorians Dance Orchestra programme was very much appreciated and Lieut Norgrove was a popular MC. At 2 am the MC thanking the supporters and wishing them good night announced that the floor was being taken over until 3am by our American Friends who wished to make a real night of it to give some of their members who are returning to their homeland a night to be remembered.

Life for young ladies

It was quite evident that social life in Shepton had picked up with the presence of the American Soldiers. Our intrepid reporter Colin Ryall interviewed five young ladies of that time to gather their recollections.

Contributors: Rose Moon, Muriel Amberton, Gwen Carter, Joyce Spacey and Christine Czerny.

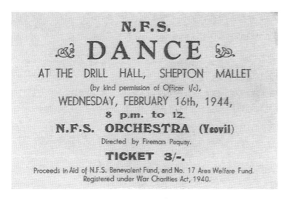

Dance ticket.

Christine Czerny (née Haskins) pictured in 1946.

Rose, an evacuee, had originally arrived in Shepton with brothers and sisters, sent by Mum & Dad from West Ham where they had lived in a nice part near a large park. Rose remembers people were surprised by how little she and other evacuees brought with them, but Rose said this was on the express instructions of the authorities. They bought simple one change of clothes and their gas masks. 'You never went anywhere without your gas mask in its cardboard box, slung round your neck on its string.' Rose remembered people being a little wary of the evacuees as some arrived unclean, their poor condition due to their poor circumstances. 'You stood there tagged with a luggage label giving name and destination'. Those intending to take in evacuees simply viewed the new arrivals and picked any they liked the look of. 'Like strays.' Pretty girls presented no problem, scruffy boys took longer to place; this meant siblings were sometimes split up, adding to their distress.

Rose at first lived at Charlton with people who made her very welcome. They really took to her, wanted to adopt her and her sister, 'Our Little Queens', but Mum wasn't having that.

Rose recalls all evacuees, when they went to school, were at first segregated at Kilver St School, but this did not last long.

Rose's family home in London was bombed on the first day of the blitz (Sept.1940), although this caused no loss of life in the family it did mean the complete loss of all family 'treasures'. Her bombed out mother came to join Rose while Dad remained to work in London.

They were allocated a cottage on the farm where her brother worked that lacked the amenities they were used to in London. It was lit by candles, water raised by a manual pump, primitive sewerage disposal. The radio powered by clumsy 'wet' batteries that had to be re-charged weekly in town. (No telephone of course, a rarity in ordinary homes even in London.) Later she lived at Chesterblade. Rose remembers the ammo (?) dumps alongside railway track from Cranmore to Shepton. (These could have been storage dumps of other types of war material.)

Rose had the nerve to tell servicemen not to whistle at her and her friend, as they were only schoolgirls. (Her friend had whispered, 'You speak for yourself.') Nevertheless they were afterwards treated with more respect.

Rose also recalled being pursued, while out cycling, by a black man on a bike, she took refuge in an Evercreech garage where her brother was an apprentice.

Muriel, (local farmer's daughter). Had evacuees stay with them on the farm, a gran and her two granddaughters.

Muriel fondly remembers the gay times at local dances. She worked in a factory producing 'dry' batteries for the war effort. About 200 worked in the factory and although everybody worked hard they all had a good time. Muriel recalled the old foreman coming along when the manager was away saying, "'Now girls, what are you all up to?' 'And there we would be putting our hair in rollers ready for the evening dance.'" The boss was a proper city type who bought each of his two sons a farm to avoid them being called up, (farming was a 'reserve' occupation) but they only worked in the factory. She gave the impression the boss was a war profiteer.

Muriel could never remember being short of food or, it would seem, a laugh.

Gwen, (née Warr) recalled vivid memories of the loss of her brother, A.S.W. Warr. He was first sent home to recuperate after being caught in a shrapnel blast; he was supplied with tweezers and disinfectant and told to remove fragments as they surfaced. He returned to duty only to be killed just a month before the War ended, but not before a last visit home. He was granted compassionate leave when he received a phone call saying his father was ill. Arriving home he found his father hale and hearty, a fact the lad duly reported at the police station. However the mix-up proved a fortunate error as it made for a last family meeting. By the time photos taken on that occasion came back Gwen had received the news that her brother never would return.

Gwen herself joined the army at seventeen, having been trained in Morse code. She made lance corporal twice but twice lost her stripe when her Army life and her social life clashed. After which Gwen gave up trying to become an NCO.

Joyce's father was policeman at Wraxall, she remembers troops camped behind the house coming in the back door leaving by front door as they lined up for hot shaving water.

Joyce remembers giving her sweet ration coupons to a young father in a 'non-combatant' troop, to send home as presents to his daughter.

Joyce recalled that the bakery for all the local American forces personnel was located at Evercreech. It was manned by white officers and black other ranks.

Joyce remembers an encounter with an American Army convoy as she made her way home. As she pushed her bike up Pye Hill she was chatted up by 'the biggest black man you ever saw' as he drove alongside her in his left-hand drive lorry. At the crest of the hill she mounted her bike and raced down the hill. She actually out paced the heavy lorry but went so fast she fell off at the bottom of the hill, fortunately into the arms of her father.

Joyce remembers visits to London and how it was full of life despite the bombing and how relieved she was when a porter returned her coat, left on the train. Such a loss would have been difficult, if not impossible to make good due to the severe wartime shortages. She was also surprised to find that industrial disputes were taking place despite the war being on.

The war made a lot of work for her father; he was on duty for long hours. At local dances he made all arrivals put their bicycle lamps in a sack only to be collected when they left.

At some small dances the music would be provided by '78's' played on a 'wind-up' gramophone, but at least this meant the latest 'American' dance music rather than the rather outdated offerings of the local bands.

Chris (née Haskins) twice widowed, her last husband was a German ex-POW who only ever returned home once, for a short visit and that a very long time after the war, when the Iron Curtain had fallen. Chris accompanied him, but that was long after hostilities…

When war broke out Chris was a schoolgirl attending Waterloo Road School and living in the family home at the bottom of Town St., No 45 (the part below Waterloo Rd. now known as Tipcote Hill).

At that time Waterloo Rd School catered for children of all ages, from the reception class to the final year. Of schools Chris recalled, "Then there was only Waterloo Rd and Bowlish; and Kilver Street. Most of the evacuees were sent to Kilver Street owing to them having more space than we had in the town ones. When you got old enough you sat your 11+ and then if you didn't pass it you went on to the senior school. That was next door, it was a separate building, it's where you've got the flats for the old people now, the first one was the girls school and second one was the boy's, the one that finished right on the hospital road."

"Segregated of course, the boys had a playground at the top, then the girls and one for the little ones which is the one still used."

Chris failed her 11+ but wanted to improve her education, "I used to go night times to the Convent, cos I was only enduring the Council School."

When asked how the coming of war affected her Chris replied with characteristic candour, "I was frightened. I remember thinking, "Oh dear!" September the 3rd 1939 wasn't it?"

Chris had every right to be frightened. Gas masks had been issued to everyone with strict instructions that they should be carried at all times, air raid shelters built. Surely this could only portend bombardment by gas and high explosive?

And then there was the very real threat of invasion. It was all very well for the boys at her school to sing,

> "Whistle while you work
> Hitler is a twerp!

      Goering's barmy, so's his army
      Whistle while you work."

but after the debacle of Dunkirk, when the Army's equipment was left in France and the Home Guard was armed with broomsticks, it was only after 'the Few' had shown that Herman Goering's boast that he would 'destroy the RAF in weeks' to be false that the very real fear of invasion subsided.

In the event the nearest bomb was a land mine that destroyed a rail bridge out at Bullimore Farm, but for a time the air raid warnings were quite frequent, 'We hid under a table under the stairs, that was our shelter. We used to keep the coal under the stairs and just back from there was the strongest part of the house and we used to stay in this little cubbyhole at the back there. I was frightened when we heard the bombers go over but they were heading for Bristol or Bath, that bomb we had was a stray, he just offloaded it before heading home. And of course Mother was very careful about the blackout.'

'We had no evacuees, we had no room.' But Chris remembers a neighbour, Mrs Linthorn, 'who lived at the bottom of Cowl Street, in Monmouth House' putting up thirteen evacuees. She would only have boys as to mix sexes, she believed, would be too much trouble. Chris clearly remembers that Mrs Linthorn kept all 'her' boys under strict control while they were in her charge.

Chris was the youngest of twelve, although tragically three brothers and a sister had 'died within the fortnight, from whooping cough and pneumonia'. That was at the end of the First World War, when her father was recovering from war wounds in a London hospital. Chris' mother had to cope on her own when she lost four of her five children, 'The only one to survive was my brother Jack' (J. H. Haskins founder of the High St. J.H. Haskins & Son.) The family was then living in Coleford, ' And my Mother didn't have any counsellors come around, but she had the whole village....Mum always said they were wonderful, they supported her.'

'We did have soldiers in our house, you'd come home and you couldn't find a seat to sit on.' They were visitors. 'My brothers went off to the war and Mother always used to say, "Well I hope someone looks after my boys", so after one of my brothers brought home a soldier he had found fallen down in the snow Mother always made him and his comrades welcome; for tea or soup, or just a sit by the fire.' These lads were part of the advance party of the Northumberland Fusiliers. The regiment trained in the area and then went abroad.

'They were Geordies and you couldn't understand them, I mean it was worse than having foreigners than trying to talk to a Geordie.'

' One was a dispatch rider called Ernie Rutter from Newcastle. He got killed, cos Mother kept in touch with his mum and Ern's mum wrote and told her he had been killed, a lot of them were killed, but of those that survived some came back and found their old girl friends and married and stayed.' Chris mentioned several names of those who had settled in Shepton. So some couples had overcome the language problem!

'Mum also helped in the British Legion. They provided tea and sandwiches for off duty soldiers in a room behind what is now the Baptist Church. It was just somewhere for them to have a chat. And Mum felt she was doing her bit.'

Asked if rationing was severe Chris said not really. The family registered at Felton's a shop at the bottom of Catsash that has long since gone. 'Mrs Felton wouldn't let you have an ounce over your ration, but she was very fair, she always made sure you got your fair share of anything that was in short supply. Mrs Felton died only recently, she must have been in her 90's.'

Chris' elder brothers were in business and so got a petrol allowance, as they visited farms on business they could pick up the odd pat of butter or a few eggs. 'Mum also supplemented the meat ration from time to time by making brawn from a pigs head. I couldn't face it but the brothers liked it.'(Pigs heads were un-rationed.)

The coal ration could be supplemented with wood, 'or you could get coke from the gas works. I remember schoolboys taking their home made carts to get coke on a Saturday morning.' (The gas works were in Cowl Street, near Chris' home.)

Other regiments came and went after the Northumberlanders and then the Americans arrived.

One incident stays vivid in Chris' mind. Chris remembers a fire in the American motor pool workshop behind the Crown Inn. Someone had put a tin of polish on the stovetop. This exploded. Chris and her sister were 'coming down the hill on our way home, in the blackout and there was this explosion. Well it was the war you know; we thought it was a bomb or something. We were scared.' Reaching the scene Chris remembers the inaction of shocked onlookers, staring in horror as personnel stumbled out ablaze from head to foot.

Chris didn't let her fear stop her doing what she could, 'Joyce and I removed our coats and wrapped then round the victims. I believe three of the men later died. We never heard if any one was held to blame for the accident, the Americans would have had their own enquiry. They had their own courts.' (Note. This incident certainly happened but didn't appear to make the local papers.)

In some other cases these courts handed down the death sentence. 'Mother told me that years ago they would ring the prison bell when they were going to hang somebody. That stopped years before the war but during the war we always knew when someone was due to be hung. You'd hear that Pierrepoint was having a drink in the Pack Horse and there could only be one purpose for his visit. He was the English hangman, why they didn't have their own hangman I don't know.'

The war ended and the Americans left and that was the last of the executions at Shepton. In fact life began to return to normal, Chris started to go out and enjoy herself the fears and tensions of war fading.

In the general conversation several of the ladies recalled that meals were available to all at an officially sponsored canteen, an Emergency Feeding Station (the British Restaurant), at the top of the High St. This was for civilians in difficulties, people passing through, displaced people, unsettled evacuees and old people finding it hard to cope. Joyce said they made lovely stews and rice puddings. For some of the helpers it was their 'war work' (labour was directed during the war), others were volunteers.

The ladies talk made it clear that they had all enjoyed a lively social life despite, or even perhaps enhanced by, the war conditions. The 'American' dance bands in particular made a lasting impression. None of them mentioned any serious food shortages, they were more concerned with the severe clothes rationing and the non-availability of cosmetics.

As the ladies talked it became clear that one of the major impacts on life in Shepton Mallet was the influx of the many different incomers the war brought. First to arrive were the evacuees, both children who came under the auspices of official schemes, then office workers as businesses re-located to avoid the bombing. Others were older people who came of their own volition (my own maternal grandparents took a country cottage, my grandmother having suffered hysterics during the Gotha bombing raids of WW I.)

The evacuees were shortly followed by 'foreign' soldiers from the North and later by the real foreigners, as Allies or POW's.

It also became clear that the war conditions gave these then young ladies much more freedom, much better prospects and far wider breadth of experience then they could have expected in depressed and depressing pre-war Shepton Mallet.

9 July 1943

'The Market Town of Shepton Mallet' a delightful little booklet by Alan C Tarbet has just come to hand. A very readable and pleasing little book nicely produced and finished. It will be on sale in the Town and the proceeds will be devoted to the Red Cross fund.

An Innovation. From an announcement appearing in another column it will be learned that at least 16 businesses are closing down for the whole of the August Bank Holiday week. It is a bold step and one said to be activated 'In consequence of the war conditions and with a desire to give staff a short holiday. Whatever may be said either for or against the scheme it is refreshing to know that for once there are a number of business people in the town who can co-operate and show something of the team spirit.

Regal 'Orchestral Wives' starring George Montgomery and Glen Miller.

Cricket. Shepton Mallet and Cranmore v Leigh on Mendip. Shepton Mallet 72, Leigh on Mendip 72. 12 aside. A very keen game was witnessed and resulted in a tie.

16 July 1943

Good News. At long last at least two post cards have come through from Prisoners of War in Japanese hands. Mrs Coward has heard from her husband that he is safe and well and Mr & Mrs Whittle have received a similar intimation from Mr Jack Gardiner.

Shepton Mallet Company Home Guard. Inter Platoon Rifle Competition. The Inter Platoon Rifle Competition for the Silver Challenge Cup, presented by Mr J P Luff JP was bought to a successful conclusion on Sunday when the Batcombe Platoon under the command of Lt Britton topped the score with 447 points. Second Shepton Mallet No 1 Platoon, third Ditcheat

Platoon No1 team, 13th Cranmore Platoon.

Shepton Mallet Urban District Council. Bus queue shelter. The Highways and Lighting Committee reported that the work on the proposed bus queue shelter has been suspended following further information from the bus company as to the date when buses fitted with gas producer plant will operate to and from Shepton. In view of the delay in carrying out the company's intentions the committee recommended that as a temporary measure the passage adjoining the Market Hall be covered with corrugated iron. (Note. There was an attempt to power buses by producing gas by burning coke in a trailer towed by the bus. This was not at all successful and the buses barely went above walking pace –especially up hill.)

Editorial. It must be gratifying to all concerned to know that the Communal Kitchen not only continues its good and useful work but for the month of May showed a comfortable profit.

Editorial. In their successful landing on Sicily, the Allies have thrilled the civilised world and given renewed hope to millions of enslaved and impoverished people.

Advert. Lorry Drivers wanted – apply Showerings Ltd, Kilver Street, Shepton Mallet.

Advert. Undertaker – Alfred Connock, Pilton 'phone Pilton 56 (night and day)

23 July 1943

Polo Match – Members of the Shepton Mallet Swimming Club journeyed to Wells last week to play in a polo match against Wells. A keen game was witnessed in which the homesters ran out winners 4 goals to 1.

Tragic Death of Shepton Mallet Motor Cyclist. Mr S G Green, a sixty-one year old motor cyclist of 18 Darshill, Shepton Mallet was killed in a road accident on Friday. His son Edwin aged 13 who was riding pillion sustained serious injuries.

Card Playing and Dancing on Methodist Premises. In the light of the decision of the Methodist Conference to allow dancing and card playing on Methodist premises under certain very precautionary conditions, the editor has had an interview with the superintendent of the Shepton Mallet Methodist Circuit with a view to discover the attitudes of local Methodists on this question…. Mr Merrit said…. He could not and would not at any time, associate himself in the slightest degree with dancing or card playing on church premises…. I am convinced that such forms of entertainment as those in question tend to destroy spiritual life.

30 July 1943

The newsagents of the town give notice that they will close their establishments on Monday Tuesday and Wednesday next week at 10am.

Advert. Baseball Match in Whitstone Park. August Bank Holiday between United States Army DTC No 1 and No2. Collection on behalf of the Red Cross penny a week fund.

Advert. A Dance Given by officers and men of the United States Army DTC will be held at the Drill Hall Shepton Mallet on Wednesday August 4th 8pm – 2 am. American Swing

Band Entertainments, refreshments, bar, door prizes. Admission, Forces 1/6d. Civilians 2/6d. Doughnuts will be served free of charge.

Note. Stan Blacker paints an interesting picture of the social life at this time and in particular of the tensions between the American Troops and local British Troops. It was a period when there were a lot of troops in the country with not a lot to do. Most young local men were away from town, stationed elsewhere and only got home on 48 hour leave. According to Stan, for some the leave was often one long session of drinking and picking fights with the American troops.

> When things had got sufficiently out of hand, the local police sergeant would round up the British lads and take them to the Charlton Road (Somerset and Dorset) Station and put them on trains back to their camps.

6 August 1943

Shepton Mallet Waterworks Company. Unusual Drought Warning. The directors of the Company desire to call attention to the serious future prospects in regard to the sufficiency of the water supply to the town in consequence of the unusually dry period for some time past.

> Water would be cut off at night and a ban on use for fountains, fishponds, lawn sprinklers, hosepipes for watering gardens, washing house or shop fronts, paths, carriages and all Motor Vehicles. Geoffrey Budd, Secretary.

300 watched the Baseball match in Whitstone Park and the collection raised £6.

13 August 1943

Combined operation. The 1st Shepton Mallet, Cheddar and Baltonsbourgh troops of Boy Scouts spent a very happy time under canvas at Rowberrow at the Annual District Camp, together with 200 scouts from all over Somerset.

Wedding at Mottingham. A wedding of local interest was solemnized at St Andrews Church Mottingham London on Tuesday August 3rd between Mr Alan W Hoskins youngest son of Mr and Mrs J O Hoskins of Park Farm Shepton Mallet and Miss Constance M Murphy of Mottingham.

Note. 'Peggy' died after an illness in 2003 but Alan still has memories dating back to those days. Arranging the wedding had not been easy. Peggy had to go back to London for the Banns and hated it there. Alan went up for the wedding and only took his brother and sister. He says you were only allowed 6 photographs and 40 guests maximum anyway. The church was bombed shortly before the wedding. They only stayed in London for three days and with the blackout and bombing going on, Alan gives the impression that he was very glad to get out of it.

They had met when Peggy came down to Shepton with the National Deposit Friendly Society at the beginning of the war. She lodged at Eden Grove, the large house in Leg Square. She took on duties as a fire watcher. Alan says that things were a lot more lively down there than out in Bowlish.

Home Guard Memories – Alan Hoskins

As a farmer, Alan was exempted from Military Service but he took on a major role in the LDV and then the Home Guard. He says that when Neville Chamberlain put out his radio call for home defence volunteers, as someone with a shot gun he felt obliged to join the LDV. He suggests that although officially the 'Local Defence Volunteers' their nick name 'Look, Duck and Vanish' may bear reference to the Secret Auxillary Units which were operating at that time, trained in tactics to stop invading forces. He is sure there was not a unit in Shepton Mallet. The units stuck to the higher ground, Dulcote, Dinder, Beacon, Creech Hill. They were in positions for observation and were connected to the Green Line Defence Chain which ran from Brean Down along the south side of the Mendips just to the north of Shepton as a sort of 'outer defensive line' for Bristol. The men from the Auxillary Units came back into the Home Guard as the immediate threat of invasion lessened.

In Shepton Mallet, at first the LDV had no equipment or Uniform at all. Arm bands arrived first then denim overalls before eventually the Home Guard got uniforms. For weapons they started off with their shotguns, but he can't remember them ever resorting to the use of pikes! Then some grease-covered rifles arrived from America. When the major invasion scare happened on the 8th and 9th of September 1940 he can remember being with his platoon at the top of Compton Road. The platoon was led by Freddy Bennett. There were 20 of them and they had only 10 rounds of ammunition between them. Freddy kept five and

Home Guard officers of the Shepton Mallet Company.

gave the other five to Alan. Quite how this was going to stop the Germans, Alan is not sure. It was good observation point and they watched someone approaching all the way from East Compton. It turnout only to be the chap who had gone to look to the Tilley's prize-winning Old English Sheepdogs.

There was provision for anti tank traps built into the roads at a number of points across the area but a printed sheet of instructions to the Home Guard Commanders issued in 1941 of which Alan still has a copy shows that the army instructed them not to erect them until given instructions. From the tone of these instructions it would appear the army were rather worried that the Home Guard may have jumped the gun and got in the way.

The Shepton Mallet Company Home Guard consisted of many platoons covering Shepton and the surrounding villages. It was under the command of Colonel Spencer from Cranmore, a major landowner. Alan can remember the day when they were on exercises on Barrendown and Colonel Spencer came across and told him he had heard that morning that his son and heir had been killed in the fighting in Italy. Major Fred Luff of Bowlish was the second in Command of the Company.

In Shepton Mallet there were three platoons. Alan was in No 1 platoon who met at the Market Hut and had to look after part of the railway line at Winsor Hill. There was another Platoon in Waterloo Road and the other was at Charlton. He also believes there was a platoon connected directly with the Railway.

Once the Home Guard was established they started to get proper weapons although some of them where rather alarming. They had to make Molotov Cocktails, glass bottles with sulpher etc. These were supposed to be dropped into invading tanks though how was never clear. Then there was the Northover Projector, a Mills bomb was fired through a mortar connected to a rifle – a rather dangerous arrangement. There was also the 'Blacker Bombard' a great big thing which they tried in Ham Woods – the explosion rather shook up Shepton Mallet one Sunday morning.

They got Browning Automatic Rifles and Tommy guns later the war. There were a few accidents. He remembers that Stan Bullard once dropped a Tommy Gun when the catch must have been off. Five rounds went rattling up Kilver Street. Alan also remembers going on a training course with the regular army in Shepton Mallet Prison learning about Lewis Guns. Somehow they got locked in for the night and it was extremely dark.

Alan himself rose through the ranks in the Home Guard. He got his commission and was put in charge of the Pilton Platoon who he says were a good bunch of blokes. He finished the war with the rank of 2nd Lieutenant. After the war he was asked if he would train the army cadets but thought that it was time to concentrate on farming.

13 August 1943 (cont)

Shepton Mallet Urban District Council. A complaint has been received regarding the nuisance created by the littering of the paths and doorways with fried chips and greasy paper, and recommended that: i) attention of the police be drawn to this nuisance, ii) that two containers be provided, one for the bottom half of the High Street and another for Town Street on the site of 64 Town Street and iii) suitable posters notifying the public that this offence will be prosecuted.

A Misapprehension. The council had taken 50% of the profits of the Swimming Club Gala held on Bank Holiday Monday in the belief that it was the 'Annual Gala which they usually took 50% profit. However the swimming club pointed out that this had been a charity gala for the Red Cross Charity.

> Mr Pullen said 'I do not think the Council ever intended to take half the profit of a gala held on behalf of charity. Mr Witcombe moved and Mr Hardwidge seconded that the council forfeit their share of the profits. (Note. The Council operated the Swimming Baths.)

Regal, Errol Flynn and Ronald Reagan in 'Desperate Journey'.

20 August 1943

Collett Park. In another column appears an announcement of a band concert to be given in Collett Park on Wednesday afternoon, by the band of the South Wales Borderers, under the baton of Mr S V Hayes. The programme, an excellent one, should prove a great attraction.

Missions to Seamen. Sermons were preached and collections taken throughout the day at the Parish Church on Sunday….Probably there is no subject to-day which has a greater pull on the public than that of 'our seamen'. The collection amounted to the gratifying sum of £17.

Missing Home Guard Ammunition. The story of three lads aged 10, 11 and 12 years, stealing a quantity of ammunition valued at £2/6/10d from a Home Guard Store was heard at the Shepton Mallet Juvenile Court on Thursday last week when the lads pleaded guilty. … All the boys admitted the theft…and told how they went to the woods and tried to get out the bullets by throwing the cartridges at stones.

> The defendants were placed on probation, two of them to reside at approved homes at the discretion of the probation officer.

27 August 1943

Allotment and Gardeners Association. Annual Show. The third annual 'Dig for Victory' vegetable show organised under the auspices of the Shepton Mallet and District Allotment and Gardeners Association was held by kind permission of Messer's Wainwright, Laver and Crees Ltd in their commodious Market Hut at their Repository Sale yard on Saturday.

Learning by experience, the exhibits proved to be the best seen in the town since the start of the war, and so keen and close was the competition that the judges found themselves 'up against it' and delayed the official opening time by three quarters of an hour. There was a gratifying entry of 270.

A week in camp. A number of the 1st Shepton Mallet Girl Guides spent a very enjoyable week under canvas at Blagdon during the second week of this month, when they were fortunate in having very favourable weather.

A great relief. Mrs Witts and her 14 year old daughter received great news on Tuesday, after a silence of two years, viz that Mr Witts was safe and well but a prisoner in Japanese hands. The good news was bought on a post card written by Mr Witts himself. Mr Witts is a sailor and his ship was HMS Prince of Wales (sunk by the Japenese in December 1941 off the coast of Malaya).

Advert. To all Farmers. The Mid Somerset Motor Co Ltd (Allen's) Shepton Mallet have been appointed and licensed under The Ministry of Agriculture and Fisheries to supply farm machinery and tractors. Apply to us for delivery dates, prices etc.

3 September 1943

A record – To Miss D Lintern the local organiser and her willing band of helpers who so cheerfully sold emblems on behalf of the National Institute of the Blind on Friday last, well merited congratulations are due…they raised the record sum of £32/9/8d.

Baptist Church. As was confidently anticipated the visit to the Baptist Church on Monday of Miss Emma Munn of the 'World Wide Evangelisation Crusade' proved a great attraction and she was accorded a warm reception by a full congregation.

Regal. 'Wild Bill Hitchcock Rides' starring Bruce Cabot and Constance Bennett.

10 September 1943

War Anniversary – The fourth anniversary of the declaration of war was, in compliance with the express wish of HM King George VI, fittingly observed on Friday with special services of prayer and intercession at the parish church.

German Fined at Shepton Mallet. Offences under trading with Enemy Regulations.
> For trading with a man in Spain who was on the Board of Trade 'Black List' a German who resides at Croscombe had four offences preferred against him at Shepton Mallet Police Court on Friday.
> He was Arnold Frederick Strauss and he pleaded guilty to unlawfully having commercial intercourse with a firm in Spain on August 5th 1942. He was an intermediary trading pharmaceutical goods and said he had not spotted the name on the list.
> The Chairman, Sir Frederick Berryman, said the bench was satisfied that there was no treasonable action in what had happened. At the same time it was important that regulations made in the interests of the Country should be complied with, particularly by persons enjoying the hospitality of this land. Fine £5 for each offence.

Note. Somewhat surprisingly there are not really that many cases of straight forward black marketeering appearing in the courts. However talking to a number of people it is obvious that there was a fair amount going on. To what extent the police were turning a blind eye, I can't speculate. It would seem unlikely considering the petty things that did end up in court. Stories I have heard range from produce stolen off allotments to misappropriation of Red Cross Supplies. Many goods related to the Americans (who had much better rations than British Military Personnel) are also reputed to have been traded. I have been given names, but as it is only second hand information and some families are still involved in the town I think the less said the better – which seems to have been the successful method of working then.

Advert. Mrs London-Griffiths West Lodge Shepton Mallet requires a capable domestic help.

17 September 1943

Helping the Red Cross. At the Rabbit Show on Saturday a 'peep' at two pence a time at two lemons from Sicily, bought in the gratifying sum of £1/3/8d for the Red Cross Penny a Week Fund.

Shepton Mallet Bowls Club. The final for the Trevor Lintern Cup of the Shepton Mallet Bowls Club was played off on the bowling green on Wednesday afternoon between Mr J Blytherin and Mr J E Plowman. The match excited much interest and a good number of spectators watched a very interesting game – won by Mr Blytherin.

Letter. Dear Sir, Can nothing be done to ease the confusion caused at the Cenotaph every time the buses leave? I am aware that there are obstacles barring the way to the erection of a shelter, but I can hardly believe it would offend the parties concerned – or deface their property- if the Urban Council were to send a man with a pot of white paint and a brush to mark out queue lines, clearly named for each of the three bus routes!
    I remain yours truly 'Also Ran'.

Shepton Mallet Rural District Council. Surveyors Report. Mr Walker also reported that Mr Doble of Stoney Stratton had offered the council a small portion of garden at the entrance to Back Lane Stoney Stratton to widen the entrance to that lane from the Westcombe Road on the condition that the council shall rebuild the wall on the new line.
    (Jim Doble a member of the project group confirms that this was because of the increased number of lorries which kept banging into the wall. The work was completed as described.)

Darshill Sick Bay. The Public Health and Housing Committee reporting on the proposal that the Darshill Sick Bay should be available for the treatment of local children. They had been told that it would be possible but only if charges were fully paid, which as the council had no means of getting the money meant that it couldn't go ahead. (This Sick Bay was the successor to the one at Pylle and was financed out of Evacuation Funds.)

24 September 1943

Letter from E H Norman, Chairman Shepton Mallet District Council, notifying people of a church service and parade for 'Battle of Britain Sunday,' 26th September.

Circus – The visit of 'Ringlands' Circus to the town on Monday proved a popular attraction, large numbers attending each of the two performances in the afternoon. The several items of the programme were well received and the clowns were really quite funny.

Shepton Mallet Petty Sessions. Albert Watts 19, Labourer, Sunset, Villa Waterloo Road, Shepton Mallet and James William Hodges 18 quarryman, Garston Street, Shepton Mallet were summoned for using indecent language on the public highway. They pleaded guilty. Fine 10/- each.

Marriage of Mr L J Edwards and Miss Helen Todd. The luxurious Congregational Church of Oakhill has seldom had its seating accommodation more taxed than on Saturday, the occasion of the marriage of two young people who by their many activities in the life and welfare of the parish have earned for themselves well deserved popularity.

(Lionel Edwards was at that time with auctioneers Wainwright, Laver and Crees. After the war he opened Chamberlain Brothers and Edwards in the town which is now run by his son. He was for 50 years secretary of the Mid Somerset Show and also long time chairman of the Shepton Mallet Carnival Committee before retiring with his wife to Bath. Lionel died in April 2004 during the preparation of this book)

Editorial. The long winter nights are now quickly approaching and within a few weeks it will be pitch black in the streets at 6.00pm. Each successive blackout season brings with it its own crop of nuisances and annoyances….By far the greatest source of annoyance is the disgusting habit some men have of making a public convenience of every doorway in the main street.

There can be no possible excuse for it and surely it must be the business of either the UDC or the Police to do their level best to stop it.

Advert. Advertiser retiring from business wishes to purchase a small country house, cottage or bungalow with nice garden and a little land suitable for poultry.

Advert. Wanted. Boys to work in Bottling Stores. Also youths to assist with beer deliveries from motor lorry. The Charlton Brewery Co Ltd Shepton Mallet.

Rose Ware and the 'Railway Way Gangers'

Note. Labour shortage was getting quite extreme by this time. Rose Ware (née Brooks remembers working on the Railways.

Her father – Mr Brooks was a porter out Charlton Station, suggested she go for a job there. As she has a withered arm from infantile paralysis she was worried but he told her to hold it behind her back at the interview, which she did. She was the first girl on the railway. In the end five of them under Walt Gunning who had lost three fingers in an accident. They worked from Wincanton to the Wellow tunnel. 'Gangers' greasing fish plates and other track work. When a train was coming they had to make sure one nut either side of the fish plate was tightened back up and get out the way. They painted signs, cleared weeds etc

They had a hut at between the two Winsor Hill tunnels where they went when it was raining. They made themselves soup with cabbages pinched from Mr Godfrey's fields – great big cow cabbages. Only one girl went into the field at a time and went to the middle of field where the cabbages would not be missed.

Of course as soon as the war was over, they were not wanted any more as their jobs were given back to returning soldiers.

1 October 1943

'Battle of Britain Sunday'…it was the first time that members of the Royal Observer Corps had been able to attend as a uniformed body and their presence on this particular occasion, with their Chief Observer, Mr EE Poles, was as gratifying as it was appropriate.

Regal. 'Queen Victoria' starring Anna Neagle and Anton Wildbrook.

8 October 1943

Workers Education Association – It was a matter of much regret and disappointment that owing to illness Mr Jackson was unable to commence his course of lectures on International Relations on Wednesday.

Shepton Mallet Petty Sessions. Alice Maclaren, Manor Farm, Chesterblade, was summoned for using a milk churn belonging to another person for a purpose other than the collection or delivery of milk. She pleaded ignorance of the law. She had used the churn for keeping paraffin in. The case was dismissed on the payment of 4/- costs.

Evelyn May Davis Manor Farm Chesterblade was summoned for permitting use of the churn for a purpose other than the collection or delivery of milk. Fine £1 imposed.

15 October 1943

Bell ringing – Not since long before pre-war days have so many fine peals and changes been heard from the church tower as those which rang out on Saturday afternoon and evening on the occasion of the Quarterly meeting of the Diocesan Bell Ringers.

A problem. The problem of securing sufficient labour to cope with this year's harvest has been very difficult to solve….farmers have had to rely to a very considerable extent on the good will and public spirit of volunteer workers many of whom have generously given up annual holiday to 'lend a hand on the land'.

Shepton Mallet Urban District Council. Fire Guard Problem. In view of the persistent rumours in circulation in the town regarding arrangements for fire watching several questions were asked by members....there was a certain amount of confusion...some apparently had been told that the arrangements for fire watching had been cancelled, others had been informed that they could report for duty, sign their names and go home.... The council...decided that the clerk should make a statement to the press setting out the position which, it was pointed out, was precisely as hitherto, no formal de-prescription having been made.

Regal. 'Yankee Doodle Dandy' starring James Cagney.

22 October 1943

Garage Proprietor Fined. Theophilus Matthews, garage proprietor, Junction Garage Evercreech was summoned for failing to keep a daily record of the quantity of motor fuel acquired against surrender of 'W' coupons and record the quantity of such fuel used for each purpose for which coupons were issued. Fined £5 & advocates fees £13/3/-

Regal. 'The Gentle Sex' starring Leslie Howard and the ATS Girls.

29 October 1943

Repatriated. Sergeant J Walshe RAF .... Last Week Mr and Mrs Walshe received and official intimation that 'Johnnies name was included on the list of those to be repatriated... On Tuesday the glad telegram arrived 'Arrived safely in England. Going to hospital for examination.' He had been shot down over Germany where for two years he lay in hospital. His wounds were severe and his progress slow, but with his indomitable pluck, he managed to keep alive.

Poppy Day Appeal. 'Because of the great shortage of materials we appealed last year for the return of poppies after 11th November. Many thousands of Poppies were returned by public-spirited people and it was possible to renovate a large proportion of these for use again.

5 November 1943

Home coming of Sergt J D Walshe.
   Mr Walshe,.... Was perhaps (father-like) the most restless of the family and somehow sensed that John would be home before Sunday. Accordingly he made several trips to the GWR Station on Saturday but to no avail. Nothing daunted he tried again at 7.30pm and on this occasion Mrs J Walshe joined him. They were richly rewarded for as the train stopped, out jumped 'Johnny' wreathed in smiles, and preceded by two hefty kit bags.
   Sergeant Walshe's plane was shot down near the Friesian Islands on September 2nd 1941. As the plane struck the water the cabin in which Sergt Walshe was the gunner, broke away and when he recovered from the shock he found himself trapped at the bottom of the North Sea. He quickly liberated himself and was soon on the surface. The night was almost pitch black but after struggling in the water gravely injured, he was attracted to a dark object floating on the surface. This turned out to be his plane and

there were the other members of the crew. They pulled Sergeant Walshe into the dingy and after drifting for nine hours the crew were picked up by a German rescue launch. He was suffering from compound fractures of the femur, smashed knee cap, broken wrist as well as other injuries.

For fourteen months he remained in the hospital and being the only 'foreign' patient found it very lonely…. Eventually he was transferred to British Prisoner of War Camps where he benefited from receiving Red Cross parcels, for which he has the greatest gratitude.

Being transferred from one camp to another he travelled quite a bit in Germany and saw some of the bomb damage, particularly at Emden where the destruction he says is terrible…

Whilst at one camp he was quite near where the RAF smashed the great German Dams and later saw how bridges had been washed away, houses and trees flattened.

The Germans he says are full of fear, but perhaps most of all fear the RAF and a Russian invasion. Prior to Stalingrad they were boastful and arrogant … but now their attitude had changed somewhat…

(Sergeant Walshe seems to have deservedly taken on the role of local 'War Hero'. He was guest at many meetings and asked to open fetes etc. Stan Blacker fills in a few details. Apparently he had lost a foot through his injuries. Before the war he had been the manager of the glove factory which was located through the arch next to the solicitors (now Dyne Drewett) at the south end of the High Street. Apparently it also occupied the building now used by Chantry Digital in Townsend. Sergeant Walshe insisted on joining the ARP Rescue party when is was set up, at that time the only member who was not in the building trade. He was soon able to join the RAF.)

Shepton Mallet Petty Sessions. Tyrell William James, farmer, Whitnel Farm, fined 5/- for allowing a horse to stray onto the highway.

For your Christmas Presents, visit the Red Cross and St John Gift Shop, Market Place Shepton Mallet. Please send us your gifts and come and buy. All proceeds for the Prisoner of War Fund. (Shepton's first Charity Shop?)

RAF Dance – A dance held under the auspices of the Market Hall on Wednesday on behalf of the RAF Benevolent Fund proved a huge success. £15/11/- raised.

A fine experiment… the WVS have arranged to open the British Restaurant at Market Hall on Friday afternoon for the benefit of people awaiting the departure of an omnibus.

12 November 1943

HMS Mendip. Two ingenious collecting boxes for war amenities fund on behalf of 'our ship' HMS Mendip have been opened, the one at the British Legion Club and the other at Messrs C J Moon. The former yielded £4/10/2d and the other £2/14/6d

Shepton Mallet Urban District Council. Post War Housing. Discussion of the needs to provide post-war housing. It is recommended that a scheme be submitted to the Ministry of Health for approval to the acquiring 83 acres…I may say that the site is over the Railway Bridge and is south of the Great Western Railway. It runs right through to the Pilton

Road. (Ridgeway)

Public Conveniences. The Committee of the whole Council further reported that in accordance with a request from the Police, arrangements are being made for suitable illuminated signs to be erected indicating the position of the Public Conveniences in the town. Mr Penelhum reminded the Council that some years ago he had repeatedly urged provision of extra lavatory accommodation.

19 November 1943

Regal. 'King Arthur was a Gentleman' starring Arthur Askey, Jack Train and Evelyn Ball.

26 November 1943

Cinema Seats Damaged. Recently two lads between the ages of 12 and 13 years appeared before the Juvenile Court charged with committing wilful damage at the Regal Cinema. They split open with pen knives the arms of the luxuriously upholstered seats and took out the rubber. The bench found them guilty, bound each lad over and placed them on probation for a period of two years. A condition of the probation was that the lads should not enter the cinema for one year.

Fewer coupons for wooden soled footwear. The number of coupons needed for wooden soled footwear has been reduced…including non-industrial clogs.

Wells. Young girl's complaint against a US Soldier. A 15 year old Wells girl's story of how she was stopped by an American Soldier, dragged through the principle street of the town and taken to a quiet spot and then ordered to lie down in the grass was told to a USA general Court Marshall held in a south west town…attempted rape. Pte Fred Fisher dishonourably discharged from the US Army and to be confined to hard labour for 10 years.

The American Military Prison

It is almost certain that this soldier would have been imprisoned at Shepton Mallet Prison which had been taken over by the American Military. This has become something of a 'cause celebre' with many articles written about the prisoners and their fate and at least two drama's based on their stories. One of these was the film 'The Dirty Dozen'. The issue of racism both within the American Army and the impact of the presence of black soldiers on British society has been much researched.

With its high grey stone walls and solid square buildings the prison certainly gave prisoners a grim

Execution block,
Shepton Mallet Prison.

aspect. The fact that so many were executed for their crimes and that there was always an issue as to whether there was racial equality in treatment has added spice to the history. For those looking for full details we would refer to Francis Disney's meticulously researched 'History of Shepton Mallet Prison' which is still available on CD. As a member of the Local History Group he has allowed us access to his notes.

In all 18 American Military Prisoners were executed, 16 by hanging and 2 were executed by firing squad. At least 10 of those executed were coloured. 10 of the crimes involved the violent rape or killing of young women, one a case with a girl as young as 7. Three offences involved murder of fellow soldiers and the balance appear to have been criminally motivated murders. Some of the murders and rapes of young women were headline stories in the sensational papers of the day.

Although the prisoners were judged and sentenced under American jurisdiction the official British hangman, Pierrepoint, was used to do the dispatching. A number of people have commented that everyone in Shepton Mallet always knew when there was going to be an execution as he used to stay in the Bell Hotel in the Market Place and could be seen drinking in the bar the night before an execution.

The executions provide the sensationalist side of the Military Prison. However there was much more to it than that. At any one time it is believed there were up to 400 prisoners held there. Some would have been for minor crimes, probably many alcohol induced. Francis Disney has recently been in communication with a former American Prisoner whose crime shows another aspect of the harsh regulation within American Army life.

In the spring of 1944 eighteen American Servicemen where charged at a Courts Marshall with mutiny under the violation of the 64th and 66th Articles of War. In that they held a protest meeting at Martock and refused a lawful order to proceed to work. Apparently it was over a relatively minor issue where the soldiers had just had enough of the regime. However the justice was harsh.

All the men were held at Shepton Mallet Prison from 17 May 1944.

Staff Sergent George Gayles	age 24	18 years
Sergeant William Fristoe	age 22	15 years
Sergeant Wilson Theodre	age 27	15 years
Technician Bernard James	age 23	18 years
Corporal Richard Geaithers	age 19	10 years
Corporal Harold Perry	age 20	10 years
Private Robert Berry	age 21	8 years
Private Jimmie Day	age 29	5 years
Private Paris Davis	age 19	8 years
Private George Washington	age 24	15 years
Private Ballard McKinley	age 19	18 years
Private Henry Davis	age 24	18 years
Private Roger Harris	age 19	8 years
Private James Felders	age 19	18 years

Private Robert Roots	age 24	5 years
Private Aaron Smith	age 20	18 years
Private Walter Johnson	age 20	5 years
Private William Withers	age 23	5 years

All confined to hard labour at such places as the reviewing authority may direct. Apparently they were imprisoned at Shepton Mallet and then continued their sentences in the USA after the end of the war.

3 December 1943

Shepton Mallet Petty Sessions. Failed to join the Home Guard. Reginald Chinnock, a 48 year old railway worker of 21 Great Barton, Kilver Street pleaded guilty…to failing to enrol in the Home Guard as directed by the National Services Officer on Sept 23rd. He said 'I did not attend as I am doing one night in six fire watching on Railway premises, I have never received any notice saying I am released from this.' It had been explained that directly Chinnock enrolled in the Railway Home Guard he would be automatically released from fire watch. Fined £5.

Depletion of staff. Owing to the depletion of staff through illness Messrs A Byrt and Son will be grateful if customers would kindly call for the papers for the next few days.

10 December 1943

Percy Hodges butcher and purveyor of 16 Cowl Street on being called to the colours has been forced temporarily to close his business. On leaving the town to join his unit he expressed his thanks to all his customers for the warm patronage afforded him during the past 20 years.

A Magnificent Achievement. The success attending last weeks shopping at Enyd's where each day a great variety of goods were on offer in aid of the Duke of Gloucester's Red Cross and St Johns Fund for Prisoners of War must have succeeded all expectations for the handsome sum of £315/5/9d net resulted. It was a great triumph for Mrs E C Addleshaw Commandant VAD Somerset 78.

Regal. 'Holiday Inn' starring Bing Crosby, Fred Astaire and Marjory Reynolds.

Advert. Shepton Mallet Waterworks Company. Cancelling the drought notice and thanking everyone for their co-operation 'but care and economy in the use of water is still needed' Geoffrey Budd. 'Water is Precious'. Save It.'

17 December 1943

Shipwrecked Mariners Association Whist drive with 19 tables organised by the indefatigable Mrs Snelling.

GTC Gain Good Report… Miss G M Roberts hon. sec Local Detachment. 'May I as secretary of the GTC beg a space for an account of the very excellent report received by the GTC after their Headquarter Inspection in October. I feel that the parents and friends of the Cadets would be gratified to know what the Inspecting Officer thought of the unit.

24 December 1943

Advert. How about that Christmas present. Try Haskins, Town St (Tipcote Hill), Shepton Mallet.

Advert. AR Bowden and Son have a vacancy for a young lady (preferably one who has recently left school) in their Grocery and Provisions department. Will intending applicants please call at 9 High Street.

An evening off. Members of three local platoons of the Home Guard under the command of Capt C R Rodway together with numerous visitors took an evening off on Tuesday from regimental duties and gave themselves an evening's enjoyment.
    Many excellent songs were contributed, in which the choruses were lustily enjoyed by a company of some 100 strong. It was a rollicking good evening.

Regal. 'Casablanca' starring Humphrey Bogart and Ingrid Bergman.

31 December 1943

Death of Dr A H Finch. It is with profound regret that we announce the death this week of Dr A H Finch who passed away on Christmas Eve….the last of the doctors of the old school. He had been in town for over 40 years and by 1907 was a church warden,

Fatal Accident on Christmas Eve. Mr Thomas James Miles 74 of 50 Garston Street was knocked down by an Army motor vehicle. He died in Shepton Mallet Hospital.

A Red Letter Day. The children of the town and district were freely entertained to a first class programme at the Regal Cinema on Christmas Eve. 'Rhythm Parade' was the star picture. Thanks to the generosity of Mr Truman Dickens… The climax came on leaving when the Americans presented to each child a huge bag of fruit and sweets. It was an exceedingly gracious act on the part of the Americans, one very much appreciated.

The Parish Church was attractively decorated for the great festival of Christmas. A huge Christmas tree, beautifully Illuminated through the generosity of the North Somerset Electric Light Company, stood beneath the Tower and was surrounded by an amazing and varied number of Christmas gifts which were disposed of by the WVS.

Regal – '6 Days with Deanna Durban' a season of six different Deanna Durban films.

Chapter 7

1944

- June 4, Allied troops enter Rome.
- June 6, D-day landings, Allied forces under Generals Eisenhower and Montgomery invade France.
- June 13, first V-1 flying bomb attack. New wave of evacuation. 1.5 million leave London by end of July.
- August 25, Paris liberated by Free French forces led by General de Gaulle.
- September 8, First V-2 rockets land on London.
- December 16, Germans mounted last offensive on the Western Front through the Ardennes towards Antwerp. It was stopped by December 27.

7 January 1944

Death of Septimus G Lemon, popular manager of Westminster Bank. For the second time within ten days, the town and district has suffered a severe loss by death and it is with deep regret that we announce the passing of Mr S G Lemon in the early hours of Monday morning. He had been desperately ill since September.

He came to Shepton Mallet from Trowbridge in 1933, then in his early 40's, in the best of health, and being of agricultural descent, his appointment here in an agricultural district proved immensely popular.

Note. By one of life's amazing co-incidences five days after I had copied this out I received a subscription for this book from a Miss Janet Lemon of Bournemouth. She commented 'If you come across anyone named Lemon during the war it will have been my parents.' I wasted no time in getting in touch with Miss Lemon who very kindly sent us some photographs and a few memories.

Septimus G Lemon was one of those names that kept coming up, usually as the Treasurer of local organisations. Given his links with farming it is of no surprise that he was treasurer of the Mid-Somerset Agricultural Society. According to Miss Lemon although they had a car it was always her mother who had to drive. Mr Lemon never learnt as he always wanted to look over the hedges to see what his farming customers where up to. He was also organiser of the Shepton Mallet War Committee Fetes held in the grounds of Summerleaze House, it is believed that the photographs of him were taken there.

The family lived above the Westminster Bank, now National Westminster, in the centre of town. According to Miss Lemon as the bedrooms were on the second floor and a long way from the staircase they were not allowed to sleep upstairs during the war. 'Two camp beds were brought for my mother and myself. My father had a single bed. We slept down in the Bank by the strong room. My father's bed was actually by the strong room. My Mother's and my beds were side by side where it was wider. Each morning these were taken down, put in a corner of the Managers Room and covered over. In the evening the opposite happened.

Miss Lemon was only 12 when her father died and knew more about the wartime activities of her mother who would appear to have been one of the very active set as befits the wife of the local Bank Manager. It is interesting to note that she also got roped in to be treasurer. According to Miss Lemon, her mother started a canteen for servicemen in what was the Congregational Church Hall, after Dunkirk, with other people who gave items to run it. She later became the treasurer of the Community Kitchen (British Restaurant) at the top of the High Street.

Lemon family in the grounds of Summerleaze House.

Because the Bank had a large lounge, when the evacuees came she started a working party for making clothes etc for them every Monday afternoon. Numerous people would come and make things. She also helped to run a shop in part of Geoffrey Budd's buildings where people would come if they wanted things for evacuees.

Scouts good turn. The local scouts and cubs spent a very happy evening on Wednesday of last week at their annual Christmas party when as a special Christmas 'good turn' they entertained the evacuated children from the Hostel at Mayfair Charlton Road….Amongst other guests were some American Soldiers who had previously been scouts in the United States.

New Year's Eve. With time honoured custom, the New Year was warmly ushered in by the ringers with a merry peal on the Church bells. All evening the ringers had been busily engaged in the tower; first a happy peal, then an exchange or two and finally the muffled peal of farewell to the old year – a brief pause and then the joyous welcome to 1944.

14 January 1944

Aboard H M S Belfast. Able Seaman Cooper whose ship took part in the dramatic naval battle which culminated in the sinking of the Scharnhorst is home on a few days leave looking very fit and full of the indomitable spirit of the boys in blue. Mr Cooper married the younger daughter of the late Mr L Woodland, who is now residing with her sister at 3 Victoria Grove, Shepton Mallet. Shepton Mallet can claim therefore in part to have had a hand in the sinking of the great battleship.

Shepton Mallet Urban District Council. Mr Pullen. "I feel myself that not enough has been said about our worthy Doctor (Dr Finch had been Medical Officer to the Council) I have known him all my life and only wish I was capable of paying a fitting tribute to his memory. I feel that our worthy Doctor gave his life for his country just as much as any man serving in

Septimus G. Lemon.

the war. For many years he had foregone any holiday and for some time past had been entitled to his retirement but had remained in office owing to the war. There can be no doubt in our minds that he worked himself right out to a finish."

Helping the Navy. Arising under any other business Mr Budd…He wanted the Council, if they would let him, make use of a window at 11 Market Place…as part of a general scheme through the county, a collection of books and subscriptions for the Royal Navy War Libraries. Continuing Mr Budd said he was going one step further and ventured to ask the Council for the loan of the model of HMS Mendip…the Council unanimously acceded to Mr Budd's request.

21 January 1944

Home Guard Recognition.. His comrades of the Home Guard together with a host of friends will warmly congratulate Sergeant Harold John Luscombe on being awarded a certificate for good service in the New Years Honours List. Sergt Luscombe was one of the original members of the LDV being enrolled on 24th May 1940. He has given continued service ever since and has qualified as a musketry instructor.

Wartime Shepton – Memories of the Market, Shops, getting to school and the Home Guard. Jim Doble of Stoney Stratton near Evercreech.

"Talking to John Newsome the other day, he reminded me his parents ran the Hare & Hounds during 1939-45. He was but a boy at the time and he was saying he has a snap of himself aged 4 years standing in the entrance porch that straddled the pavement. This led me to recall how the main bar was entered to the left of the entrance hall and stairway, where I could remember the farmers on Friday market days congregating for a drink and to do business with the millers' representatives. The room was half divided by a partition towards the square bar in the far corner, where Daphne Hoddinott served the drinks, mostly beer or gin and occasionally the odd rum, as whisky was almost unobtainable.

Some used to lunch upstairs, where the food was hoist up with a dumb waiter from the kitchen below. But the afternoon usually ended by paying the millers' bills, ordering what little rationed animal feed was available and haggling perhaps over the price for a few tons of farm grown corn and hoping the agent would stand the drinks!

Friday was the day the country folk came to town. The farmers would first go to the market with calves and cattle. The Ministry of Food controlled everything. The poor calves went for processing while good calves would go straight to the slaughter house for veal, as did the old cows, called 'barreners' and a few beef cattle to be killed and the meat distributed to butchers to sell in the rationing system.

It is a job to remember that Haskins car park and garage were a cattle market. Wainwright, Laver & Crees auction ring was housed in a draughty high shed clad with iron sheets, where the cattle were brought from the rows of railed pens to be weighed and documented and the long low shed where the calves were sold on the spot.

Wives also came along for the weekly shopping trip as the car could be used legitimately on the meagre petrol ration to attend markets. In those days Shepton shops provided almost everything one needed within the rationing system. Widdecombe's shop would fit out the men if they didn't make to Philip Hall – or was it Tommy Laing? - and the Misses Thorne catered elegantly for the ladies – but Henley's were cheaper! There were an abundance of grocer's shops, with Arthur Hobbs on the corner, the International Stores downtown and Bowdens somewhere in between. Syd Mapley and Harry Britten vied for butcher's trade and there were hairdressers aplenty – where some farmers had their shave for the weekend on market day – from Darby Miller to old Helliker by the Market Cross. Penn's jewellers nestled at the end of Paul Street almost opposite Moon's bakery and restaurant and all were outnumbered by the couple of dozen pubs and inns scattered across the town.

In the early days of the war I used to cycle the four miles into Shepton to catch the 5d return bus to school at Wells – adults had to buy a 9d pink ticket! There were about a dozen of us boys going to the Cathedral School who used the bus as it was closer, but a large number of boys and girls from Shepton used the train as Tucker Street station was closer to the Blue School. We boys used to wait by the traffic lights until the bus came down the High Street and picked us up, heading along Commercial Road past the again busy Anglo Bavarian building and by the old cloth mills at Darshill that had also sprung back into use.

At first, I parked my bike up the alley way where Britten's had their dis-used slaughter house in Little Ostry, but ended up trundling it up the little lane at the back of Dr Bishop's house and into the yard behind Milliards' cycle shop. I was kitted up with water proofs as it seemed to be raining more often than not and was always glad of the run down Cannards Grave Road by the Cenotaph in time to catch the Bristol Company's bus by 8.30. I seem to recall workman letting metal sockets into the road there for anti-tank defences to be inserted when fear of a German invasion prompted a chain of defences along the Mendip Hills. At that stage we always carried our gas masks and identity cards. Twice I recall roadblocks; one on Prestleigh Hill when I was cycling and another when the bus was stopped at Croscombe, then cards had to be shown before they let you through.

The most frightening experience I had cycling to and from school was one afternoon at Cannards Grave Road. On my way home I heard a stuttering plane engine over the high cloud, then an almighty thud- and looking over my shoulder I saw a plume of earth in the distance across at Bodden where a bomb had fallen. Current advice was, 'Take cover', but I put my head down and pedalled like the wind for home!

That night a string of bombs were jettisoned near Evercreech, killing a number of cows, blowing some telephone wires to smithereens and waking everybody. On other occasions I recall lying in bed and hearing bombs whistling overhead – one landed close enough to rattle doors and windows violently - though we were later reassured that if you heard that whistle you were safe!

Shepton, in spite of the War, seemed a friendly place. Nearly all the shop-keepers lived above the shop and there was an old-fashioned air of respect wherever you went. I was friendly with Dave Hobley and often used to visit his upstairs home. There were many rooms on those two floors, some with ironmongers goods stored and others where he and his widowed mother lived. One thing they didn't store there was the explosives they supplied to the local quarries. They had a special van that had the cab and goods compartment separate for safety's sake, in which they took the ICI product early in the day and then old Mr Woolley from Croscombe used the van on his rounds selling paraffin and general ironmongery.

Across the road Mr Lemon, the Westminster Bank manager, lived overhead and possibly Mr Hobbs did the same over his grocers shop, though Reg Byrt the Journal printer next door couldn't because his presses were installed above the stationer's shop.

Entertainment was a bit scarce, but I remember the long gone Regal Cinema that was built in 1934 being the source of some luxury with its comfortable seats . I used to cycle in sometimes to see a film, and we were always keen to see the Pathe newsreels that provided pictorial news years before TV was common – though wartime news was usually rather limited and only showed the bits to cheer us up!

Just before D day our Home Guard platoon from Evercreech spent one night guarding the Waterloo Road viaduct. Six or eight of us would take turns to do 2-3 hours on duty and snatch sleep on the bunks provided in a wooden hut. Another chap and I walked the length of the structure several times in the near dark. We were stood at one end when we heard crunch, crunch in the distance and wondered what we could expect, was it friend or foe? We were about to raise our rifles when out of the murk we made out a hedgehog creeping over the sleepers and ballast and realised that when it touched the stones we heard a crunch! We were quite relieved that our fears developed into nothing more sinister.

There were two platoons in Evercreech; one based on the railway staff at Evercreech Junction and the other in the village. If you didn't volunteer when the time came you were drafted to the Junction, which entailed a two mile bike ride – so most of us joined the village gang!

By 1942/3 kit was in good supply and we were issued with khaki uniforms complete with great coats, heavy boots, service gas masks, rifle and bayonets, tin hats and Somerset Light Infantry badges for our hats.

Basic soldiers' drill and rifle handling was regular for a few hours several nights a week as everyone had a day job. We sometimes deployed in the fields gaining experience of using cover, learning how to co-ordinate and support each other in small bunches while gaining observational skills. Mostly at weekends we would be loaded up from time to time in Feaver's coal lorry for extra training, such as a visit to the Beacon butts for rifle shooting practice. Our two sergeants were old WW1 soldiers, so they knew how to keep us in order and tell us what to do. Once we took our only spigot mortar for practice with live ammunition to a quarry. The mortar shell was dropped over the spigot, which had been already aimed at the distant rock face, and upon contact automatically fired, exploding when it hit the stone. One, I recall, caused some consternation as it fell in clay and our officer and sergeants had to recover the thing while still unexploded, which they succeeded in doing!

On another occasion we were taught how to throw grenades, called Mills bombs. They looked like a small pineapple with a handle held safe with a pin. This all happened on Creech Hill on the old golf links where some rudimentary trenches had been dug, We had to hold the grenade tightly with the handle in our grasp, remove the pin, throw the thing, watch where it had landed and then duck. I suppose cricketers would have been good at this, but we had little practice thereafter – but I kept the pin ring as a key ring for many years.

Armistice Day always meant a church parade and occasionally we would be called to muster in the village square at a minute's notice to see how quickly we could respond. Like Dad's Army we were never engaged in any real fighting, but we did have useful training that could have been better than nothing had an invasion occurred."

A remarkable achievement. Speaking at last week's meeting of the Shepton Mallet Urban District Council, Mr F J E Pullen gave particulars of a competition organised under the 'Dig for Victory' Campaign. Third had come Mrs Padfield and rightly she was proud of the high position she had achieved. Mrs Padfield is in her 70th year and affords a fine example of good health and hard work. May she long be spared to continue her good work.

Letter from Mr C H Langdon Griffiths of the National Deposit Friendly Society saying they had done their best to 'recruit local children to our office'. "It seems to us who have to examine the children a tragedy that they should leave school with such an entire lack of the most elementary education… How do these children spend their school life up to the age of 14 years of age? Attendance at school in Shepton Mallet is presumably compulsory as it is in other parts of the country… One wonders what effect the new Education Bill will have upon the school curriculum in Shepton Mallet. Will the children merely remain at school for another year in the top form, satisfied that no further progress can be made."

28 January 1944

The Home Guard. Advert for dance 3/- a ticket. Suggested that people not interested in the dance could send 3/- 'it would perhaps be a pleasing gesture to send the treasurer of the local company Home Guard a gift of 3/-. It would no doubt be gratefully received and acknowledged, and would afford some little encouragement to the men who freely give week-by-week of their time – time which if they could please themselves they would probably much prefer to spend in their own homes or about their own business.

Last weeks education letter received five responses all defending the schools. Pointing out that there was a range of abilities and if the National Deposit interviewed 'D' grade pupils without consulting the heads it was no wonder that they got a funny impression. People also pointed out that the 'cream' was taken out of Shepton Mallet by the 11 plus.

(Note. The Grammar School had been shut in 1929, much to local annoyance. There were scholarships for brighter pupils from Shepton Mallet at the Blue School in Wells and at Sexey's and Sunnyhill Schools in Bruton.)

4 February 1944

For the Hospital. An enjoyable foursomes Snooker match was played one evening last week at the Constitutional Club between Squadron Leader Hore and Lt Tibbs US (Visitors) and Mr S Mapley and Mr R V Showering. The visitors lost by a narrow margin and as a result donated £1 to the Shepton Mallet and District Hospital.

11 February 1944

Regal. Betty Hutton and Eddie Bracken in 'Star Spangled Rhythm'.

18 February 1944

Eggcellent. A hen owned by Mrs W Lintern, Longstowe has laid an egg weighing five and a half ounces. This has been disposed of for the British Red Cross Prisoners of War Fund and the amount of £7/1/- realised.

Shepton Mallet Parochial Church Council. The annual meeting of the Shepton Mallet Parochial Church Council was held in Peter Street Rooms on Thursday evening with the Rector, A S Gribble presiding supported by Mr G R Keates and Mr E E Poles joint hon. sec's. There was a gratifying attendance including Rev D V Galloway assistant Priest.

> "There have been several days of special observance and on these occasions there have been large congregations. The youth organisations have held regular church parades as also have members of H M Forces until their departure from the town. That the regular congregations have also been good is endorsed by the fact that the Church expenses have again been very well met."

25 February 1944

Unique – Last week we recorded that an egg laid by a hen belonging to Mrs W Lintern of Longstowe weighed five and a half ounces. On being carefully opened it was found to contain not only a yoke and 'white' but also a second egg complete with shell about the size of a pullet's egg.

3 March 1944

Shepton Mallet Petty Sessions. Ernest Frederick Coles Dairyman High St Shepton Mallet was accused of a number of offences, obtaining an excess quantity of milk. He bought his milk from his father's dairy farm and topped up his needs from Prideaux Dairy (Evercreech). He had sold more milk than accorded him in his permit and failed to keep an accurate record of milk received and quantity sold.

> Prosecutor Mr Ames suggested a deliberate attempt to evade the order. The witness stated that he started work at 6.00am each day and finished bottling milk at 7.30pm. He then had to do his books. He handled over 800 bottles of milk a day and only had one lad to help him.
>
> He said his records of purchase were on his father's farm and all the milk he sold was entered in the sale's ledger. The defending solicitor criticised those operating the scheme. Any breach was unintentional. He suggested that rather than prosecuting they should be doing more to help and advise. Fined £9/10/-.

10 March 1944

Regal. 'Clive of India.' Starring Ronald Coleman and Loretta Young.

Advert. Refined Business Lady requires Full Board residence with nice family within 10 – 15 minutes walk from the town of Shepton Mallet. Write box RB Journal Office.

Rat Menace. Every man, woman and child is asked to be a 'Rat Reporter'. Rats are a growing danger. 'Every year rats and mice together are responsible for destroying or fouling 2,000,000 tons of food' it has been stated by the Ministry of Food.

17 March 1944

Sunday Evening Concert at the Regal arranged by the Home Guard. Starred Miss Eileen Vaughan (BBC, ENSA etc) musical comedy soprano. Possessed of the sweetest of voices and blessed with a charming manner she took the house by storm.

24 March 1944

A Gallant Gunner. This week Mrs A M Oatley has received a very bright and cheerful letter from her son Sergeant Maurice Dredge RHA who is serving in the Middle East. Enclosed were interesting 'snaps' of the official handing over of Tripoli, the Prime Minister and General Montgomery, and a commendation card. 'Your name has been brought to my notice for your gallantry in action. I thank you for your devotion to duty and for the high example you have set. Signed H R Alexander. General Commander in Chief MEF

Shepton Mallet District Hospital. w/c 18th March 1944. Admitted 11, Discharged 10, Outpatients 43. The matron wishes to thank Mrs Pond-Jones and Mr C Amor for their very acceptable gift, proceeds from the dance held in aid of the hospital at the NAAFI on 18th March. The Matron would be very glad if any kind friends could supply her with chicken as they are urgently needed for the patients at the hospital.

31 March 1944

Shepton Mallet Rural District Council. The Public Health and Housing Committee reported that as a result of further meetings of the Area Committee it had been decided to engage six rat catchers instead of three. The chairman remarked that there seemed to be a great deal of overlapping in regard to rat catching. Miss Bethell. "Do they kill them?" The Chairman. "I do not know. They are killing a lot of cats and dogs."

Congratulations. Shepton's grand old man, Mr John Parsons of Cowl Street, celebrates today his 95th birthday. Townsmen generally will congratulate him and wish him well.

A pleasant surprise. In a letter received from her husband Mrs Young was thrilled to read that he (serving with the Royal Artillary in the middle east) had met his brother in law Mr Tom Boyce …strolling one evening into the YMCA he was overjoyed to meet Tom who is serving with the RAF.

Marriage of Miss Edith Brooks. Many friends assembled in the Congregational Church last week to witness the marriage between Mr Ralph Wallace RN and Miss Edith Brooks eldest daughter of Mr & Mrs L Brooks. Following the ceremony, a reception was held at the residence of the bride's grandmother at Bowlish. Later Mr & Mrs Wallace left for their honeymoon in Cornwall.

> Ralph Wallace served in a Navy section that was based in Shepton Mallet for most of the War. They rebuilt and tested marine engines (and according to family legend also tested torpedos in the local quarries at Waterlip.) They had workshops in Mid-Somerset

Motors Garage in Commercial Road and also used a house adjacent to Summerleaze in Hitchen Lane and Old Bowlish House for accommodation. It is reputed that the cellars at Old Bowlish house were nearly always flooded, it is right beside the River Sheppy, so they kept ducks which were a useful supplement to their diet.

(Note. Ralph and Edith's son, David Wallace was for many years secretary of the Shepton Mallet Cricket Club. Her sister Rose Ware and nephews Len and Tom both helped with this project.)

Regal. 'My Friend Flika' starring Roddy McDowell, Preston Foster and Rita Johnson.

Shepton Mallet Gas Company. The increase of 3/- a ton in the price of coal imposed on February 1st 1944 compels the directors to give notice hereby that the price of gas will be increased by three farthings per therm. Fred W Delafield Secretary.

Shepton Mallet Petty Sessions. Pedal cycle offence. Roland A Hatcher (farm worker) of Waddon Cottage Lamyatt was fined 5/- for being one of two persons unlawfully carried on a pedal cycle. The other rider had run off.

7 April 1944

Advert. Seed potatoes. Allotment members can obtain seed potatoes on Saturday afternoons during April from 2pm – 5pm at the rear of the Co-operative Butchers Shop, Peter Street.

Shepton Mallet Snooker League Grand Finale. Members of the Shepton Mallet Snooker League concluded their second season in triumphant fashion at the Bell Hotel. The president, Mr Alfred Williams, one of the founders and most enthusiastic members of the league presided.

Farewell Presentations were made at the close of school at Kilver Street School on Tuesday afternoon to Miss Cromwell and Miss Fowler who have both resigned on retirement. It was appropriate that their going should be fittingly marked, for few can doubt that during their turn in office, a very good influence has been bought to bear on the school.

Regal. 'Jitterbugs' starring Laurel and Hardy.

14 April 1944

The Shepton Mallet Discussion Group invites all and sundry and particularly our friends in the U.S. Forces to a film programme entitled 'An evening with Britain' a survey of Britain at War, on the farms, in the schools, with merchant seaman, in city and countryside. Council Hall 7.30pm

Sea Scouts Exhibition at London Scottish Drill Hall, Buckingham Gate SW London. A party of Shepton Mallet Lads accompanied by scout master C Amor, propose visiting the exhibition today and are also looking forward to participating in the parade on Trafalgar Square on Sunday and attending service at St Martins in the Fields.

Shepton Mallet Urban District Council. Playing at War. Mr Hardwidge called attention to the dangerous condition of a length of wall in Town Lane by the river. Part of it had now been pulled down but in another place stones were being thrown into the river making a crossing from one side to the other.

Mr Pullen. "They have been practicing war down there, and have made a pontoon bridge – very effective too." (Presumably local children)

Following discussion the matter was referred to the surveyor.

21 April 1944

Fashionable Wedding at the Parish Church. The marriage at the parish church of Capt Peter Gerald Hounsfield ....to Miss Doreen Margaret Hall (junior commander ATS) younger daughter of Mr Berkeley Hall JP and Mrs Hall of Bowlish Villa, Shepton Mallet attracted widespread interest, the more so because of the uncertainty almost to the very last, as to whether these young people would be able in these 'advanced' days to obtain the requisite leave....she was attended by Miss Pamela Hall....the best man was Mr John Dyke the bridesmaid's fiancé.

28 April 1944

One and a half columns of the front page were taken up with a list of the gifts from the previous week's wedding. Almost everyone of note in the area had given a cheque. Sir Frederick and Miss Berryman had given National Savings Certificates. Traders and other local residents had given household things like table mats.

(Note. One of the reasons for the prevalence of cheques as gifts was the growing shortage of good gifts to buy.)

Advance notice of 'Salute the Soldier week' hon. sec. A W Chidgly.

5 May 1944

Advert for 'Salute the Soldier Week' 'Tommy's got a target – Victory...peace, and he'll make it, will Tommy Lad!'

Harold 'O' Saunders from Manor Farm, Downhead was summoned for causing unnecessary obstruction with a motor car in Market Place....a traffic block from Town Street to the Hare and Hounds. This was mainly due to a private car standing near Mr Barnes shop. The car was left 3 ft from the kerb...(the defendant said) 'I have only been to a shop and the bank and was detained. I did not think I would be so long.' Fined £1.

Regal. 'Dear Octopus' starring Michael Wilding and Margaret Lockwood.

Advert for Shepton Mallet Urban and Rural District Councils Conference and Exhibition, 'The future of the Countryside' Council Hall, Market Place, Shepton Mallet Friday 26th May

12 May 1944

A strange co-incidence. Almost at the same time as we announced last week that Major Aynesly Delafield who had been in India for nearly two years had with other officers the honour of being presented to Lord Mountbatten, official intimation was received by his father Mr F W Delafield that he had been wounded. Further particulars are awaited.

Shepton Mallet Urban District Council. Proposed Post War Development. Need for permanent industries. Action which had been taken with a view to the industrial development of the town after the war was reported to the monthly meeting of Shepton Mallet Urban District Council…a sub committee of Messrs W A Price, G C Budd and F J E Pullen was appointed.

Post war housing. Looking to provide 100 houses in two years as part of the post-war programme. Mr Pullen ' In Shepton Mallet the situation is very bad, and if something was not done before next winter there would be quite a number of homes scarcely fit to live in.'

Behaviour in Collett Park. Messrs Pullen and Price complained of the behaviour of a certain section of the community in Collett Park and also in Park Road. Mr Price said he understood that last week a little girl in the park narrowly escaped injury through people riding bicycles there. He suggested that some more prominent notice boards be displayed announcing that cycling was prohibited in the park.

19 May 1944

Salute the Soldier Week, Target £150,000, amount raised to date £86,398. Sharp to time 3 o'clock the procession proper moved off and what a procession! Quite one of the best of the series – a really marvellous show. Headed by two stalwart police constables and the band of the Kings Dragoons, it came over the railway bridge and into High Street. Behind the band was a smart contingent of the Royal Navy at the slope and with fixed bayonets led by an officer with sword drawn. They were followed by detachments of the WRNS well led, marching splendidly and looking very fit.

> Next came the lads of the Royal Air Force in their familiar blue together with a strong muster of the WAAF bearing themselves admirably. A short interval and then came two strong contingents of our gallant Allies, troops of the USA with standard bearer. They bore themselves well and were a most welcome contribution to the procession. Then came the band of the Wells Home Guard followed by the bandsmen themselves looking spick and span and far from being 'browned off.' The Army Cadets followed and marched well. Then followed detachments of the NFS, ARP Wardens and Rescue Squads, Red Cross, St Johns, ATC with their band, GTC, Land Army, Scouts, Brownies and Guides the whole totalled over 600.

Note. Throughout the war the Army Cadets was an active organisation giving a basic training to local youngsters. Evacuee George Bartlett was one such youngster towards the end of the war.

"My memories of the Cadet days in the war are not that clear. Things I recollect are mainly the long treks and the drill. In fact, come the ending of the war we carried rifles and as a youngster these were heavy. We often went out on a recce – to capture a empty building. Thunder flashes were used which put the living daylight up me. Blanks were fired and one lad got hold of a 303 bullet and fired at a selected target. No one was injured.

We were told at school – look out for any suspicious object that resembled a bomb. My friend and myself found this object. I told my friend 'wait here while I run to get a policeman. I remember running a very long way but no police were available but a local man came back with me to the bomb area. You have to remember this was wartime and very exciting.

Our bomb turned out to be a high tension battery which was used to power radios."

Shepton Mallet Petty Sessions. Maintenance order made by Ivy Cothel Young 25 against husband Cyril Edward Young. It appears that it was stable marriage until Mrs Young had to register for National Service and became employed at the National Deposit Friendly Society. She made friends with other girls with whom she worked and used to go out in the evening with them sometimes. The husband objected to this.

> In her evidence Mrs Young alleged that her husband objected to her going out to dances and the cinema although at times he accompanied her. He was also jealous of her association with an American friend but she had never been out with this American friend except in the company of other girls when they went to dances or parties.
> The defence - I have yet to come across a case where there is 100 % guilt on one side and no guilt on the other.'

26 May 1944

Shepton Mallet Urban and Rural District 'Salute the Soldier Week' Target £150,000 Total Raised £200,294…the achievement was no mere walk over but rather dogged perseverance and determination in which officials and general public played their parts magnificently. It was a week of united effort, good team work and excellent comradeship. Strenuous though it was and tired as were the participants when the curtain rang down on Saturday night few would gainsay that they were feeling better for a week's diversion and a real round of social engagements.

Regal. 'Sherlock Holmes and the Voice of Terror' starring Basil Rathbone and Nigel Bruce.

2 June 1944

The Whitsuntide passed of very quietly in the town and was essentially a 'stay at home' holiday. The Regal Cinema, cricket and Fairfield provided the principle forms of entertainment. The gardens too claimed a fair measure of attention. Fortunately no mishaps have been reported.

Shepton Mallet Petty Sessions. Evercreech Farmer's Offence. Leonard G Creed, farmer Westbrook Farm, Evercreech was summoned for failing to keep two pigs moved by licence separate from all other pigs for 27 days. Two pigs he had taken to Yeovil market but which had not been sold. Fined £1.

9 June 1944

Red Cross Cadet Units inspected by the County President. The youth detachments Somerset 512 and Cadet units 2026 and 2348 had the honour of being inspected by Mrs Ridley OBE the County President….the President addressed them saying how pleased she was to meet the Shepton Mallet Junior Red Cross. She thought they had made excellent progress in their work…she was especially interested to see they were flying the Junior Red Cross Standard, as it was the first one she had seen.

16 June 1944

Advert. Homely Garden Party at West End House, Saturday 17th from 3pm – 7,30pm.

Admission 6d Children 3d. Proceeds to Baptist Church.

Shepton Mallet Urban District Council. Post War Housing. Prefabricated Houses. Miss Bishop had been asked to attend an exhibition in London of a factory made house. Miss Bishops report. "I inspected this house as thoroughly as was possible in the time allowed...I realise that it was planned as a temporary dwelling only (though I gather it is meant to last for some years) but even as that I do not consider it as satisfactory...I will not go into the question of the outside beyond saying that it looks like a cardboard box...Inside it all looks bright and cheerful but the ceilings are far too low. The hall is far too small to take a full sized perambulator and the WC faces the door....One of the biggest faults in the house is the failure to provide any sort of convenience for home washing...I also consider a back door is essential."

Mr Pullen "For better of worse we shall have to have them and have to put up with them." There were also praises of Miss Bishop for being able to think of the needs of families when she herself was a spinster.

23 June 1944

For King and Country. News has been received this week of two Sheptonians who have been in the thick of it in recent fighting. The one in Italy and the other in France. The former is Driver Ware son of Mr & Mrs R Ware of 24 Downside and the latter William John (Billy) Hill son of Mr & Mrs E Hill of 14 Garston Street. Both are now safely in England and are making satisfactory progress.

Advert. Shepton Mallet Bowls, Croquet and Tennis Club. Tennis section. All persons interested in tennis are invited to attend a meeting in the Pavilion, Frithfield on Tuesday 4th July at 8 pm. Provided sufficient support is forthcoming, two courts should be ready for playing the next day. A F London general secretary, Grove House Shepton Mallet.

30 June 1944

Roll of Honour. Sympathy is extended to Mrs Veysey of 35 Cornwall Road in the sad news ..of the death of her son Royal Navy Stoker, First Class Roland Thomas Veysey who died in a hospital in Italy from an appendix abscess.

7 July 1944

Local Corps GTC Fine Achievement. In connection with the International Youth Council in Britain....five wireless sets offered to youth organisations who had put up the best record in War work and service to their town in the first three months of 1944. Hundreds of Youth Clubs and service organisations entered for the competition including the 554 Company Girls Training Corps, Shepton Mallet, thinking no doubt that their claim would be swamped in the great flood of entries for such a coveted honour. One can well imagine then the pride and elation felt by the girls when the glad news was received last Saturday by the Commandant, Mrs D Lawless, that their Company was one of the successful entrants.

Advert. Mid Somerset Agricultural Society advertising for 'Volunteer Helpers for Hay and Corn Harvest...financial arrangements for such help are between helper and employers...

14 July 1944

A splendid record. Mr Jack Baker of Quarr, himself an old soldier, has every reason to be proud of his family, nine of whom are serving their country. He has one son in France, another in the Middle East, one in the Far East, two somewhere in England, three in the Home Guard and a daughter in a factory of National importance.

Summonses against Mid-Somerset Motor Company. Offences under Petrol Regulations. Nominal fines imposed. The Mid-Somerset Motor Garage Company Shepton Mallet were summoned at Shepton Mallet Petty Sessions for a number of offences under the Petrol Regulations…unlawfully surrendering to a supplier, coupons for motor fuel at a time other than that at which the fuel authorised was supplied. Failing to keep a record in relation to motor fuel whether used for consumption or in each motor vehicle let out on hire. Failing to keep a daily record of the quantity of motor fuel acquired against the surrender of coupons marked 'Misc' and 'Z'.

> Leslie John H Allen 'Cairo', Charlton Road, Shepton Mallet was summoned as a Director of the company.
>
> The main problem seems to be that Mr Allen had given the fuel coupons to a petrol garage in bulk ('banked') so that his drivers - some of whom were not considered trustworthy – did not handle them, There was no question of fuel being obtained without coupons. On this offence the magistrates fined 1/- and refused the prosecutors appeal for costs.

21 July 1944

A budding agriculturalist. In connection with a six month series of literary competitions recently organised by the Farmers Weekly 16 prize winners, 8 boys and 8 girls, have been invited to attend a short experimental course at the Northamptonshire Institute of Agriculture in August. Included in the list is the name of Molly Dennett of Yew Tree Farm, Preistleigh a pupil at Waterloo Road Senior Girls School.

Down on the Farm. Colin Ryall interviews Norton and Mary Corp who remember what it was like to be 'young farmers during the war

In the past Shepton Mallet owed much of its prosperity as the town that served the surrounding farms so for this interview I talked with a couple who had been in farming all their working lives.

When war broke out Norton was a boarder at the Cathedral School, Wells. Even this establishment was affected by the war. Two schools had been evacuated to Wells but many of the younger masters had 'joined up'. Thus many of the teachers were superannuated and struggled to cope with the extra workload. Both staff and pupils were relieved when American servicemen volunteered their help with the school's sporting activities.

'As part of the war effort the school kept pigs, fed on the school waste. Us boys saw to them, we country bred boys coped but some of the evacuees had never been out of London before, they found it hard going, some never took to it.' (The general population was exhorted to put any suitable waste in special 'pig bins'.)

Norton was certainly untroubled by the pigs as he had always been expected to help out at home, on his father's farm at Lottisham. In fact this requirement led to his education being cut short. Farming in the 30's was still labour intensive but this caused no problems when other forms of work were in short supply. The war changed that very quickly. Farm workers disappeared into the forces or well paid factory 'war work'. Of necessity Norton's school career was cut short, his services were needed at home and so Norton left school before his fifteenth birthday. 'Not fifteen quite, I left a bit early because there was nobody much helping with the hay making and that in the summer.'

Milking was still done by hand. 'Women made the best milkers, we had five or six from around the farm.'

Milking.

'Like most farms then we made butter and cheese; during the war all we produced had to go to a Ministry Depot. It was weighed and graded and we got a fixed price.'

Besides milk and milk products the farm produced cider on a considerable scale.

'We supplied many of the pubs in and around Shepton. That was good cider then, made from our own fruit, all the old Somerset varieties, Kingston Black, Redstreak, Yarlington Mill and many more. And they used to get through it! We'd take two pipes a week to the Horse and Jockey during hay making. After they'd worked in the quarries by day and then the fields of an evening they couldn't get enough cider.

'I remember we had a round house, a mule walked round and round driving the apple mill, it took a deal of swearing at and a bit of stick to keep that old mule moving!'

'Then we had a stationary engine and that took a deal of starting, you had to put a bit of burning rag in the air intake and then crank it over. By belts from the main shaft it drove the various machines in the cider house. It powered the hydraulic press to extract the apple juice. Grandpa was so keen to get the last drop out that he'd put extra weights on the safety valve. More often than not the seal would rupture and by the time the repairman had fixed it Grandpa was out of pocket anyway!'

'When the war came we had Land Army girls to help out. I'm amazed how they took to farm work. Some had never been out of their home city. One girl from Liverpool, Lena, when asked to bring in a cow that had been put in a far field on its own came back crying and reported, 'It's no good farmer I can't get that beast to move!' Not surprising really as

Land Army girls – Winter 1942.

upon inspection the animal proved to be dead! However Lena proved to be a good worker. 'We still keep in touch', Norton mentioned.

The girls chose to take on farm work rather than go into the forces or a factory. They were given basic training by the Ministry at Steanbow, West Pennard and lived in a hostel in Baltonsborough.

'Some really took to the work, tractor driving and ploughing, which was much heavier work than now. The tractor had to be cranked by hand to start it, and there were no hydraulic lifts on the ploughs.'

Not all were so dedicated however. It was noted that one girl regularly arrived late and left early. It was discovered that she was more interested in looking after the soldiers in charge of a searchlight based near the farm. She would cook them breakfast and tea. They were living under canvas and no doubt enjoyed the female attention.

'Father had one of the first tractors in the district, a British Fordson, pretty basic. That did an immense amount of work; it was on the go nearly every day. The Ministry forced every farmer to plough so much land. Of course many were against this as they thought it would ruin their pastures.' (The intention was to increase food production and reduce dependency on imports.)

But it was one of the consequences of war that farmers came under much more government control. Shepton Cattle Market operated throughout the war but prices were controlled. A panel of respected farmers would grade an animal and it would then be offered at a fixed price. The intention was for the farmer to get a fair price and for the consumer not to have to pay an inflated price. Norton recalled that at this time many cattle would arrive at market having been driven in on foot. 'Dealers would rent a field near the market for the cattle to rest up before being put up for sale.'

Although Norton made no mention of it, there was the temptation to sell farm produce on the black market where much higher prices were obtainable.

'If we filled the form in we were allowed to have a pig for ourselves. We arranged to go halves with an Uncle. Our pig was slaughtered first and split head to tail, but when the other pig was duly butchered and we received our half it was the fore-half of the pig! Needless to say that was the end of the pig sharing and Father didn't have much to say to Uncle for some time!'

'Then of course there were plenty of rabbits about. I can remember rows of rabbits hung up in Shepton Market.' However rabbit was poorly regarded and not to everybody's liking.

So although farmers were nominally subject to rationing like everybody else being on the farm meant there was always plenty of food. This was of great benefit to one group of visitors to stay with Norton's family. 'Lady Ryder organised places where aircrew on leave could stay. Having completed a tour of operations they would arrive in a very exhausted and dispirited state. At first we wouldn't see them for days on end; they'd stay in bed. After a few days they'd be down for meals and by the end of their stay they would have bucked up no end.'

'As a young boy I didn't realise what a tremendous strain repeated 'ops' put on these young men, some only a little older than myself.'

They liked the cider. 'I remember one November when we were cider making they tried the apple juice. This is a very pleasant drink but they drunk too much and it gave them the 'trots' something dreadful.'

Norton's own experience of armed service was limited to being a messenger boy for local Home Guard. 'I don't know about 'armed'. I can't remember any of the local unit having rifles until very late in the war, if then. The men were issued with uniforms. 'With Double Summer Time you could be working 'til near midnight. I remember Father putting his uniform on after work, going on watch all night and then coming home to milk at 6am. Some of them got very bad tempered, I kept out of their way!'

Although watches were, kept not much exciting happened; no parachutists or aeroplanes came down in Norton's area. 'Oh, one dark night the dispatch rider attached to the search light crew rode his bike into a ditch on the farm. He ended up with the motorbike on top of him. When asked a few days later how things were the sergeant replied, "Don't worry the motorbike's fine". That was about it!'

'When there was call out I had to ride round and knock everybody up. One chap used to turn up in a pick-up truck converted from an ancient bull-nosed Morris Cowley. When asked, "What's going to do with that?" he said, "I thought we could mount a machine gun on it"!

'Some hope! We were expected to repel Jerry with a pitch fork!'

Such vehicles were not uncommon on farms (without machine guns!) During the war a strange mix of ancient and modern machinery was pressed into service, mostly ancient. Homemade hybrids were put together. 'I remember one chap replaced a car's back wheels with mower wheels. He made several of those and they worked quite well. He was a clever chap, his father was a blacksmith.' And of course horses were still made great use of.

Several times Norton would start a recollection with the phrase 'If we filled the form in.' So many things came under government control. You had to justify your petrol allowance and although you could get a new tractor, rubber tyres were unobtainable. 'If you had some you kept them. Father put the ones he had on each replacement tractor he got.' Most tractors worked with steel 'tyres' fitted with steel spikes; these were covered with steel bands for road travel.

Electrification came to the farm during the wartime, 'But we had to supply our own poles. Father and a helper went up to the top of Ditcheat Hill and cut down some firs. They would come with the electricity if we could get the poles. By this time we had a German prisoner who used to come in every day. A lorry would pick them up from their camp and come round and drop them off at different farms or factories, wherever they were working. This German prisoner we had was a really good chap, a nice fellow. We had a spokeshave and he skinned the firs, made proper poles out of them and we put these up. Grandfather went round the people in the village, well not a village really, the farms around, to share with the expense and four of them said they would, so we got the Electricity Board in but when they'd finished two of them pulled out. He didn't take very kindly to that! Grandfather wanted it for the cider making, I suppose that's what made it worthwhile.'

'There were a lot of Italian and German prisoners; our regular chap would always turn up with his Wellingtons slung around his neck. When work was done he'd change back into his shoes and again sling the boots round his neck. When his boots were on the ground there one day Bill Longman, the chap who was doing the cider making, went to move them and there was a bottle of cider in each boot. So Bill thought 'I'll have him', so he took the cider out and put in some coloured water! He never took any more cider after that! Still you couldn't blame the bloke really', Norton ended with a chuckle.

Farming did move on apace during the war. Immediately pre-war many farms relied almost entirely on muscle power, whether animal or human, but by the end of the war significant progress towards the mechanisation that is now general had occurred.

'How we managed I don't know!' reminisced Norton, thinking back to those far off days.

The other change was the increase in Government controls. Any modern-day farmer will tell you of the enormous amount of paperwork farming involves. A lot of this was introduced during the war and has continued to grow ever since.

28 July 1944

Shepton Firm 'Takes a Risk' and delivers the goods. Corn Merchants Dilemma. At the Shepton Mallet Petty Sessions on Friday, Messrs Allen and Foster Ltd, Corn Merchants of Park Road, Shepton Mallet pleaded guilty to supplying rationed foodstuffs otherwise than against the surrender of ration documents. There were nine cases in all and a fine of £1 was imposed in each case.

> They had been supplying farmers without collecting the coupons – allowing the farmers 'overdrafts. What had happened was that the defendants had undoubtedly had been more zealous to meet the wishes of farmers than to observe the orders which had been issued by the Government to restrict this.
>
> No question of 'Black Marketeering' but getting a competitive advantage against other feed firms. The defence pointed out that it was 15 tons out of 1500, 1% of turnover. Farmers did not always keep their promises to hand over the coupons when they received them. They pointed out that stock either had to be fed or slaughtered and the slaughtering might be slow by starvation. Bench declined to make an order for costs.

(Note. As someone who spent many years working in the feed industry the motto always was 'you can't feed excuses to animals'.)

Shepton Mallet Petty Sessions. Refused to take Evacuees. The first summons in the District for a considerable time for failing to comply with a billeting order. Richard J Padfield, a 74 year-old retired mason of 14 Whitstone Road, Shepton Mallet, was summoned for failing to billet a woman and two children who had been bombed out in London. He pleaded not guilty.

He and his wife lived in a 5 roomed house but he claimed it was inconvenient, only one lavatory and the cooking was done on an open fire. Fined £1.

(Note. It could well be that there were renewed problems following the V1 rocket attacks on London)

Regal. 'Jane Eyre' starring Joan Fountaine and Orsen Wells.

Editorial. 'So tight has the censorship clamp been screwed down upon the news coming out of Germany during the essential days of the past week that even now nobody knows for certain what happened, whether a genuine attack was made by bomb against Hitler or whether it was a 'Frame up' to enable another purge to be put into operation.

Shepton Mallet Petty Session. A case against a Market trader dismissed. 'It was alleged that he made it a condition that in order to obtain tomatoes customers must also buy three lettuces.'

4 August 1944

Flag Day. A very successful flag day in aid of the PDSA organised by Mrs S Ware and Mr C Amor was held in the town and district on Friday when many willing helpers worked indefatigably in the selling of emblems and in other ways to make the day a success. Mr & Mrs Webb kindly organised a competition and made mascots which added considerably to the fund.

Constitutional Club. Visit by Mr Melbourne Inman a professional billiards player raising funds for Red Cross. He won two exhibition matches but his opponents did very well, Mr Inman being obviously ill at ease and far from his best. This no doubt was due to the distressing news he had shortly before play commenced viz that his home had been bombed out. The company was sympathetic.

Regal. 'In Which we Serve' starring Noel Coward, Bernard Miles and John Mills.

11 August 1944

The Price of Victory. The news from the Western Front has been good this week but locally here at home there have been sharp reminders that progress is only purchased at a great cost. Two local lads…have made the supreme sacrifice viz Cecil James Bailey son of Mr & Mrs Bailey of New Street and John Henry Baker sixth son of Mr & Mrs J Baker of Quarr.

War Charities Fete. Record Attendance. What could possibly have been nicer than the war charities fete at Summerleaze on August Bank Holiday Monday? When literally hundreds of happy folk, apparently care-free folk, assembled to enjoy the lovely grounds, to meet each other in friendly fashion, and to support as liberally as their means would allow a charity which really commends itself to all….

> One of the most popular attractions during the afternoon and evening, especially to young folk, was the Wainwright Railway and it was a fine one, well worth every penny of the six penny admission fee. It was all electric with a tremendous track with double and treble lines, shunting, sidings, station, signal boxes and all complete. The erection of the railway and its multifarious accessories must have entailed an immense amount of work, and certainly it kept the staff, Masters David, James and Charles Wainwright, fully occupied for days whilst the superintendent of the line Mr C D Wainwright must also have had a busy time – A good show lads.

Shepton Mallet Urban District Council. Post-war housing 'Originally the site had been 85 acres which had now been cut to 25 acres. The question of the roadway approach was an important one. It was proposed to effect an entrance through Compton Road and to work on a turntable principle.

> (Note. As it so turned out – one of the most inconvenient decisions ever taken. The Ridgeway is a major housing estate with very poor traffic flow.)

18 August 1944

British Restaurant. The following is an appreciative little note handed into the offices of the 'Journal' this week:- 'Many thanks to the volunteers who opened the British restaurant from 8th -12th August. Good cooking appreciated by all.'

National Fire Service. Today, Friday, makes the third anniversary of the National Fire Service and to commemorate this occasion parade services are being held….In keeping with other firemen…the local men will attend the service at the Parish Church at 11am

Farewell and good luck. The Rev D V Galloway, curate, after a stay of nearly three years, leaves with his family today for the Rectory at Clutton and he takes with him the sincere and hearty good wishes of the parish wherein he had made himself so genuinely and universally popular.

Fifty years service. Our readers will join us this week in offering their hearty congratulations to Mr Arthur Brown a member of the 'Journal' office staff upon completion of 50 years service.

Regal 'Four feathers' (coloured) starring John Clements, Ralph Richardson and June Duproy.

Advert. To Let Large 3 Bed roomed caravan. Situate at Charlton Filling Station. Apply Allen, Shepton Mallet.

25 August 1944

Mentioned in despatches. The many friends of Edmund (Ted) Boyce A B Royal Navy who for the past two and a half years has been serving on one of the most famous of aircraft carriers will learn with satisfaction that he was mentioned in despatches in the King's Birthday Honours List and has since received the oak leaves.

Mr Boyce who saw service throughout the last war is now in his 28th year of service in the Royal Navy. After finishing his time he was out of the service for three years but was recalled at the outbreak of war since when he has been in the Battle of Malta in the North Africa campaign and in many other interesting engagements, including the bombing of the battleship Tirpitz in a Norwegian Fjord. Two of his sons, Roy and Jack, are also in the service.

Failed to enrol in the Home Guard. Farmers Excuse's at Shepton Mallet Court. *******, farmer of Easton Farm Pylle, was fined £15 at Shepton Mallet Petty Sessions on Friday for failing to comply with a Ministry of Labour directive to enrol in the Home Guard.

His reason was that although he had no objection, he did not have the time to do it. The farm was in the name of the defendant's father who, however, was suffering from chronic rheumatism and only able to do light work. Management of the farm therefore fell on the defendant. There were 195 acres to be looked after including 70 arable. At present there were 60 cows in milk as well as 40 – 50 pigs and other young stock. The labour of the farm consisted of the defendant, two farm workers and the defendant's two sisters. Defendant was the only tractor driver. He never finished work until somewhere about 8.30 in the evening summer or winter.

1 September 1944

The marriage of Miss Pamela Hall. The Parish church was once again the scene of a very attractive and fashionable wedding on Saturday afternoon when for the second time within a comparatively short period Mr Berkeley Hall gave away a daughter in marriage.

Once again the paper devoted two whole columns of the front page to the wedding and the gifts.

Air raid test. An air raid test will be carried out on Monday next as follows: Raider Past 10 am, Alert 10.05 am. Raider Past 10.10 am.

Servicemen who lose a limb or limbs may obtain free and post free a leaflet setting out the arrangements for limb fitting, discharge and pension and resettlement in civil life, Relatives may also apply. British Limbless Ex Service Men's Association.

Roll of Honour. News has been received of the death in Italy on August 1st of Pte L Preece aged 31 who died of wounds. 'Leonard' will be readily remembered by his many friends in the town. Formally he was in the provision and grocery trade and served his apprenticeship at Messrs Leaver Bros. Later he joined the staff of the Shepton Mallet Co-operative Society. He had been overseas for upwards of two years….Every sympathy is extended to his mother of 14 Victoria Grove and also to his widow Mrs Preece of Evercreech. By a strange co-incidence 'Leonard' lost his father under similar conditions in the last war.

Regal. 'Kings Row' starring Ann Sheridan, Ronald Reagan, Betty Field and Robert Cummings.

Shepton Mallet Water Works Company. Town Water Supply Warning. – once again restrictions in place. 'The company re-washers cold water taps free of charge.'

Note. Unlike the first few years of the war the editorials at this time give very full details of the progress of the war and the number of deaths of soldiers.

Soldier's tragic death whilst seated in lorry. Shepton Mallet Police Court inquiry into the death of Gunner Ralph Arnot who was shot while seated in a lorry having a few minutes conversation with comrades before settling down for the night in the back of the lorry.

It would seem he was accidentally shot with a rifle which was accidentally loaded with live ammunition. Hearing adjourned.

Advert. Shepton Mallet and District Rabbit Club Annual Open Show (under BRC rules) The Produce Shed, West Shepton. Judges Mr Wyatt and Mr Purnell.

8 September 1944

Personal Tributes to Capt M H D Williams. The many friends in Shepton Mallet of Col V D S Williams of Hornblotton House, learned recently with profound regret of the severe loss he has sustained by the death in France of his son.

The Bishop has approved the appointment of the Rev'd H T Hillier as assistant curate of Shepton Mallet....Mr Hillier has not been ordained long....he was wounded in France during his service in the last war.

Editorial. Britain's most depressing of all war time restrictions, the 'Blackout' will be almost banished on Sept 17th when Double Summer Time ends. The great news was announced on Wednesday night by Mr Herbert Morrison, Home Secretary and Minister of Home Security, together with big cuts in Civil Defence and Fireguard duties. At the same time, the War Office announced the end of compulsory drills and training of the Home Guard as from Monday September 11th.

15 September 1944

Good News. The many friends of Pte Bryan Jones son of the popular landlord of the Kings Arms Inn will be pleased to learn that after officially being reported missing last week in France, he has written home saying that he is fit and well. Apparently, while pushing ahead in one of the great surges he was taken prisoner, but after two weeks the British turned the tables on his captors and he was rescued. At one time Pte Jones who is serving in one of the Highland Regiments was a member of the local Home Guard in which he was held in high esteem.

Regal. 'Action in the North Atlantic' starring Humphrey Bogart, Raymond Massy and Alan Hale.

Advert. Onions for sale. Approx four and a half hundredweight of pulled and dried onions for sale. A D Stockdale. Clerk to the Urban District Council.

Independent Traders Alliance. Wells, Shepton Mallet, Glastonbury and Street Branch. A meeting for all independent traders will be held, Council Hall, Shepton Mallet, Tuesday next 19th Sept at 7 o'clock. Speaker Mr Edward Gallop. 'The importance of Maintaining Private Enterprise'

22 September 1944

The Town Band. Dear Sir. Sheptonians will be aware that as most of its members were called away the Town Band ceased to function for the Duration. Some months ago however Mr C Attwood got some boys to take instruments and after many try outs he has succeeded in bringing out a few who are making good progress…..Now the few old members who are left are assisting and there are excellent prospects the band will soon be able to make a start in public….. F J E Pullen.

Repatriated. News has been received that Fusilier J G Holdsworth was amongst the latest batch of prisoners of war to be repatriated from Germany and has arrived in the country…. Fusilier Holdsworth, who married Miss Ena Templeman of Church Lane, was taken prisoner by the Italians at Gazala.

Street Lighting. It was a great pleasure to see the street lighting go on again in the town on Sunday evening, the first time since the outbreak of war. Shepton Mallet is one of the first towns in Somerset to have its street lights at the higher standard permitted by the Ministry of Home Security…Many children who saw the lights for the first time in their lives were thrilled by the experience.

Editorial. 'Hats off to the Council and its officers for a very nice bit of work….far reaching sight of the Council for getting the street lighting up to standard before other towns.'

Offences under the Food Rationing Scheme. Mrs Ellen Amelia Rayes. The Green Tree Inn, Ditcheat was summoned for failing to keep an account record of meals and hot beverages served in her establishment between April 4th and June 24th 1944, for failing to secure that the total quantities of rationed foods permitted to be used were not exceeded and thirdly for obtaining rationed foods otherwise than in accordance with the terms of a buying permit.

George Baker, grocer the Post Office, Ditcheat, was summoned for supplying Mrs Rayes with rationed foods otherwise than in accordance of the terms of a permit.

Mrs Rayes said her husband had been in the RAF for two years and she had never understood the forms and just entered the figures he had used.

Defence said anyone running a catering establishment was bound to fall foul of some

Coal advertisement.

of the rules. There were six bedrooms in the Hotel and up to 12 residents. Mrs Rayes worked from 8.00am to 10.30pm with little assistance. He mentioned the courage of Mrs Rayes trying to run a business in these times. Fined £1 on each charge, no order as regards costs.

29 September 1944

Admitted to Hospital. Mrs Mitchell of 52 Garston Street has been notified that her youngest son Corpl J Mitchell has been admitted to hospital seriously wounded. Corpl Mitchell is 28 years of age. He joined the Army when only 16 and has thus put in 12 years of service.

Safely Home. News has been received by Mrs E Manship of 34 Victoria Grove that her son CMS Ralph Manship Royal Engineers, who was seriously wounded in Belgium has arrived home safely in this country and that following excellent progress in hospital is now continuing to make good in a 'not-so-far-away' convalescent home,'

6 October 1944

An Honour. This week news has been received by Mr and Mrs R Vincent of Victoria Grove, Shepton Mallet that their youngest son Pte Gordon Vincent serving with the Worcester Regiment has been selected as a body guard to his Majesty the King. In civilian life, he was a full time member of the local National Fire Service.

13 October 1944

Threw a stone at a train. At Shepton Mallet Juvenile Court on Thursday last week a 14 year old evacuee pleaded guilty to endangering the lives of passengers on the railway by throwing a stone through a railway carriage window. PC Talbot stated that he made enquiries and interviewed the lad concerned who admitted being in Collett Park and throwing a stone at the train. He was fined 10/- and ordered to pay 11/9d damages.

An Anglo American Alliance at Shepton Mallet. Much interest was evinced in an Anglo American Alliance solemnized in the Parish Church of St Peter and St Paul by the rector Rev A S Gribble on Wednesday afternoon when Mr Fred W H Bennett gave his only daughter Rita, in marriage to Charles Meyers of Minnesota USA

The happy pair are both well known in the town. The bridegroom was in addition to his best man, supported by a considerable contingent of the DTC stationed in the town.

A lasting Alliance. Colin Ryall interviews a former American Soldier, Otis Doye, who married a local and settled in Shepton.

I arranged a chat with an old friend, Otis, sometimes known as 'Tex'.

Otis had first come to the UK as an American serviceman in 1942. Otis was not a GI but a regular; he had joined the US Army in 1936, in his hometown Shreveport, Louisiana. So on this occasion I had high hopes of discovering what life was like for a coloured soldier serving in Shepton Mallet during the War years but once again my the interview didn't go as expected.

Otis is now 86 years old and his memory far from perfect but he had no trouble recalling his participation in Operation Redball. This was the massive transport operation to keep the invasion forces in Normandy supplied. From huge storage dumps prepared in the run-up to D-day (6th June 44) convoys of 'artics' conveyed anything and everything the fighting men who had opened up the Second Front required. From 'toothpaste to a tank', as Otis recalled. These storage dumps were dispersed all over southwest England, some around Shepton. It was Otis and his fellow drivers who moved all these supplies firstly to Southampton, later in France up to the forward area. This was an immense, all-out effort; as each driver finished his shift a fresh driver would take over his seat in the tractor unit. Some loads could be dangerous in the extreme, Otis could recall being distinctly nervous when he was in danger of being 'blown sky high' moving high explosives, even though these were loaded onto specially sprung semi-trailers.

Otis Doye.

Fortunately Otis never heard of any of disaster involving these although he did witness a huge fuel tanker exploding after a collision, the accident probably due to the near exhausted state of the drivers involved. Otis recalled the comradeship of those days, how the whole convoy would stop to help one broken-down vehicle.

Otis said he and his comrades did very well for their own supplies, especially the officers, 'plenty of whisky.' But the ordinary soldier did 'OK', 'Oh boy! We had fun in those days', he grinned.

When asked how he got on with the locals Otis replied, 'Mighty fine man! I married one didn't I?' He actually had more trouble with his own officers (white) ' Some were OK, but some were bad, real bad', Otis recalled. However when I got round to life in Shepton I was disappointed, Otis was never stationed in Shepton but Stonehouse in Gloucestershire.

When I asked how come he ended up in Shepton, Lou, Otis' wife took up the story.

('I was Lucy, Lucy Bartlett, but he's always called me Lou.')

Lou was born in Kilver Street when it was a self contained community (it had its own shops, pubs, P.O. and school, now all demolished or converted) but when war broke out Lucy, as she was, was working in an ice-cream parlour in a Weston-Super-Mare hotel. With the coming of war all young women became liable to be called up but Lou's boss got her call up deferred for six months. During that time Lou's ice-cream parlour became a bar for the officers who had taken over the hotel. 'And a right mess they made of it', Lou commented. When her boss could not get an extension to her deferment Lou had to go where directed by the Government. This could have been into the forces or, as in Lou's case, into any civilian work needed for the war effort. Lou was sent to an ammunition factory in Stonehouse producing 'tracer' machine gun bullets.

Lou did not find this work to her liking and so when she was released 'temporarily' from it to nurse her sick mother, she stayed put in Shepton, even after her mother recovered. She never went back even though she had met Otis while employed at the factory, on a day off in Cheltenham. 'Me and a friend were in a bookshop, Otis and his friend blocked the exit and only let us out after agreeing to a date', Lou fondly recalled.

As the end of the war came into sight Otis and Lou were married. Otis recalled nearly missing his own wedding day when he found there were no trains running, (a not uncommon occurrence when schedules were disrupted by enemy action, wartime shortages, or by priority being given to military transport) but he was lucky enough to get a lift right to his destination.

After the war Otis returned to the United States to be discharged in San Antonio, Texas (this, together with his pronounced Southern drawl, is why Otis is known as Tex). Lou stayed at home as due to her mother's renewed incapacity her father wanted her to look after the family. To enable Otis to return, Lou went to see Mr Burnell, a director of Charlton Brewery, from whom she obtained a promise of work for Otis. It was only with this promise of work that Otis was allowed to return to the UK, which he did as soon as possible.

I first heard how Otis came back across the Atlantic related in the Field Inn (now closed) and remember the wry comment of one old wiseacre present, 'Oh aye', he said 'That'll draw you further than gunpowder will blow you!' I wondered if he realised that Otis had indeed risked being blown to 'kingdom come', but he was to endure to enjoy a happier fate.

Otis and Lou first set up home in a now demolished cottage in Garston Street, at a rent of 5/- (25p) per week. However they soon moved (1950) to one of the new council houses on the Ridgeway Estate, where they have lived happily ever since.

Otis and Lou's story shows how people's lives were changed by the war, for Otis and Lou with a very happy outcome. Incidentally it also illustrates how before the advent of the Welfare State daughters were expected to make care of the family their priority, putting it before their own work or marriage.

Lou was not the only Shepton girl to marry an American serviceman; most expected to follow their husbands home 'stateside', but at least one Shepton girl was disappointed. The sister of one of the contributors herein never heard from her husband once he had returned across the Atlantic. 'I think he was a bigamist', was the sister's opinion.

13 October 1944 (cont)

Shepton Mallet Urban District Council. Mr Price calling attention to the overgrown state of the graves in the Cemetery despite people paying for their upkeep. The Surveyor said that due to the shortage of labour he had only had the grass cut once during the season but hoped to put staff on it now that road dressing had finished.

Mr Pullen also called attention to the overgrown state of the country lanes in the district. He referred particularly to Rubble Lane which had now become impassable. Mr Lintern explained that the County Council was now the Highway authority. It was however the responsibility of the occupiers of adjoining land to cut back the overgrown hedges.

(Note. Rubble Lane is a track off Forum Lane north of Bowlish. It is now little more than a footpath,)

Shepton Mallet Rural District Council. At this time they were very preoccupied with water supply for the villages, East Cranmore, Hornblotton and West Bradley are amongst those mentioned.

The editorial comments on the urgent need for rain.

Advert. Get your utility furniture at Haskins. We offer you the best advice and information on utility furniture. Bring your permits and your bedding and linoleum tokens to us and inspect a complete stock of utility and other furniture. Nursery furniture is supplied without units.

20 October 1944

Missing. Mrs Drew of the Horseshoe Inn Bowlish has received official intimation that her son Edwin John Fowler ('Chick') is reported missing as from September 28th.

Regal. 'Flesh and Fantasy' starring Charles Boyer, Betty Field, Edward G Robinson and Robert Cummings.

27 October 1944

A gruelling experience. Mr & Mrs Emery of 33 Victoria Grove have received the good news that their second son Pte Kenneth Emery of the 4th Wiltshire Regiment serving in the second Army is making good progress following the terrible experience of being twice buried within a week as a result of German trench motor fire. His life was spared by the good work of his comrade who twice dug him out. Sad to relate his chum has since died.

Roll of Honour. The many friends in the town of Mr and Mrs E C Cannings (formerly of 115 Whitstone Road) have learnt with deep regret of the loss they have sustained by the death in France on October 5th 1944 of their son Frank at the age of 20 years.

Letter. From General Jaggard Major DADPR Sn Commander. Sir the de-requisitioning of private and public property is very much in the public mind just now. May I be allowed through your columns to point out that everything possible is being done by the military authoritities to get rid of requisitioned property as soon as is practical.

Regal. 'The Phantom of the Opera' starring Nelson Eddy, Susanna Forster and Claude Rains.

Advert. Barnes and Sons. Fine selection of the finest quality garden bulbs. Daffodils / Tulips.

3 November 1944

Letter. 'Dear Sirs, We the undersigned – past and present members of the Shepton Mallet Rescue Party - are anxious to meet the person who sent an anonymous White Feather post card to our leader. We suggest next Saturday at 21 hours in the depot at Monmouth House, Five minutes will suffice.

ARP Rescue Party, circa 1943.

Our leader is much respected; he has done his job for more than five years and was the founder of the party. During the first 21 months of the depot – a miserable place – was next to his house and he could have slept in his bed. In spite however of a serious physical disability he did his duty every third night and on every siren. We were a voluntary party and did not even get subsistence.

During the critical period we were called out often to stand by and we went in the early hours to Weston (twice) Bristol and Bath. At the first named we were highly complemented for the work we did.

There is much more we could say in defence of a splendid leader and a gentleman and he could defend himself, but not against the dastardly attack. We have noticed the Council are asking for informers against rats, whereupon they will take steps to exterminate this pest be it male or female.

Signed L F West, E E Trott, F D Taylor, C J Jones, W Shore, C Carver, S W Prince, E G Dupe, J Whitmore

Stan Blacker still has very clear memories of this period and the Rescue Party in particular.

Mervyn Pullen, who ran a local builders, (son of FJE Pullen) was asked to form the ARP Rescue Party in 1939. Its members were all supposed to work in the building trade. Their projected rescue task - to pull people out of bombed buildings. Stan, then only 14, was working for Pullen and joined from the start until he was old enough to join the Royal Marines. The original depot was in Pike Lane in a garage adjoining the Pullen's house and builder's yard. They only had very basic equipment and little uniform.

Things improved in 1941 when they moved to a depot at Monmouth House which was demolished to make way for the Hillmead estate in the 1960's. They then had full uniforms and were paid 1/6d per shift. The rescue party was on duty one night in three. Parties based in Wells and Glastonbury served the other nights. Stan can remember their trips to Weston when there had been heavy bombing on the Bournville Estate. They pulled out many dead but also one person alive and a live dog!

All the members of the rescue party were incensed by the white feathers received by Mervyn Pullen. He was a very severe asthma sufferer and would not have been accepted by any medical board for active service. He also worked in a reserved occupation. 'Mind you' says Stan, 'I can think of a dozen Shepton families who were draft dodgers. But not Mervyn Pullen.'

We have a photograph of the rescue party which from its membership can be dated to 1943. Standing Ern Dupes, John Taylor, Jack Whitmore, Gilby Wilmott, Les West, John Jones. Seated Don Taylor, Mervyn Pullen, Capt Hemmings (Area organiser ARP), Nip Shore and Chris Jones. Joe Carver was absent haymaking!

Editorial. The Home Guard officially 'Stood Down' on Wednesday, and though perhaps on grounds of happy comradeship there may be expressions of regret, on the whole, how glad the men must be to have done once again with parades,

> The Home Guard have done a grand job of work, and the county owes them a debt of gratitude it can never fully repay.

10 November 1944

The Town Band. A word of thanks and encouragement to members of the Town Band who put in their first public appearance on Sunday since the war….. they did exceedingly well, and the town will watch with interest and pride its further progress.

Methodist Church. The Women's Social Hour Annual Rally was held at Shepton Mallet on Tuesday when the chair was taken by Mrs T F Merritt. The report was presented by Mrs Gillard and this reflected the splendid work done by the ladies of the Social Hour during the past year.

> A substantial sum of money has been raised. The total of knitted garments made for the forces since the war (began) has now risen to about eleven hundred, Miss Foxwell being the organiser for this effort.

17 November 1944

In German Hands. Official intimation has now been received by Mr and Mrs Tom Martin of Beard Hill that their son George Alex Martin, previously reported missing in Italy is a prisoner in German hands.

Shepton Mallet Urban District Council. Rat Catchers. Considerable disquiet that they were not getting value for money. People were being paid £6 per week as rat catchers but actually only spending 10% of their time ratting as they were unsupervised.

British Restaurant had made a loss for the second month running. Whole Council resolved to tell the Ministry of Food that they could no longer see the need for the restaurant.

The Council interviewed Mr Weatherhead ARP Organiser about the use of the Council Hall for Dances. Mr Weatherhead said he would raise no objection provided such dances were not held too frequently.

Regal. 'Thank your Lucky Stars' starring Bette Davis, Errol Flynn and Ann Sheridan.

24 November 1944

Letter saying the British Restaurant is essential. People on essential work are coming into town every day and there is nowhere else a mid day meal can be obtained.

In German Hands. Mrs R Gilham of the Pack Horse Inn has now received news of her son Gunner Clifford Sheldon who has been missing since September 26th. He is a prisoner of war in Germany. Gunner Sheldon was with the airborne forces at Arnhem.

Well represented. The local ATC were well represented in the Somerset ATC Football team which met Wiltshire at Salisbury on Sunday in the Southern Command ATC Knock out Cup. Three local players were in the Somerset side. K West (Captain) K Dark and Plumbly. They ran out winners 5 goals to 2.

Advert. The Duke of Gloucester's Red Cross and St Johns Fund for Prisoners of War etc. The Gift Shop in aid of the above fund will be opened on Friday December 1st at the White Rose Dairy, High Street, Shepton Mallet. Toys, Books and many other useful Articles will be for sale.

Editorial. If evidence was needed of the amount of time and work members of Shepton Mallet Urban District Council gratuitously put in….. Included in the long list of business was, post-war housing, bus services and shelters, facilities for Cannard's Grave School children, rats and mice, the British Restaurant and the letting of the Council Hall….
> It is not always appreciated how many hours Councillors spend in governing the well being of the town and it is sometimes overlooked that their only reward is adverse criticism over matters in which they have little or no control.

1 December 1944

Roll of Honour. Mr & Mrs H J Luscombe have been notified that Corpl Harold Luscombe has been killed in action in the Central Mediterranean on 16 October whilst engaged in a gallant attack on an enemy strong point.

Shepton Mallet Scouts Annual Meeting. Report stated there are 31 scouts and 48 cubs. Meetings have been well attended and the Scout Hall is open most evenings for the use of boys and to keep them off the streets.
> Three more boys trained by our Sea Scoutmaster sat for the Royal Navy and are now serving together with others who joined the Merchant Navy.

Shepton Mallet Petty Sessions. Raymond O Snook, farmer of Glebe Farm, Binegar was summoned for using a motor tractor in respect of which a road fund licence had been taken out at a certain rate, for a purpose which brought it within a class to which a higher rate of duty was applicable.

Farmers converted old car chassis into 'tractors'. In this case Mr Snook had used it to collect an arm chair from his mother's in Shepton Mallet. He claimed it was part of a journey where he was hedging some land at Long Hill. Fined £3.

Advert. Four schoolboys Aged over 12 required for Newspaper Delivery, Small rounds, Apply Chalker Town Street Shepton Mallet.

8 December 1944

Shepton Mallet Company Home Guard officially Stand Down…. How then should they celebrate their 'stand down'. Little wonder then, human nature being what it is that the men unanimously 'plonked' for a good old fashioned sing song in preference to a ceremonial parade. It was held in the Old Cinema on Thursday evening and proved in every way a huge success.

> The strength of the company consisted of well over 400 Officers, NCOs and men divided into nine platoons, three of which operated in the town and the remainder being located at Croscombe, Pilton, East Pennard, Ditcheat, Evercreech and Cranmore. Large contingents came from these outlying platoons and celebrated with comrades in no mean fashion.
>
> Amongst the officers present were the commanding Officer Lt Col H G Spencer TD, Major C B Rodway Company Commander, Capt W H Norgrove 2nd in Command; Lieutenants FWH Bennett, HAF Tilley, W T Moody, W Napier, A H Scutts, J D Judd, E J Montgomery; 2ndLueitenants WEJ Allen, A W Hoskins and J E Hawkins together with Sergt Major Giddings.
>
> Col Spencer's speech included "The Prime Minister himself has said 'There is no doubt at all that the greatest deterrent to the invasion of this country by the Germans was undoubtedly the Home Guard. If it had not been for the existence of these soldiers in every hamlet throughout the country there would have been nothing to stop the German Airborne Troops until they could assemble in large numbers by when it would have been too late."

A Grand Effort. The Shepton Mallet Girl Guides under the inspiring leadership of Miss Pearce have since the beginning of war collected the magnificent total of 25 tons 12 cwt of paper – well done.

15 December 1944

White Gloves presented. There was no business at the fortnightly Petty Sessions on Friday and the clerk Mr J H Addleshaw, handed to the Chairman Mr C D Wainwright a pair of white gloves – the customary way of denoting that the area has been free of crime.

Roll of Honour. Widespread sympathy is extended this week to Mr & Mrs Ernest Penny in the sad news of the death of their second son 'Trevor' while on duty with the Fleet Air Arm. 'Trevor' was a fine specimen of a healthy English lad, full of enthusiasm, energy and the joy of life.

Welcome Home Fund – A very successful whist drive was held in the Council Hall on

Monday in aid of the British Legion Welcome Home Fund when 23 tables were in play.

Popular Home Guard Officer Married. A wedding of more than usual interest was witnessed by a large congregation of relatives, friends and well wishers at the Parish Church between Miss Hilda May Tripp, daughter of the late Mr & Mrs Thomas Tripp of the Field Inn and Lt F W H Bennett son of the late F W H Bennett of Bristol.

Regal. 'Stage Coach' starring John Wayne, Claire Trevor and Thomas Mitchell.

Shepton Mallet District Hospital Bring and Buy Sale was declared open by Lady Paget. 'As you know Shepton Mallet Hospital was originally started by my father in law the late Sir Richard Paget in collaboration with Dr Craddock of Shepton Mallet and my mother in-law laid the foundation stone in 1879. Though she is now almost 97 she still takes an interest in the welfare of the hospital.

> You may know the story of the old lady who said to her friend, "I think this austerity campaign has gone far enough – if the Ministry of Health starts to ration illness we will have no pleasures left."

Shepton Mallet Urban District Council. Queue Shelters. GWR still unwilling to allow shelters. Reopening discussion with Mr Wainwright.

The County Council has said it could not provide provision for school transport for the children of Cannard's Grave as it would set a very expensive precedent.

Showerings Ltd asking Town Development Committee to support them in an application to the Ministry of Food for permission to install a new pressing plant without which they could not carry on as their old pressing plant was worn out.

22 December 1944

A grand job of work. Civil Defence Sub Control to close down. An epoch of the war has ended this week with the closing down of the Civil Defence Sub-Control at Shepton Mallet which covered an area of four Urban and two Rural Districts and whilst its officers and staff will continue to stand by in their own homes, we venture to hope that it will never again be necessary for them to be called upon for active duty.

> In the early days of the war when Mr A E Wetherhead was the ARP organiser one recalls the names of Major Garton, Capt Partridge, Col Williams and Mr Berkeley Hall. Mr Wetherhead then became Sub Controller which position he has performed in an honorary capacity ever since with Mr J Cockrane and Mr R S Short as his deputies. Mr F J E Pullen and Mr W I Gadd have also been associated with the control since its foundation.
> The post has been run very quietly and efficiently and the whole staff have worked on an entirely voluntary basis. The smooth working of the organisation has been contributed to greatly by large numbers of telephonists, plotters and messengers who, by the faithful and constant attendance day and night have put up a record of remarkable achievement.

Editorial on the closure of the ARP Control. There is one other unit, which continues on full duty and whom generous and unstinted praise is due viz the Royal Observer Corps. Inaugurated in 1938 it has been doing duty ever since and its members will be at their post

Royal Observer Corps post on Ridge.

as usual on Christmas Day. The Corps has had a long and strenuous innings and during the winter months suffers much privation and no little hardship.

At least five of its members have given unbroken service since 1938 viz Messrs E E Poles, A Angwin, S C Bailey, A R Bowden and R Moon while C S Clifford, H Miller H Fish and D Simmonds follow closely on.

(Note. This was amended the following week to say that C S Clifford was one of the originals. He was the father of Donald Clifford who until he recently retired carried on his father's Jewellery Business in the town.)

29 December 1944

The Town Band spent a busy time over the Christmas holiday for not only did they play out before the festival but on Boxing Day 'did the rounds' visiting Pilton and district.

Marines Wedding. The marriage was solemnized at the Parish Church on December the 18th between Nora Kathleen eldest daughter of Mr & Mrs Russ 109 Whitstone Road and Stanley George, youngest son of Mr & Mrs Blacker of Garston Street. The bridegroom wore the uniform of the Royal Marines and Mr Mervyn Pullen acted as best man.

The couple later left for Sheffield where the honeymoon was spent.

Note. Both Stan and Kate are still well approaching their diamond anniversary. The honeymoon was spent in Sheffield at the parents of a soldier friend of Stan's who had originally been going to be the best man but had been taken prisoner of war in the fighting in France.

Kate spent the war in the Voluntary Library which operated from the Council Offices before it was later moved to the old Cinema. She was presented with a 'Freedom of the Library Certificate' for her efforts. She also served in the National Fire Service. She said she was one of many waiting for their husband's return. Stan was demobbed in July 1946 and Kate went on the down to Templecombe on the Somerset and Dorset Railway to meet him.

Since the war Stan has been a leading light in the British Legion. Along with others such as Gordon Vincent they have kept alive the memories of those from Shepton Mallet who gave their lives in the war and those who served.

Talking to Stan and Kate one gets a better understanding of some of the social strains in Shepton Mallet at the time. The real class differences, the tensions between the British and Americans and the feeling that the Americans got the best of everything. The tensions among the British troops where some saw plenty of fighting whilst a good number never even went abroad. Also the memories of draft dodgers. Stan reckons there were around a dozen families in Shepton who made strenuous efforts for their sons to avoid service in the Army. He cites a local family who moved towns a number of times to avoid the call up.

Stan was recently interviewed on the TV programme Two Men in a Trench for his memories of firing the massive guns that fired shells across the English Channel at 'Hell Fire Corner'.

West End Institution. The West End Institution was once again for the Christmastide turned into a veritable fairy land with luxurious embellishment exquisitely executed by members of staff and patients. One of the spacious rooms was converted into a small cottage with flowers and ornamental gardens.

American friends presented to the Institution packets of sweets sufficient for every patient.

Children's Home. The matron and staff of the children's home in Waterloo Road, as their custom, did their level best to bring added happiness and good cheer to the young people in their charge during Christmastide. The hall, big dining room and play room were profusely decorated with holly and evergreens and presented an attractive and picturesque appearance. The children were early astir and great excitement prevailed. Mr F J E Pullen and Miss K Thorne, members of the committee, kindly attended and helped serve the sumptuous fare.

Chapter 8

1945

- January 17, Soviet troops capture Warsaw
- March, Allies secure bridge at Remagen and cross the Rhine
- April 18, Mussolini captured and hung by Italian partisans
- April 21, Soviets are at Berlin
- April 30, Hitler commits suicide
- May 7, Unconditional surrender of all German Forces to Allies
- May 8, VE (Victory in Europe) Day

5 January 1945

Downside Inn Thrift Club completed another successful year when during Christmas Week it paid out to members the handsome sum of £581/14/6d

Letter from F J E Pullen talking about the wonderful old cricket field to the right of Station Approach. Lost to the town some time after 1902 but he believes may rightly belong to the town under a bequest. He was trying to find a way of getting some of the land back as part of the long running bus shelter dispute.

Military Medal. Bombardier Cyril Bernard Carter son of Mrs Carter of 36 Rock Place Shepton Mallet has been awarded the Military Medal for conspicuous bravery in the field and for devotion to duty while serving on the Western Front. The Bombardier is well known in local circles and before the war was a prominent member of the Shepton Mallet Football Eleven.

Regal. 'This Happy Band' starring Robert Newton, Celia Johnson and John Mills.

12 January 1945

A reply to Mr Pullen from Mr J H Addleshaw (the local solicitor) Although from 1699 the field was part of the Strode Charities and from 1757 was under the control of the Trustees of the Strode's Bread and Almshouse Charity, it had been sold by the trustees in 1909 and therefore the Town had no rights. – The paper reproduced the notice of sale from 1909.

Ongoing row in letters to the paper over the fact that the members of the Home Guard would not have rights to join the British Legion.

Advert. Scottish and Irish Seed Potatoes. Please order early as supplies are limited. Good eating potatoes in stock. Allan Feaver and Son, Coal, Corn and Seed merchants Evercreech. Phone Evercreech 5.

Shepton Mallet Urban District Council. 'Bus queue shelters. The Highway and Lighting Committee reported that letters had been received stating that ….no objections would be raised to the erection of bus shelters at Townsend…. The Committee resolved that

a) Mr Wainwright's offer of 20 yards frontage to Station Approach Road be accepted on the condition that if another 5 or 10 yards be needed it will be granted.

b) That the surveyor prepares and submits to the Military Authorities plans and details of the proposed shelters.

The Council also decided to curtail public parking in the Market Place between the corner of Church View to the Town Council Office due to congestion.

19 January 1945

Red Cross Cadets. A most enjoyable evening was spent by well over 100 Red Cross cadets and friends in the council Hall on 10th January when a 'bumper' party was arranged by C B Rodway (Cadet Divisional Officer) assisted by Mrs Laing and Mr C Amor. Games and dancing were enthusiastically participated in by all and a marvellous programme of dance music was gratuitously provided by Mrs E G Moores which was very much appreciated.

> (Note. Once again the name of Mr C Amor who has appeared as Scout Master and fund raiser throughout the war. In June 1945 he was sent for trial accused of indecent behaviour with a number of Boy Scouts.)

The paper was already running letters debating the Post War general election.

Death of retired Post Master Mr H Hacker who had been an enthusiastic member of the Royal Observer Corp and the Shepton Mallet War Savings Executive Committee.

Advert. In aid of the Royal Navy War Libraries. A dramatic entertainment in the Council Hall Shepton Mallet at 7.30pm. Programme includes three one act Plays presented by the Drama Section of the Stoke St Michael WI and George Sidney will provide an Exhibition of Conjuring.

26 January 1945

Billiards. The Billiards tournament which has excited so much interest at the Constitutional Club during the winter months is drawing to a successful conclusion. The finalists are Mr A Bond last year's winner and Mr Geoffrey Williams.

Shepton Mallet Brains Trust sits in the Council Hall. A novel and most enjoyable evening was afforded townsfolk on Tuesday when a 'Brains Trust' sat at the Council Hall to answer questions previously received by the question master. The organiser of the 'Brains Trust' was Mrs Addleshaw who hit upon the happy plan not only of assisting the Red Cross but providing an entertaining and instructive evening.

> A few random questions. Is there any truth in the old adage 'spare the rod and spoil the child?' How far do you agree with the statement that a career for married women is detrimental to home making and housekeeping? It is said that a mans best friend is his mother. Why not his father?

2 February 1945

Snow, Wind and Rain. Seldom has the district experienced a more severe spell than that prevailing since Christmas and now following a week of intense cold, snow and fog a most welcome thaw has set in. So intense has been the cold that on Monday and Tuesday children attending school out of the town were sent home, it being almost impossible to heat the schools. With the thaw on Tuesday after a comparatively heavy fall of snow on Monday, the town and district was deluged in slush, and in many instances there was much damage done by flooding. While it lasted however, the snow provided ample sport for young and old, and it has been a long time since so much tobogganing has been enjoyed.

Shepton Mallet Rural District Council. Tinned Foods. The Medical Officer of Health it was stated had reported to the Public Health Committee concerning the condition of tinned foods, stating that it was desirable that the public should be particularly careful in the use of tinned foods at a time when old stocks are being released from store,…. He recommended that consumers should look under the paper wrappings to see that there was no rust on them.

Regal. 'Robin Hood' starring Errol Flynn, Olivia De Haviland and Basil Rathbone.

Both the UDC and the RDC. Debates on the new Education Act. It was proposed set up local divisions to control education with no role for the Districts Councils. To be fair there had been no control before and the councils seemed to accept it as a 'fait accompli'.
   (Note. Education had for some time been a County Council responsibility but presumably the UDC's and RDC's felt they had had more influence.)

9 February 1945

Shepton Mallet Petty Sessions. Shot Homing Pigeons. Local Butcher Fined. John W Yeoman, butcher 17 Victoria Grove, Shepton Mallet, was summoned for killing a homing pigeon, he pleaded guilty.
   Harry Comer, ex police Sergeant, witnessed … he spoke to the defendant and asked him if he had no more sense than to kill a tame pigeon. Yeoman replied that he thought they were wild ones…..Comer also told him that it was a serious matter to shoot a homing pigeon as so many of these birds were being used on war work. 'I would rather have given £1 to the Shepton Mallet Hospital than shoot a tame pigeon' said the defendant. Fine 10/-

Note. Henry Esain a farmer at Binegar can remember that they had a number of semi tame pigeons around the farmyard which used to roost under the eaves of one of the cow sheds. One evening during the war a policeman called and instructed them to catch and kill the pigeons because they could have interfered with the pigeons involved in war work.

Letter from William Aldridge former Head Master of the Grammar School which had been shut for a decade and a half calling for it to be re opened now that the Education Act gave everybody the right to a secondary education.

Editorial. Urban District council 50 years ago. The Shepton Mallet Urban District council has this week been celebrating its Jubilee marking the occasion by a dinner at the Hare and Hounds on Tuesday evening.
   Fifty years ago the then governing body, the Shepton Mallet Local Board, as it was called gave place to the newly elected Urban District council.

The Council at its Jubilee Dinner on Tuesday marked the occasion by presenting to Sir

Frederick Berryman an illuminated address in appreciation of his 50 years continuous service to the town as councillor. In his speech Sir Frederick said. "….quite frankly Shepton Mallet people are all right. They could be slow, careful and deliberate starters but once they got going they were good workers and good stayers….."

16 February 1945

Shepton Mallet Urban District Council 'Bus Shelters. ….. Reported that the surveyor had reported that the probable cost of the queue shelter would be around £60 and that he had arranged with Mr Wainwright to show him the plan. It was also reported by the clerk that Mr Wainwright would confirm in writing the arrangements made with Mr Norman and the rent he will require after seeing the plan.

Cribbage Tournament. The local hospital has recently benefited to the extent of ten guineas as a result of a friendly cribbage tournament held at the Charlton Inn.

Post War Housing. The committee of the whole council reported amongst other matters in relation to post war housing that it had been resolved that 75 per cent of the houses be fitted with gas cookers and washing appliances and in the case of the remaining 25% of the houses it was to be left to the ingoing tenants to choose whether electric of gas appliances be installed.
  Councillors wanted to know if you were giving 25% the choice why not all of them.

Regal. 'There's something about a soldier' starring Tom Neale and Bruce Bennett.

Letters. A lot of support for the suggestion of reopening the Grammar School.

23 Feb 1945

Shepton Mallet Petty Sessions. Chased by Police officer. ***** *****, farm worker, Roemead Farm Gurney Slade was summoned for riding a pedal cycle without lights at Croscombe at 8.05pm on February 4th.
  PC Talbot said he saw defendant riding without lights. On seeing him defendant rode away at fast speed towards Wells. He followed him for half a mile and then saw ***** turn into a side road. Entering the side road he found ***** stopped. Asked for an explanation defendant said, 'It's no use. I am beat.' ***** had no lamps on his machine. The Chairman 'You were on your pedal cycle?' 'Yes Sir.' A fine of £1 was imposed. Note. Reopening the case for the defence sixty years later the defendant points out that the reason he was caught was because he was having trouble with the gears on his bike. As he was only a sixteen year old at the time he earnt 7/6d a week and batteries cost 8/- a pair. He also points out that earlier in the war he was in trouble with the police for not having his bicycle lamp properly masked. Improvising, he had stuck some tape across the front but apparently it still allowed the light to point upwards.
  Due to the serious nature of these crimes the defendant has asked to remain anonymous!

Alleged False Pretences at Shepton Mallet. Married Women Sent to Prison. Two married women, one with young children, were sentenced to two months imprisonment at Shepton Mallet Police Court on Thursday on charges of false pretence. They both pleaded guilty to obtaining money and clothing coupons by making false statements to the Public Assistance

Authority at Shepton Mallet on July 3rd 1944. The accused said they were evacuees from Sussex.

2 March 1945

Air raid warning. The quarterly 'sound' test of the Air Raid Warning will be made on Monday next and the public are hereby warned of the practice.

British Legion Grand Dance. Old Cinema March 9th 1945. in aid of British Legion Earl Haigs Fund. With the Western Serenaders Dance Band.

A meeting will be held in the Council Hall, Shepton Mallet Wednesday March 7th at 4pm to make known the scheme for helping bombed out people in Lambeth with household goods. The chair will be taken by the Rev A S Gribble. Help urgently wanted.
   (Note. Presumably this is in response to the V2 rockets destructive campaign.)

Letter from C G Bunce, 6 Great Ostry complaining about shop keepers putting goods in their window which aren't for sale. 'Apples for example are sorted and the good ones put in the window, but when customers ask for them they are told they can have only some speckled, mouldy rubbish kept inside, half of which is waste.'

Letter. W P Price. Chairman Shepton Mallet Town Development Committee responding to 'Sleepy Shepton' accusations pointing out the strenuous efforts which had been carried on over a long time to get industry to Shepton Mallet.

Regal. 'Buffalo Bill' starring Joel McCrea and Maureen O'Hara.

Shepton Mallet Rural District Council. Darshill Sick Bay. It was reported that an intimation had been received from the Ministry of Health to the effect that the County Council would be taking over the Darshill Sick Bay premises for use as an ante-natal hostel for expectant mothers.

9 March 1945

Fire. Shortly after 5 am on Friday the NFS received a call to Kent (West Shepton) where an outbreak of fire had been discovered at the residence of Mrs Gammon an evacuee from London. The discovery was made by a neighbour, Mr Grimshaw, who with Sergt Illman and the aid of a garden hose affixed to a water tap succeeded in keeping the flames under until the arrival of the Brigade. Happily there were no personal injuries but Mrs Gammon lost much furniture salvaged from London.

Regal. 'Cover Girl' starring Rita Hayworth, Jean Kelly.

16 March 1945

A Country Dance Party will be held at the Council Hall on Tuesday March 20th 7.30 – 10.30pm. Miss M Pullen will M. C.

St John's Ambulance Brigade. Popular Social at National Deposit Canteen. Saturday March 17th 7.30pm, tickets 1/6d, including light refreshments and Wilton's Band.

The Council Hall, Market Place, Shepton Mallet will be open every Friday until 30th June

1945 between 11am and 4 pm to provide waiting room facilities for the General Public. A D Stockdale, Clerk to the Shepton Mallet Urban District Council.

(Note. Why? Was this in response to the shutting of the British Restaurant?)

A 'ladies' night', the first of its kind ever organised by the local Buffalo Lodge was held at Lodge Headquarters on Wednesday and was strongly supported by both sexes.

Shepton Mallet's New Rate. Increased County demand expected…Mr Berkeley Hall who moved the adoption of the report said he could not pretend to do so with any pleasure. There was a proposed increase of 3/- which was wholly accounted for by an anticipated increased demand from the County Council. Although it was anticipated that local requirements showed an anticipated decrease of a penny ha'penny rate.

There was nothing they could do about the County rates…… A large element of the increase 1/7d was for education.

Shepton Mallet Urban District Council. Needs of Ex-Service Men and Women. Preference in Council House Tenancies. Resolution that ex-service men and women should have preferential treatment in the granting of tenancies in Council Houses and in post-war council employment were passed at the monthly meeting of Shepton Mallet Urban District Council on Tuesday evening. The resolutions were proposed by Mr W A Price who is hon. secretary of the local British Legion.

Mr Pullen backed by Mr Hall were worried as to what the housing part would imply. Preference had always been given where there were children. Mr Price argued that was unfair on soldiers who had had no opportunity for five years to raise a family. (!!!). However that did not appear to be the feeling of the Council. Final wording included 'other circumstances being equal' special preference will be given to ex-service men and women.

The Council agreed that the local Branch of the British Legion should be asked to accept the responsibility of the Council to provide a 'Welcome Home Fund' for all ex-service men and women in the town …..irrespective of whether they were members of the British Legion.

Note. Although outside the scope of this study it appears that there was some controversy about the way this fund worked. Stan Blacker says he received only 32/- but was not really looking for much, others have commented that their fathers were disappointed how little they received. There is also rumour that a lot of the fund was loaned to Pilton and not returned. Perhaps a subject for research in a study of Post War Shepton?

From about this time there is an increase in large advertisements in the paper which cut down on editorial. It was still in a four page format.

23 March 1945

Home again. The many friends of Sergeant Tom Walsh RAF were delighted to see him home again, safe and well, during the weekend. The lads from overseas are gradually drifting back and it is really good to see them for the most part looking uncommonly fit and well. Others home recently were Mr Albert Short and the Messrs Dix Bros. They are glad to be home but after their experiences abroad find things very quiet and dull in the home town.

Editorial on last week's rate increase reports Mr Hall saying 'One can only hope that when the full programme is put into operation, increased grants will be made to local authorities', but even so presumably that will have to come out of the taxpayer's pocket.

In pursuance with the National Policy, the Council is going forward with its post war housing schemes, and again, the outlook for the poor wretched ratepayer is, to say the least of it, bleak. Costed out proposed Ridgeway Housing Scheme at £200,000 – something to be getting on with.

30 March 1945

Dance. Allotment Association, Council Hall, Friday April 6th 8 – 12pm Admission 2/6d.

Ministry of Agriculture and Fisheries Domestic Poultry Keepers Club inaugural meeting will be held at the Peter Street Rooms on April 14th 1945

A summoned meeting of the Loyal Mechanics Pride Lodge No 5318 MUIOOF will be held on Monday 9th April 1945 at York House to receive statement of accounts for 1944. William A Corben, secretary, 50 High Street.

Advert. Regal Theatre Shepton Mallet Sunday 8th April 1945. Emory's T Jones presents A Grand Concert (in aid of the blind) 'Hubert' supported by the Band of RAF Station, Pucklechurch, The Melody Makers Dance Orchestra, The Mendip Quartets, U S Army Spot, Compered by 'Jarge Balsh'. (Advert space donated by Mr S Oatley, Haulage Contractor.)

6 April 1945

Soldier Suicide. Tragic Discovery at Shepton Mallet. The discovery of a soldier with a gunshot wound in the head and a sten gun between his legs was described to the coroner Mr C Leslie Rutter at a Shepton Mallet inquest on Tuesday afternoon. The dead soldier was QMS Robert Cecil Hall aged 43 of Cardiganshire. He leaves a widow and one son aged 4 years.

An 'Old Time Dance' in aid of the Shepton Mallet Town Band was held under the auspices of the 'Gay Nineties' on Wednesday last week. Music was provided by the Western Serenaders.

British United Aid to China. – An inaugural meeting is being held in the Council Chamber, Market Place Shepton Mallet on Thursday April 12th. Invitations to attend have been sent to the clergy, heads of schools and all organisations.

Bravo Shepton. Mr & Mrs Millard have had good news this week of their elder son Lt Ronald J Millard who has been in the thick of the fray with his regiment in Burma. They learn that he is well and that he has been awarded the Military Cross for gallantry in action on the 3rd February 1945. The many friends of Mr and Mrs Millard will rejoice with them in their good news and offer sincere congratulations.

Soldiers bound over. Three soldiers ….were bound over at Somerset Quarter Sessions at Taunton last week for breaking and entering the workshop of Mr F W Bull shoe-maker of Whitstone Road, Shepton Mallet stealing 25/- and shoes, boots and laces value £5/16/ 5d. The men stated they had been to a dance and acted under the influence of drink. An Army officer said they were all 'quite good fellows.'

Letters from Mr F E Coles and W A Simmons. Mr Coles having disposed of the White Rose Dairy, High Street, Shepton Mallet saying how it will carry on his high standard. 'Milk will continue to come from the noted TT Herd of Guernsey and Shorthorn Cattle at Manor Farm, Emborough.

13 April 1945

Shepton Mallet Urban District Council. Appeal to people to take over 11 vacant allotments. Mr F J E Pullen thought this a serious matter….Having regard to what the Ministry of Agriculture had said recently, it should be realised that the country was facing a serious food situation in the coming winter.

Good Friday Circus. The Council had received objections from the Rector, Father Metcalfe and Mr H T Turner about a circus to be held on Good Friday. It appeared that Cook's Paddock has been let while its owner was away from home without it being realised it was Good Friday. Circus would only cancel if paid £40 which was out of the question.

NAAFI advertisement.

Regal. 'One exciting night' starring Vera Lynn, Donald Stewart, Frederick Leister.

Advert. 'Earn a serviceman's thanks – Join the NAAFI. The official canteen organisation for H M Forces now, and in peacetime, women are urgently needed to serve in the forces NAAFI Canteens.

Advert. Full Circle. When the volume of war traffic rose like a tidal wave in 1939 the railways were called upon to transport double their normal loads at once. They did and are still doing it.
    When the all clear is given, the same ingenuity, the same working organisation will restore civilian trains and travel to luxurious pre–war standard – or better. GWS – LMS – LNER – SR.

20 April 1945

British Legion's farewell to the Royal Navy. As a token of their esteem of the local naval contingent, the British Legion Club gave a social evening to the Officers and ratings on Thursday last. A snooker four-some knock out competition, skittle match, also darts and shove halfpenny and a splendid supply of refreshment. Mr SC Clifford (Club President) voiced the Legion's regret at the impending departure of their Naval friends and wished them well and hoped they would all return to renew the good comradeship which had been a feature of their stay in the town. Lt-Commander W G Powell suitably responded.

Military Cross for Major B M Durie. Townsmen generally, and their numerous friends far and wide, will rejoice with Mr & Mrs C Durie of Chashill (?) on the homecoming this week of their son Major David B M Durie and will congratulate them upon his having been awarded the Military Cross.

Major Durie was one of three West Country Officers in charge of the infantry which captured Neiderheicke, the first German village to fall to British Troops on November 18th....

The Citation stated that he commanded his company throughout a 4,000 yard advance with the greatest gallantry, coolness and determination while continuously under fire.

A very pretty wedding was solemnized at the Baptist Church on Wednesday last week between Miss Betty Lillian Carter youngest daughter of Mrs A Carter and the late Mr A J Carter of Rock Place, Shepton Mallet to PFC John Weir of the United States Army.

27 April 1945

Shepton Mallet Urban District Council. Mr Norman re-elected as Chairman for the tenth year, Mr Berkeley Hall re-elected as Vice-Chairman.

The Independent Trade Association. Fighting the menace of Monopolies. A serious threat. Mr Gallop (Chairman of the Bristol Branch) said that the most serious threat which the independent trader had to face was from the growth of monopoly. The battle for their rights against vested interests was a very big problem.

V E Day Celebrations. The VE- Day Committee reported that it was unanimously of the opinion that VE Day – the day on which the Supreme Allied Commander declares that organised resistance in Europe has come to an end, should be regarded as a day of thanksgiving rather than a festive occasion and therefore recommended that the Clerk be instructed to discuss with the rector what arrangements can be made for the holding of a United Service for all denominations on the evening of that day.

Note. Fat chance – it quickly became apparent that VE Day was to be considered a very festive occasion.

4 May 1945

An extra half hour – the licensing Justices have granted an extension until 11pm to all licensees in the SMPS Division on the occasion of VE Day. No formal application need be made.

Still smiling. This week has bought a cheery letter from Sgt Jack Pursey (Burma).....Always something of a wit Jack concludes, '....I should like a pint of Charlton Beer; that's a thing we miss out here.'

Roll of Honour. Since last week news has been received that two Sheptonians have made the supreme sacrifice. Sgt Harry Barnes and B S M Cooksley. The former....died of wounds in Burma on 18th April and leaves a wife and four young children.

Regal. 'Western Approaches', the stirring drama of the Merchant Navy

Advert. 'The War Savings League for the South Somerset Constituency Committee has been abandoned in view of the imminence of a 'Major Campaign' to be introduced immediately after Victory Day.

11 May 1945

V E Day. Following days of suspense and expectancy it was announced on Monday evening that Tuesday would be VE Day and that the Prime Minister would make a statement at 3pm which would be followed by a broadcast by HM the King at 9pm. Over the weekend, people everywhere had had their ears almost glued to the wireless for fear they should miss the announcement.

Editorial. Thanksgiving 'Lift up your hearts'. 'We have won a mighty victory in Europe; Right has finally triumphed over Might. It is the Victory of the ordinary man….
    Victory for us will mean dedication to remake the world of truth, justice, honesty and freedom for which they died…. The hideous work of destruction is ending in the west. Now we can begin to create, to build anew….. Together we can do it.

Regal. 'Snow White and the Seven Dwarfs', Walt Disney's Technicolor Fantasy.

To our readers. The 'Journal' has been published on time this week thanks to the unfailing loyalty of the members of Staff who forwent their full holiday on V E Day and the following day (Wednesday). To recompense them for this loss the 'Journal' office will be closed on Saturday and opened again on Tuesday.

Home Guard. - A church parade will be held for the thanksgiving service Sunday 13th May which it is hoped all members will attend. Assemble at Commercial Road 10.30 am. Anklets to be worn.
    Note. These were the leather tabs worn over the tops of shoes or boots.

Letter. Thanksgiving Sunday, Dear Sir, at the wish of His Majesty the King, Sunday next 13th May is to be observed as a Thanksgiving Sunday.

The Urban District Council will, at the Rector's invitation, attend with me a special service at the Parish Church at 11 o'clock in the morning and it is hoped that as well as the public generally, the Public Organisations in the town will be represented…..E H Norman, Chairman of the Shepton Mallet Urban District Council.

Civil Defence Services – Attention is called to a letter of thanks which appears in another column to the Civil Defence workers in which the County Council, through its Chairman, to thank the voluntary organisations for their splendid work during the past five and a half years.

Conclusion

Of course that is not the end of the story. The war hadn't finished and some of the horrors of what had been happening to prisoners of war in the Far East were still to become apparent. There was also the small matter of the atomic bomb to come. But somehow all that was further from home.

In Britain the public had decided they wanted a new beginning and with the summer elections were to dump Winston Churchill and bring in a Labour Government pledged to introduce the welfare state. However in trying to cope with the years of post war shortages there were many who wished we were still at war.

Shepton Mallet was also to suffer in the post war depression but things had changed, Clark's shoes took over an army camp, Showerings started a massive growth and within a few years the town was undergoing an economic boom. Many of those who had come to the town during the war stayed.

Interesting times were ahead. But perhaps that is a subject for future study for the Shepton Mallet Local History Group.

Bibliography

There were two main sources of information for this book. The memories of the contributors and the Shepton Mallet Journal.

Other works which have been referred to include:

H M Prison Shepton Mallet – F Disney BEM
Somerset at War 1939 – 1945 – Mac Hawkins
Somerset v Hitler – Donald Brown
The Anglo – Fred Davies
Shepton Mallet Camera – The Last 100 Years – Part one 1900 – 1950 – Fred Davies
The Story of Croscombe – Keith Armstrong

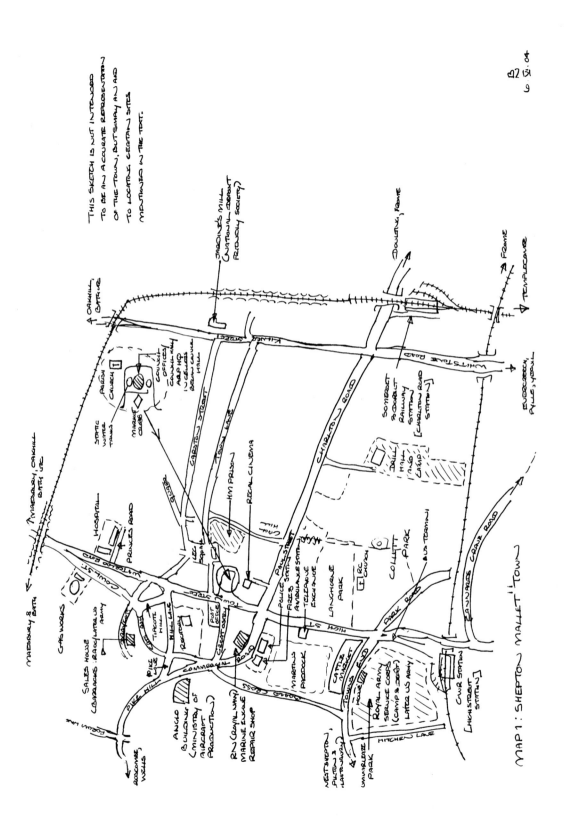

MAP 1: SHEPTON MALLET TOWN

THIS SKETCH IS NOT INTENDED TO BE AN ACCURATE REPRESENTATION OF THE TOWN, BUT SIMPLY AN AID TO LOCATING CERTAIN SITES MENTIONED IN THE TEXT.

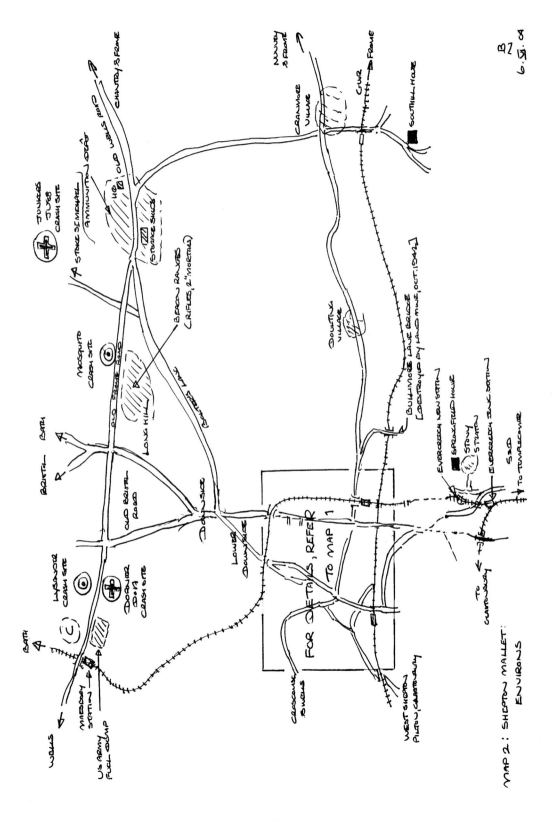

MAP 2: SHEPTON MALLET: ENVIRONS

Appendix 1

The Role Of Honour 1939 – 45. Taken from The Book of Remembrance, Shepton Mallet, Compiled by Mr Fred Hill and Mr Stan Blacker (a copy of this is kept in the Parish Church)

'Bid them rest in peace'

Private Cecil J Bailey,	age 27	10 July 1944	France
Lance Corporal John H Baker	age 29	16 July 1944	France
Sergeant Henry J Barnes	age 35	18 April 1945	Burma
Private Francis C Cannings	age 20	5 October 1944	Holland
BSM Kenneth B Cooksley	age 28	23 April 1945	Germany
P O Walter W H Cox	age 35	21 November 1940	at sea
Sergeant Alfred B Dix (RAF)	age 28	10 April 1943	Libya
Aircraftsman Kenneth V Gay	age 19	30 September 1939	France
Gunner Percy R Hayter	age 21	12 July 1940	Belgium
Aircraftsman Douglas W T Head	age 17	23 February 1940	Britain
Gunner Gilbert N Higgins	age 36	18 March 1942	Britain
Pilot Thomas P K Higgs	age 23	10 July 1940	Holland
Private James William Hodges	age 19	28 July 1945	Burma
Private Clemance S Jenkins	age 24	10 October 1944	Holland
Able Seaman Herbert E C Jones	age 19	14 August 1943	at sea
Able Seaman Louis C Lambert	age 31	19 December 1941	at sea
Seaman John G Lockey	age 18	17 January 1942	at sea
Corporal Harry Luscombe	age 24	16 October 1944	Italy
Aircraftsman Ellerton R Maggs	age	20 March 1944	Britain
Able Seaman Fred Manship	age 33	14 May 1942	at sea
Aircraftsman Thomas Mason	age	25 June 1940	Britain
Private Sydney W Morgan	age 19	24 February 1945	Burma
Gunner Thomas J Moulton	age 33	26 September 1943	Italy
Leading Airman Trevor W Penny	age 20	7 December 1944	at sea
Private Leonard M C Preece	age 31	1 August 1944	Italy
Private Kenneth H Southwood	age 23	3 November 1943	Italy
Private Gerald T E Stevens	age 21	3 December 1942	Tunisia
Lance Corporal Harry G Sweet	age 38	8 June 1940	Britain
Signalman Sydney J Taylor	age 20	2 October 1942	at sea
Stoker Ronald T Vezey	age 17	18 June 1944	Italy
Private Kenneth L Ware	age 20	8 February 1945	Holland
Private Albert S W Warr	age 19	1 April 1945	Holland
Signalman Leslie S Witt	age 33	6 April 1943	Burma